TRANSFORMING MICROFINANCE

Series Preface

Regnum Resources for Mission provides helpful material to mission practitioners, in both foundational and practical topics.

The paper used for the text of this book Forest Stewardship Council (FSC) Certified

TRANSFORMING MICROFINANCE
A CHRISTIAN APPROACH

Edited by Makonen Getu

Regnum Resources for Mission

Foreword by Larry Reed,
Director of Microcredit Summit Campaign

Copyright © OCMS 2013

First published 2013 by Regnum Books International

Regnum is an imprint of the Oxford Centre for Mission Studies
St. Philip and St. James Church, Woodstock Road, Oxford, OX2 6HR, UK
www.ocms.ac.uk/regnum

09 08 07 06 05 04 03 8 7 6 5 4 3 2 1

The right of Makonen Getu to be identified as the editor of this work
has been asserted by him in accordance with the Copyright, Designs
and Patents Act 1988.

All rights reserved. No part of this publication may be reproduced, stored in a retrieval system, or transmitted, in any form or by any means, electronic, mechanical, photocopying, recording or otherwise, without the prior permission of the publisher or a license permitting restricted copying. In the UK such licenses are issued by the Copyright Licensing Agency, 90 Tottenham Court Road, London W1P 9HE.

British Library Cataloguing in Publication Data
A catalogue record for this book is available from the British Library

ISBN: 978-1-908355-31-7

Typeset in Palatino by WORDS BY DESIGN
Cover design by WORDS BY DESIGN
Printed and bound in Great Britain
for Regnum Books International by 4edge Limited, UK

The paper used for the text of this book Forest Stewardship Council (FSC) Certified

regnum

Dedication

To all microfinance clients and practitioners.

Contents

	Preface and Acknowledgements	ix
	Foreword	xiii
1.	Christian Microfinance: An Introduction *Makonen Getu*	1
2.	Background History of Modern Microfinance *Makonen Getu*	15
3.	Opportunity International Case Study *Makonen Getu and Genzo Yamamoto*	37
4.	Vision Fund International Case Study *Nathan Brown and Richard Reynolds*	91
5.	Five Talents Case Study *Tom Sanderson*	121
6.	HOPE International Case Study *Peter Greer amd Anna Haggard*	155
7.	Faulu Kenya Deposit Taking Microfinance Institution Case Study *John Mwara and Jacqueline Nyaga*	189
8.	Microfinance Criticism and Christian Response *Makonen Getu*	215
	The Carpenter's Fund: Brief Profile	247
	Select Bibliography	249

Preface and Acknowledgements

The modern microfinance industry has been in existence for over 40 years. This book gives a brief historical account of the different phases it has gone through. It has moved from an industry: (i) which predominantly offered a single-product, credit, to an industry offering multiple products consisting of loans, savings, money transfers, insurance and non-financial products and services; (ii) wh ich practised a supply-driven approach, whereby MFIs imposed their modus operandi without much regard to the voices of clients, to an industry that increasingly applies a demand-driven approach, whereby competition has created an environment in which clients' voices and satisfaction have begun to matter; (iii) in which NGO MFIs, where no one owned any stake were dominant to an industry in which several regulated commercial MFIs with shareholders and borrowers are increasingly featuring; (iv) an industry in which only mandatory savings were mobilized as security and incentives, to an industry in which voluntary deposits are also mobilized and used for on-lending purposes; (v) which relied on a manual accounting and reporting systems whereby accurate, complete and timely accounting and reporting was difficult to make for effective decision-making to using a state-of-the-art management information system not only for accounting and reporting but also for the delivery of services; (vi) involving a multi-million portfolio to multi-billion dollar industry; (vi) which relied heavily on grant funding to an industry which relies on equity, borrowed (debt) capital and deposits; and (vii) in which MFIs operated in a more scattered manner, where little or no mutual learning took place to an industry in which networking, co-ordination and information-sharing has been made possible through global, regional and national coalitions; (viii) serving a few million clients to an industry that serves a client population of about 200 million; (ix) which strove to prove itself to an industry with global recognition crowned with a Nobel Peace Prize; (x) which was hardly criticized for almost three decades to an industry where its credibility as a poverty reduction tool has begun to be questioned.

The microfinance industry has often been portrayed and perceived as homogenous: the microfinance institutions involved are seen as sharing the common motivation of contributing to poverty reduction through the provision of financial products and services. Moreover, they all apply the basic model of a group solidarity and individual lending methodology. A closer look, however, suggests the contrary. There are as many valid characteristics that point to the prevalence of heterogeneity as much as homogeneity: some are regulated microfinance banks; some are regulated deposit-taking institutions; others are unregulated non-governmental microfinance institutions. The products offered and the ways services are delivered differ accordingly. Religious orientation is another important source of difference. Some of the MFIs are secular while others are faith-based, including Islamic, Hindu, Buddhist and Christian institutions. The vision, mission, values, principles and standards that motivate and drive secular and faith-based MFIs are different as the latter seek to be guided by their respective religious orientations. Differences also appear between the various faith-based MFIs.

Without purporting to be exhaustive, the book attempts to clearly portray the mission and values of five CMFIs and how their foundational beliefs inform their work on a day-to-day basis with the clients they serve. The Christian microfinance sub-sector has been the least studied and the least known by the public and it is hoped that this book will narrow that gap.

Let me now take a few moments to thank some people for their various contributions. The writing of the book started with the provocative question put to me by Dr. Wonsuk Ma, the CEO of the Oxford Centre for Mission Studies: "How come that we don't have a book on the work done by Christian microfinance institutions, and yet we have many of them participating in the industry? Can you do one?" Although I had been thinking about the same for a long time, it was Dr. Ma's question that became the immediate trigger. I want to thank him for the challenge that led me to action and the encouragement he subsequently provided.

I also give thanks to the authors of the various chapters for agreeing to work with me on the book project and for their consistent commitment, support and patience in bringing it to completion.

Several people, including Dennis Ripley, my supervisor, Steve Nelson, Hope Schultz, and Dr. Nancy Horn have read parts or the entire draft and provided invaluable comments, without which the book would have not been what it is. My thanks also go to Ralph Bates for his editorial assistance. Jonathan, Brenna and Laura have also proofread and edited individual chapters and deserve thanks.

Preface and Acknowledgements

I also extend my appreciation and thanks to The Carpenter's Fund led by Dick Omohundro for the generous financial support towards the publication of the book.

Last but not least, I thank my wife, Lea Getu, for her full support and the sacrifice she made as I spent many early mornings, late nights and even holidays working on the book.

Makonen Getu
Oxford
May 2013

Foreword

Do faith-based organizations implement their microfinance programmes differently than their secular counterparts? Does their faith orientation make it more likely that they will avoid mission drift and remain true to their original values? These are the provocative questions that this book explores by looking at several Christian organizations involved in providing financial services to those living in poverty.

I have looked at this question from both sides now. For 23 years, I worked for one of the organizations highlighted in this book. For the last six years, I have worked with industry-wide microfinance initiatives, which led to my current role as Director of the Microcredit Summit Campaign. In my experience, the establishing of microfinance programmes that serve people in poverty, foster positive benefits in their lives and operate according to positive social values, is hard work. Faith-based organizations have an advantage in doing this, in that their faith gives them a common set of values to build from and measure themselves against. They also have a disadvantage as their faith orientation may limit the staff and funders willing to work with them.

What this book does well is to clearly lay out these advantages and disadvantages and show how they play out in the work of real life programmes of organizations made up of people seeking to follow the example of Jesus. I commend each of the organizations in this book for taking on the challenging and rewarding task of living out their Christian values as they work in challenging environments to bring lasting and holistic change.

The bold hypothesis that this book lays out is that a holistic approach to microfinance that includes a spiritual dimension will generate better and longer lasting results for clients than approaches that neglect the spiritual dimension of poverty. I also want to encourage these organizations to continue on the path that this book begins. The next step will be to gather evidence of the results that they see from their approach. By laying out their case so clearly, these organizations can now test this hypothesis against the evidence.

In his book "The History of Christianity," Paul Johnson describes the role played by monasteries in developing agricultural production in the Middle Ages. As monasteries formed, they appealed to the king for land to house their orders. The kings gave them non-productive land, usually swamps or thickets where no crops could grow. The monastic system of hard work, discipline and scholarship taught them how to tame the land and make it productive. Their careful records led to many agricultural and scientific discoveries which the monks passed on to other farmers. This led to an agricultural boom throughout Europe that led to a rising standard of living for the continent. Eventually, the scholarship and documentation of the monks would also lead to the discovery of the field of genetics by Gregor Mendel, a monk growing peas in Austria.

My prayer is that faith-based organizations will play a similar role in microfinance and the wider field of economics. Working with a client base that others assume to be unproductive, these organizations can combine hard work, discipline, scholarship and faith to bring about a new understanding of how the spirit and values combine with finance. The result could be a new form of economics that sees lasting improvements in the lives of "the least of these", as the true measure of success.

When I was working at Opportunity International, I got to know about a group of our clients that could teach value-based economics to the rest of us. Twenty women living in a barrio of Barranquilla, Colombia, had joined together in a Trust Bank, a group of borrowers that jointly guarantee each other's loans. This group had named themselves the "Gift of God Trust Bank." They met weekly to make their loan payments, participate in training and to discuss common problems or issues that they were facing in their community. At one meeting, the group's leader brought up an issue that had been bothering her:

"For the past few weeks, on my way to this meeting, I pass by a woman that is living in such poverty that my heart breaks," the leader said. She looks like she has just moved in from the rural areas, trying to escape the guerilla war that is going on there. She has a baby living with her, but she has no place to stay. She found an old rusty shopping cart and some plastic. She tied the plastic between the cart and the tree, and that is the shelter she and her baby live under."

The leader then put the issue to the group. "This woman's condition reminds me of how bad it was for all of us when we first moved to the city, before we found out about this Trust Bank and before we had our own businesses. Isn't there something we can do for this woman and her baby?"

Foreword

The women spent some time throwing out ideas and considering options. Eventually, they had a plan. They agreed to all chip in half of their accumulated savings, which came to about $100. But since these were entrepreneurial women, they did not stop there. They went to the richest person they knew, a doctor who made regular visits to their barrio, and asked him to match their gift. After he agreed, they took their $200 to the lumberyard and explained to the owner what they were doing. He agreed to sell them hardware at his cost, and let them take any of his scrap lumber away for free. The Gift of God group took their lumber and supplies to where the woman and her baby were living by the tree and built her a small shelter with a solid floor that could keep her and her baby dry in the rain.

When the women of this trust bank told us what they had been able to do, what stood out most was the joy on their faces as they explained how they, poor refugees from a ravaged land, had been able to use their own savings and skills to become the gifts of God for someone who was worse off than they were.

To the servant who invested well the owner says, "Well done, good and faithful servant...Enter into the joy of your Master." (Matthew 25:23). The Gift of God Trust Bank knew that joy. My hope is that the work of these faith-based organizations will lead many more into that experience of joy.

Larry Reed
Director
Microcredit Summit Campaign

CHRISTIAN MICROFINANCE: AN INTRODUCTION
MAKONEN GETU

Makonen Getu (Ph.D.) is Vice President of International Business Development at Opportunity International. Makonen has also taught at both under- and post-graduate levels in development studies at Stockholm University and the Oxford Centre for Mission Studies, where he currently examines and supervises Ph.D. scholars. Makonen has published several books, pamphlets and articles on topics related to development, foreign aid, microfinance, HIV/AIDS, human trafficking, faith and development.

PURPOSE

During the last 4-5 decades, microfinance has been implemented throughout the developing world as a poverty reduction tool by various NGOs, microfinance institutions, grassroots associations and governments fully supported by international donor agencies. A large number of these players constitute faith-based microfinance institutions (FBMFIs). The purpose of this book is to provide a forum for five CMFIs to share on their own terms and in their own language why and how they implement their respective microfinance programmes.

METHODOLOGY

In addition to the introductory part, this book is made up of seven chapters. Chapter two provides a brief history of modern microfinance. Chapters three, four, five, six and seven present case studies[1] of five different CMFIs while chapter eight provides a response to microfinance criticism from a Christian perspective.

Prior to the writing of the book a study plan was formulated by the editor outlining the common themes of each case study and presented to each author for review. The study plan covered several areas including history, vision, mission, core values, organizational structure, clients served and products offered, technology applied, interest rates and fees charged, lending methodology, funding, impact, Christian standards and challenges. Although not necessarily in the same order, the authors cover all the aspects listed here in their respective papers.

The case studies are neither evaluative nor critical. They are neither based on rigorous research nor are the authors external researchers. The studies are descriptive in nature and are written by practitioners close to the programmes described. Moreover, the data used has been gathered internally using first-hand experience, reports, programme and policy documents, minutes, training manuals, and evaluation/impact studies. These features are likely to cause some degree of subjectivism and bias. Some parts might even sound somewhat "promotional" as the authors struggle with the problem of balancing passion and objectivism.

The overall intention of the book is not to produce a vigorously researched impact study on Christian microfinance (CMF). It is rather to create a space for the practitioners of CMFIs to express why and how they do microfinance. The strength of this book is, therefore, in the descriptive introduction of the CMF practice as a sub-sector of the microfinance industry in the way CMFIs perceive and do it. It is about how CMFIs see themselves, their work and their contribution. In this way, the reader will know about what CMFIs are doing and how they are doing as they tell their stories and get a better understanding of the role Christians play in fighting poverty through microfinance that the current literature fails to delineate in a distinctive manner. The information provided will also correct some possible misconceptions people have about the microfinance industry in general and CMFIs in particular.

Abstracts

The five CMFIs covered in this book are: Opportunity International, Vision Fund International, Five Talents, Hope International and Faulu Kenya.[2] Opportunity has been in business since the early 1970s and is, therefore, the oldest and by far the biggest, while the other four emerged at different points in the 1990s. The table below provides a summary of programme statistics in respect of each CMFI.

The paper in chapter three by Makonen Getu and Genzo Yamamato presents the microfinance programme of Opportunity International (Opportunity). Opportunity has been in the business of helping people living in poverty to expand and start businesses and create employment for their neighbours, and generate income for themselves and their families since 1971. Co-founded by two Christian philanthropists, Al Whittaker from USA and David Bussau from Australia, Opportunity gave its first loan to a client in Bogota, Colombia and currently serves over 4 million voluntary depositors and borrowers through 53 Implementing Members in 23 countries across Africa, Asia, Eastern Europe and Latin America involving a portfolio of over $542 million repaid at the rate of 95% and a total savings portfolio of about $114 million. About 6 million people have received both financial and non-financial training and about 4 million hold insurance policies. About 93% of the active clients are women.

Category	Opport-unity	Five Talents	Vision Fund	HOPE	Faulu Kenya	Comments
Loan portfolio	$542 million	$2.5 million	425 million	$41 million	$54 million	
Loan clients	2.8 million	30,000	686,336	149,946	80,155	
% loans to women	93%	74%	66%	82%	41%	
Average loan size	$179	$71	706	$246	$457	.
Repayment rate	95%	94%	98%	96%	6%	Faulu uses PAR rate and not ERR
Voluntary Savings portfolio	$114 million	$1 million	$8 million	$12.7 million	$51 million	HOPE also records $3.2 million SCAs savings
Voluntary Savings clients	1.2 million	36,000	252,477	316,385	239,664	HOPE also records 151,353 SCAs
Insurance policy holders	3.6 million	38,000	N/A		19,000	
Clients trained	5.5 million	64,000	N/A	617,784	50,000	
Staff	17,600	150	5,950	1,239	700	

Programme statistics of the 5 CMFIs

Motivated by the love of Jesus Christ and led by its core values Commitment, Humility, Respect, Integrity, Stewardship and Transparency, Opportunity engages about 18,000 professionals and support staff globally to bring about lasting transformation of lives among people living in poverty using microfinance as the means.

Like most of the MFIs in the industry, Opportunity focused on providing credit and related financial as well as non-financial training during the first 30 years of its existence. In the 21st century, however, Opportunity has moved from:

- Offering a single financial product to offering a comprehensive range of products consisting of loans, savings, money transfers, and insurance
- Running non-regulated microfinance NGOs to establishing and operating 11 regulated commercial banks and deposit-taking institutions in which it has majority ownership, (iii) being urban-based to being rural-based
- Focusing on the trading and service business sector to having a multi-sector approach and providing services to support agriculture including value chains, housing and land, health, education, water and sanitation, energy and cottage industry
- Focusing on women to including minorities, disabled people, people with HIV/AIDS, children and youth
- Focusing on micro-entrepreneurs to including SMEs
- Not offering insurance products to establishing and operating the world's leading micro-insurance agency known as MicroEnsure (a subsidiary solely owned by Opportunity) which provides services not only to Opportunity's clients but also to the clients of other MFIs and organizations
- Employing a basic MIS to applying the latest technology in delivering its services not only to the poor in easy-to-reach places, but also in the difficult-to-reach areas with cheaper, faster and reliable delivery channels, including mobile vans, ATMs, POS devices, GPS mapping of smallholder farmers, customized CRM systems, and cell-phone banking,
- Focusing on developing individuals to developing families and communities

The authors also present some of the major challenges faced by Opportunity. These include understanding and engaging client needs ever more deeply, optimizing human resource management internally, network standardization and consolidation, strategic expansion, facilitating and measuring transformation as well as external factors including policy environment and economic recessions.

Also presented are Opportunity's Christian values and standards: Opportunity's vision, mission, core values, motivation, services, accountability, and impact measurement are all rooted in and driven by Christian principles. Opportunity's work is in response to God's calling to serve people living in poverty through the facilitation of sustainable and wholistic transformational development.

The authors conclude that despite the challenges, Opportunity has been able to make substantial achievements by: (i) applying a client-centric approach, (ii) investing in innovation and technology, (iii) investing in organizational development and capacity building, (iv) focusing on transformation, (v) partnering with other service providers, and (vi) building good relationships with donors and host governments.

Chapter four by Tom Sanderson presents a description of Five Talents' microfinance programme. Five Talents (FT) was established by the worldwide Anglican Church in 1998 with a vision to help the poorest and empowering them in practical ways to bring hope. The inspiration was derived from the Parable of the Talents in Matthew 25:14-30 and its mission is to fight poverty, create jobs and transform lives by empowering the poor in developing countries through innovative savings and microcredit programs, business training and holistic development.

Since its inception in 1998, FT has impacted about 500,000 people, directly and indirectly, through its basic business training, savings and small loans. Currently FT operates through 11 local partners in 11 different countries and has 40,000 clients globally with an outstanding loan portfolio of about $3 million and accumulated savings of about $1.2 million. FT primarily provides savings and loan products offered through groups. Since FT is not a licensed deposit-taking institution, the savings are mobilized by informal groups known as Accumulated Savings and Credit Associations (ASCAs) and Village Savings and Loans Associations (VSLAs) formed by the clients themselves.

FT's role in this regard is to formalize and professionalize smaller microfinance NGOs to help them reach or move towards operational sustainability. The other products consist of financial literacy and business training. FT does not provide insurance products itself. However, some of its partners have linked up with local insurance providers to protect loans in the event of death or serious injury.

Tom Sanderson points out that while FT recognizes the number of people served as important its principal focus is on livelihood impact, transformation and serving the excluded and provides examples of impact on children, clients, employees, families and gender and markets. In this regard, FT's tag-line has become *"smaller, poorer, riskier"* providing smaller loans to poorer people in more risky circumstances.

Sanderson also describes the Christian distinctives as manifested in FT's work as follows: FT was a church-based initiative, the name Five Talents drawn from the Parable of Five Talents signals its Christian identity, the board of directors and staff profess the Christian faith, the motivation and energy is inspired by Jesus' compassion and priority for the poor, prayers, witnessing as appropriate opportunities arise and working with and through the local Anglican Church.

In the last part of his paper, Sanderson discusses three challenges faced by FT: (i) debt forgiveness expected by clients struggling with the repaying of their loans emanating from the prayer, "Lord forgive us our debts as we forgive those who have debts against us", (ii) human capacity related to the problem of finding qualified branch managers, loan officers, accountants and board members particularly in rural areas and (iii) financial constraints as raising donations required for expansion, new branches and new programs often outstrips resources.

In chapter five, Richard Reynolds and Nate Brown describe the work of VisionFund International (VFI). This is a subsidiary of World Vision International (WVI) established in early 2000 to manage and own all the microfinance institutions initiated and supported by WVI in 35 countries. Although some of its partners provide savings and insurance services, VFI is primarily focused on the provision of credit. Over 80% of the loans are for business. Other non-business loans include housing loans (approximately 10%) and school fee loans where clients can demonstrate a clear impact on the lives of children. VFI is part of a child-focused organization and seeks to enhance sustained wellbeing of children and fulfilment of their rights within families and communities.

The microfinance intervention is planned and implemented as an integral part of World Vision's wider effort to enhance community development within the context of its Area Development Program

(ADP). The primary purpose of WVI is to promote human transformation, seek justice and bear witness and the microfinance services provided through VFI to support businesses is an additional expression of God's love and witness to His Kingdom. By September 2012, VFI had served about 700,000 active borrowers of whom 68% were women.

The products for which the loans are used include: agriculture/livestock, trading and services, cottage industry, housing and school fee loans. Voluntary savings mobilization is seen as complex and risky and is therefore not a common practice. The same applies to insurance services that are limited to the provision of life insurance whereby the loan amount is repaid in case of death.

Non-financial services are carried out by both the WVI national offices and the VFI-managed MFIs. The former provides general training on community development (health, nutrition, HIV/AIDS, malaria, and family life), relief and emergency matters while the latter focuses on client education related to financial literacy and business skills. Each of VFI's partners has its own well-developed MIS utilizing everything from simple spreadsheets to sophisticated multi-faceted systems. In some countries, such as Kenya and Uganda, mobile banking is being used to make payments while the utilization of mobile devices for collecting data is being piloted in Tanzania and Cambodia.

The three lending methodologies employed by VFI include: community banks of 15-30 members, solidarity groups of 3-6 members and individual loans. As regards impact, the authors demonstrate that VFI's over-arching goal is to achieve sustained well-being of children within families and seeks to see that girls and boys enjoy good health, are educated for life, experience the love of God and that their neighbours and are cared for, protected and participating. VFI sees these as necessary measures of success but not sufficient. Indicators that express the power of God's love, community well-being, regard to God's creation – also need to be considered.

Some of VFI's Christian distinctives include seeking to follow Jesus in all that it does, being from diverse Christian traditions – Catholic, Orthodox and Protestant, incorporating Christian witness in its operations, supporting the spiritual development of its staff, viewing products and services as one piece of holistic development, establishing

God-honouring relationships, seeking to provide hope to clients with its products, understanding and valuing a diversity of beliefs and faith traditions, encouraging and incorporating prayer in the lives of staff, and being complementary to the church. The main challenges the authors identify as facing VFI are cultivating a diverse staff from varied faith backgrounds, maintaining its Christian identity amidst a diversity of opinions, and reducing the potential for fraud.

Chapter six by Peter Greer and Anna Haggard, presents Hope International's (HOPE) programme. HOPE officially registered its first microfinance institution in 1998, when Calvary Monument Bible Church from Central Pennsylvania realized that its "hand-out" project implemented since 1991 in partnership with a sister church in Zaporozhe, Ukraine, was found "harmful" to long-term sustainable development and decided to embark on a "hand-up" initiative and one of the leaders, Jeff Rutt, offered 12 individual loans to entrepreneurs in the Church. HOPE's primary purpose is to use microfinance as a tool for alleviating physical, spiritual and social poverty and is committed to share the Gospel of Jesus Christ unashamedly, respectfully, and sensitively. It includes Christian teaching and principles in every aspect of its work.

The paper describes the different stages of HOPE's growth and conception, their view of poverty and core values which are rooted in broken relationships and God's love respectively. In addition to spiritual and financial education, HOPE offers a variety of services to economically active people living in poverty engaged in savings and credit associations, micro-enterprises and SMEs through ROSCAs, ASCAs, and SSGs (Straight Savings Groups)[3] for savings and through community banks, solidarity groups and individual loans. Today, HOPE serves 450,000 clients through its network of microfinance and church-based savings programmes in 16 countries. About 88% of HOPE's clients are women.

The paper also points out that proclaiming and obeying Jesus Christ is at the heart of HOPE's mission and demonstrates in detail that some of its Christian distinctives: (i) a prayerful dependence upon the Holy Spirit for eternal impact, (ii) including spiritual integration and effective outreach in specific country-level planning, (iii) recruiting Christian staff, (iv) a commitment to spiritual formation for its staff and clients, (v) partnering with the local church, (vi) a commitment to funding its mission in ways that enhance the proclamation of the Gospel.

As regards challenges faced by HOPE, the paper shows that these emanate from HOPE's choice of working in hard places and its Christ-centred identity. In the former case, the challenges include (i) foreign exchange risk due to fluctuating currency values caused by economic instability, and (ii) difficulty in getting approval for registration caused by political instability and civil war. In the latter case, the challenges include (i) difficulty in accessing funding from corporations and secular foundations caused by HOPE's overt Christian mission, and (ii) difficulty in recruiting employees who are both a technical and mission fit for its Christian niche and particular dedication to working in challenging environments.

John Mwara's and Jacqueline Nyaga's paper, chapter seven, presents the operations of Faulu Kenya (FK). This paper is somewhat different from the other four papers as it deals with a local CMFI with a programme within one country. FK started in 1991 as a programme of the American-based NGO, Food for the Hungry, to offer financial services on a sustainable development approach and became the first regulated deposit-taking MFI in Kenya in 2009. The vision is *giving Kenyans hope and a future* and the mission is *to listen and empower Kenyans by providing relevant financial solutions* in line with its Christian ethos. The first core value relates to the *Lord Jesus Christ* that is exemplified by hard work, love, compassion and commitment in the transformation of lives by being plugged in to God himself.

The authors give a detailed account of the different financial and non-financial products offered through group and individual methodologies. Currently, FK serves over 396, 650 urban and rural-based customer accounts through 101 service outlets comprising 27 banking branches operated by more than 800 staff members. By November 2012, FK had an outstanding loan portfolio of $54 million and $41 million in deposits. During 2010-2011, over 19,000 lives were covered under FK's health insurance scheme and a total of 50,000 were trained in financial education. In 2011, the gender composition of FK's clients stood at 55% and 45% for males and females respectively.

In terms of sectors, FK targets micro, small and medium businesses in the manufacturing (e.g., metal, food and cloth works, light industries), agriculture, commerce, and service sectors, of which the latter two constitute about 93% and agriculture about 7%. The success of FK has partly depended on its continued investment in modern technology including an e-loan product in 2009, mobile phone banking in 2010, the T24 banking system and other key channels. Its marketing and branding strategy with the tagline, *"Your Bridge to Success,"* has also contributed to its recognition as a significant market player in the Kenyan financial sector.

Despite its overall success, FK has faced several challenges some of which relate to (i) stagnated business performance following the post 2007 general election and recurring drought, (ii) poor infrastructure in the areas with the highest target customers making reaching the unbanked difficult, and (iii) staff capacity gaps created by transformation to a deposit-taking business model as most of the staff had a credit-only microfinance background.

In chapter two, Makonen Getu provides a brief history of modern microfinance in general and in chapter eight he presents a response to current microfinance criticism from a Christian perspective by using the five case studies in a synthesized way.

DEFINITIONS

For practical purposes, CMF is defined as a microfinance programme motivated, designed, implemented, monitored and evaluated with God's love and purpose at the centre and is undertaken by Christian organizations and individuals to provide the economically active poor with access to financial and non-financial services in their fight against poverty. In other words, CMF is about the provision of financial and non-financial services to people living in poverty to enable them to expand or start economic and social businesses to create income and employment opportunities for themselves, their families and communities with a vision, mission, values, standards, and practices rooted in Jesus Christ's call to love and serve people living in poverty. As discussed below, the core business of CMF can be synthesized as providing individuals, families and communities with opportunities for deep seated transformation. A CMFI is, therefore, an institution that is implementing microfinance programmes with a Christian ethos as a means of realizing sustainable transformational development in response to the call of Christ. It is the work of CMFIs that constitute CMF.

However, CMFIs are not:
1. Discriminatory – they love, respect and serve all people regardless of religion, creed and gender,

2. Proselytizers – they do not evangelize[4] nor attempt to use financial services to coerce conversion,
3. Denominationally affiliated – they embrace ecumenism,
4. Exclusivists – they work among and in partnership with non-faith-based MFIs and other development players by actively participating in and contributing to all types of microfinance movements and networks at global, regional and national levels.

MOTIVATION AND VALUES

The microfinance work of CMIs is motivated and inspired by the love of Jesus Christ. All they do is in response to God's call to serve people in poverty by giving food to the hungry, water to the thirsty, clothing to the naked and shelter to the homeless.[5] Herein is the root of the mission of CMFIs: to fulfil God's will for people living in poverty through the provision of financial and non-financial services in accordance with Christian values and principles which inform and direct the way they do business. To cite some, Opportunity's core values relate to commitment, respect, humility, integrity, stewardship and transformation. HOPE's corporate cultural statement includes: prayer, allegiance, service, stewardship, innovation, optimism and nurturing. These are principles to help HOPE in conducting business in a Christ-like manner. VisionFund's core values include seeking to follow Jesus, a commitment to people living in poverty, valuing people, stewardship, partnership and responsiveness.

SPIRITUAL DIMENSION[6]

Although there is now a general recognition that poverty is "multi-dimensional" in nature, the conventional focus is still on the material dimension. CMFIs view poverty as having not only material and social dimensions, but also a spiritual dimension. CMFIs' raison d'etre is wholistic and sustainable transformation of lives and communities in line with Christian values and principles. As such, CMFIs contend that poverty can be effectively reduced only through a wholistic development approach which addresses both material and spiritual poverty, not only the former as is conventionally the case. Poverty alleviation measures, including microfinance, therefore, seek to improve the spiritual and mental well-being of people living in poverty. Why do CMFIs find the spiritual dimension such an important component of human flourishing? There are three main reasons:

1. Christian faith instils in people new values that, in turn, improve character, attitudes and behaviour. It enhances the level of integrity, responsibility and performance among people.[7] As a result of the spiritual transformation they experience, clients often become more effective in their business, and more transparent and reliable borrowers. In other words, business performance (economic transformation) and spiritual transformation are complementary and intertwined. CMFIs do not perceive these as two opposites but as two sides of the same coin.

2. The stronger and deeper their Christian faith, the more motivated they are by the love of Christ, the more love, forgiveness, mutual care and mutual trust clients extend to one another. Human relationships are restored and strengthened resulting in reconciliation, harmony and peace among community members and groupings, thereby creating a favourable socio-economic environment for sustainable transformational development.

3. While this is the conceptual rationale CMFIs seem to lay for the positive impact of spiritual transformation as part of the poverty reduction effort, many of the CMFIs neither engage in direct evangelization nor do they see that to be their niche. They rather demonstrate the love of Christ primarily through deeds and lifestyles.[8] The staff members of CMFIs, particularly loan officers, witness the love of Christ among clients by the way they lead their lives, including humility, commitment, integrity, stewardship, respect and care. Loan officers are expected to demonstrate these Christian virtues and traits in more tangible and concrete ways. Respecting appointments and commitments made, treating clients with respect even when things get rough, listening to and valuing clients' voices and practicing ethical living, visiting and praying for them when they are sick or are mourning and celebrating. All these are part of living out the love of Christ in a tangible way among clients being served.

CHURCH COLLABORATION[9]

The local church has been given an increasingly growing attention by donors and local governments as a vital partner in development. CMFIs recognize the socio-economic role the church has played throughout history, past and present. The church has made and is making critical contributions not only in the spiritual but also in the economic, social and political realms of societies. This is being increasingly recognized by both local governments and donor agencies which are all seeking to partner with the church in the fight against poverty. Because of their faith orientation, CMFIs do see themselves as intimately aligned with the church and have a natural inclination to collaborate with it in more effective and transforming ways in the delivery of services among people living in poverty.

This is done in both direct and indirect ways. While some do it in both ways, others do it only indirectly. Some of the direct ways include channeling funding and recruiting clients through the church, giving loans to finance church projects and developing church capacity through training activities, including financial education.

Some of the indirect ways relate to contributions made by CMFIs' staff and clients. As more staff are employed and trained, they bring to the church the skills that they gain through CMFIs and make more financial contributions through increased tithes, offerings and donations. The same goes for clients whose skills and incomes increase as a result of their participation in CMF programmes, which, in turn, enable them to make increased tithes, offerings and donations.[10]

The CMFIs benefit from the work of the local church as well. The church that specializes in teaching the Gospel contributes to spiritual transformation among CMFIs' staff and clients through internal church activities and outreach. CMFIs also have access to the physical and organizational infrastructures and strong community links of local churches to increase their outreach.

In short, CMFIs are not only in the business of disbursing and collecting debts, mobilizing savings, transferring money and providing insurance services and giving training. They are also in the business of enabling individuals, families and communities to produce more, have more and become better materially, socially and spiritually. CMFIs place people and transformation at the heart of microfinance. Their work contributes to the strengthening of the work of the local church and the work of the local church, in turn, strengthens the combined transformational impact of CMFIs on the lives of people living in poverty.

BACKGROUND HISTORY OF MODERN MICROFINANCE
MAKONEN GETU

Modern microfinance has now been implemented globally as an anti-poverty intervention for over forty years. The global effort to provide access to financial services among people living in poverty has gone through several distinctive but overlapping phases. This chapter is devoted to providing a brief history of microfinance as a background by presenting the emergence and circumstances of the various specific dominant features characterizing the industry at a given point in time. The division of the history into different phases does not imply a situation in which one phase is completely done away with and is replaced by another one.

THE PRECURSOR (1960-1975)

> *The history of financial services for the masses is surprisingly long and rich. For centuries, intelligent, ambitious, and empathic men and women have toiled at this task. Microfinance is an heir to their labors.*[11]

In his book, *Due Diligence*, David Roodman provides an excellent exposition of the rich history of microcredit. Starting from the early days of the 17th century when the author and nationalist, Jonathan Swift, embarked on providing microcredit services in response to the crushing poverty that gripped Ireland, well-doers across the globe and over the centuries have worked to provide financial services.[12] In Africa, the provision of credit to micro-businesses and/or informal activities in Africa is said to date back to the 15th century with the *susus* of Ghana and the *tontines* of West Africa.[13] This chapter serves to give a brief account of how modern microfinance started and evolved over the last four decades.

Soon after World War II ended, the world was divided into socialist and capitalist blocs leading to the Cold War. This was also the time when several colonies were gaining their independence and intensifying their struggle for freedom from the various colonial powers, mainly the British and French. Primarily driven by the struggle for sphere of influence, Western Europe under the auspices of the United States of America, started extending foreign aid to the developing world. The post-war achievements of Western Europe, made possible through the implementation of the Marshall Plan that was funded by foreign aid provided by the US government, served as a source of encouragement and inspiration.[14]

The infrastructure-focused Western aid to the developing world failed to generate results on par with those seen in Western Europe and several developing countries were faced with widespread food crises. In response, one of the key interventions made by Western donor agencies in the 1960s and early 1970s related to the implementation of the "Green Revolution" which included the application of modern technology, high-yield variety seeds, fertilizers, pesticides, and irrigation as an effort to increase food production.[15] This was popularized and spread following the success of the research conducted by Norman Borlaug, an American scientist, who developed a high-yield variety of wheat in Mexico in the 1940s enabling the country to move from a wheat importer to an exporter in the 1960s.[16]

The high cost of innovation related to the Green Revolution resulted in exclusion for people living in poverty. A donor-funded subsidized credit scheme was established, therefore, to cater for the needs of the poor farmers through the provision of cheaper agricultural loans. This effort was crafted to aid in increased agricultural productivity and food security. The scheme was operated mainly by state-owned rural development banks and, in some cases, co-operatives that received concessional loans for on-lending to customers at interest rates that were below the market. The lending programme failed to achieve the intended objectives because the lenders suffered huge losses partly because interest rates were too low and cost structures were high and partly because they were poorly managed, resulting in high default rates. In most cases, the loans ended up in the wrong hands including those of well to do farmers, politicians and bureaucrats. Much of the total loan capital disbursed was never recovered.[17]

Although the Green Revolution increased overall agricultural production by "betting on the strong", the problems of people living in poverty remained unsolved. As credit schemes became politicized and corrupt, people living in poverty were sidelined. The subsidized credit scheme, managed and implemented by government-led financial institutions, including rural development banks, was generally recognized as a failure. A study by Mercy Corps summarized the phenomenon as follows:

> Between the 1950s and 1970s, governments and donors focused on providing agricultural credit to small and marginal farmers, in hopes of raising productivity and incomes. These efforts to expand access to agricultural credit emphasized supply-led government interventions in the form of targeted credit through state-owned development finance institutions, or farmers' cooperatives in some cases, that received concessional loans and on-lent to customers at below-market interest rates. These subsidized schemes were rarely successful. Rural development banks suffered massive erosion of their capital base due to subsidized lending rates and poor repayment discipline and the funds did not always reach the poor, often ending up concentrated in the hands of better-off farmers.[18]

The exclusion of people living in poverty from the formal financial sector and their continued borrowing from the local money-lenders at exorbitant interest rates led to widespread criticism and discontent arose from academics and donors. The view advocated by the critics related to the operation of credit schemes in a more business-like manner, including charging commercial interest rates, holding borrowers responsible for repayment and lenders for their own bottom lines.[19]

The continued exploitation of people living in poverty by the local money-lenders, the failure of government-led and subsidized credit schemes and the debate on the concept of running credit operations in a business-like manner set the precursor for the emergence of modern microfinance. When the microcredit initiative was taken by pioneers like Muhammad Yunus, partly to liberate people living in poverty from the exploitation of local money-lenders and partly to prove that people living in poverty were "credit worthy", the leading donors involved in credit operations at the time were prepared to accept the new lending approach and work in favour of people living in poverty.[20]

THE INNOVATION PHASE (1975-1995)[21]

Mohammad Yunus recognized the severity of the level of poverty in his country and the cruel exploitation of the poor by loan sharks. Inspired by their creativity, Yunus started lending his own money to vendors in 1976 in the village of Jobra, Bangladesh, as an experiment with the aim of helping people living in poverty to free themselves from the local money-lenders. The borrowers repaid their loans successfully and proved to the world that people living in poverty were "bankable." Yunus then established the loan products, terms, sizes and methodologies tailored to meet the conditions and needs of those living in poverty. Eventually, the Grameen (Village) Bank was established in 1983.[22]

The innovative tools and methodologies developed and practiced by Grameen can be described as follows: loans were given to those living in poverty both individually and in groups. Despite the small variations, the various group-lending methodologies meant that the borrowers self-selected members they knew and trusted to co-guarantee each other's loans in order to avoid default in the event a member failed to pay his/her loan. Loan sizes were smaller for group borrowers than individuals in order to make repayment affordable and less burdensome. This also meant that loan terms were shorter for the former than the latter. Subsidized interest rates were removed and commercial interest rates and fees were introduced. Savings were required for accessing loans. Since women were typically more responsible for household economy and the well-being (food, health, and education) of children, and more responsive and successful at repaying loans than men, they became the main targets of microfinance programmes.

Loans were initially as small as $30 and $50. As groups repaid loans, over time the loan size increased. Cycle-based loan increases served as incentives for borrowers to fully repay their loans in a timely manner to be able to access a higher loan size. Loans were applied for and repaid as a group on a weekly basis. The first term was set to be 4-6 months increasing up to 12 and then 36 months depending on loan sizes. Loan sizes were higher to borrowers in solidarity groups and to individual clients who borrowed on the basis of loan guarantees and paid on a monthly basis. An incentive was established to graduate group borrowers into individual clients in order to accommodate the desires of clients who needed higher loan sizes to grow their businesses.

The above mentioned innovations were meant to (i) make access to financial services easier and cheaper to the clients and (ii) enable the MFIs cover their costs in order to become sustainable (self-sufficient) and increase their outreach. These innovations were adopted and practiced by other organizations in Bangladesh and throughout the world. The

Bangladesh Relief Assistance Committee (BRAC) established in 1972 and the Association for Social Advancement (ASA) established in 1978 were the first two major Bangladeshi NGOs that followed the Grameen model. Although organizations such as ACCION (1961), Opportunity International (1971), and Bank Rakayat Indonesia (1972), and others started giving loans before, the Grameen Bank of Bangladesh, led by Professor Professor Mohammad Yunus, was at the forefront of this revolutionary breakthrough. "The microcredit movement grew organically in the 1980s out of the early work in Bangladesh and small Latin states. Ideas spread through written reports and word of mouth."[23] While the initial spread of modern microfinance ideas and initiatives in Asia and Latin America took place more or less simultaneously in the early 70s, the innovation reached Africa and Eastern Europe about 20 years later in the early 1990s.

Other major innovations included the Self-Help Groups (SHGs) and Village Savings and Loans Associations (VSLAs). These were grassroots savings-led initiatives that created space for small informal savings and loans transactions run by and for the poor themselves. Members come together and make themselves socially and economically accountable to each other.[24] Unlike the village banking groups invented by Grameen whose primary task was to administer loans given to the group by external sources including MFIs, SHGs and VSLAs, they were about managing small savings mobilized by and lent to the group members themselves. The SHGs' approach was developed in India around the mid-1980s by Mysore Resettlement and Development Agency (MYRADA) when the co-operative societies it created during the period of 1983-85 broke up because they were too large and heterogeneous to lead and manage effectively. People preferred smaller and more homogenous ones and the large co-operatives were broken into groups consisting 20 members each becoming responsible for managing both savings and loans within the SHGs.[25]

The VSLAs methodology was invented by CARE International in Niger in 1991 following a handicrafts project aimed at helping women, developing into the *Mata Masu Dubara* (Women on the Move) programme and then spread across the rest of Sub-Saharan Africa and Asia. Africa is the birthplace of the VSLAs that are predominantly rural-based and, like village banking groups, each self-managed group consists of 20-35 members who could be classified as the lower segments of society.[26] Unlike conventional microfinance, the VSLAs model "attempts to build sustainable *traditions* rather than sustainable *institutions*."[27]

Even more informal grassroots mechanisms for pooling small savings of members related to what are known as Rotating Organization of Savings and Credit Associations (ROSCAs) and Accumulating Savings and Credit Association (ASCAs). In the case of the ROSCA model, members agree to contribute equal amounts of money and the total amount collected is received by any member at a mutually agreed frequency (weekly or monthly) on a rotational basis until the cycle reaches a point where every member has had his/her turn. The utilization of the money is fully determined by the member. The practice is a short-lived mechanism and often closes as soon as each member has got his/her share. There is no group intervention. Unlike ROSCAs, ASCAs were into mobilizing savings not for handing over to a member for individual purpose but for investment (group enterprise, establishment of interest-bearing revolving loan fund or group funeral fund).[28]

In village banking, conventional group members pay interest rates and fees that go to external lenders. In the case of SHGs, VSLAs, and ASCAs, the interest income remains within the groups and any interest income earned is shared between members at the end of the year or goes to group projects in the event that profit has been made. On the other hand, they receive external donations/grants to boost their capital base. These are also organizationally less complex and operationally less expensive to run as they rely on voluntary labour and involve limited local expenses.

The new tools and standards were received as a revolutionary way of reducing lending costs and ensuring a high repayment rate. Successful microcredit initiatives were implemented mainly in Asia and Latin America with high repayment rates proving that people living in poverty were "bankable." The average cost of lending decreased and the rate of interest revenue generated by service providers increased.[29] In the words of Johnson and Rogaly, the "... innovative features [of microcredit] in design have reduced the costs and risks of making loans to poor and isolated people and make financial services available to people who were previously excluded."[30]

As an anti-poverty intervention, the microfinance industry went from being run by public institutions to being run by NGOs. Concrete economic evidence proved that people living in poverty were "bankable" and "credit worthy". With high repayment rates and financial discipline, people living in poverty proved that they were better borrowers than those in the formal sectors. They were both willing and able to repay their loans with interest. Given the opportunity, those living in poverty had the ability to run profitable businesses. They did not need 'hand-outs", but rather a "hand-up". The provision of credit and related training was shown to be a powerful means of alleviating poverty. More and more people were enabled to create and sustain employment, increase their incomes and improve their standard of living through credit-funded microenterprises with a high on-time repayment rate.[31]

The evidence was so strong that bilateral, multilateral and private agencies began to show an increasing interest in microfinance as a development tool and started pouring money into microfinance programmes. Some studies showed that the funding from donor agencies increased from about $10 million in the 1970s to $100 million in the 1980s and to $400,000 million in the first half of the 1990s.[32] Following the donor recognition of the emerging role and popularity of the industry, CGAP was created in 1995 by 33 government and private agencies at a meeting hosted by the World Bank. The goal was to work together in expanding access to financial services for the poor in developing countries "with a mandate to coordinate international donor policy towards microfinance."

THE COMMERCIALIZATION PHASE (1995 TO PRESENT)[33]

NGO microfinance institutions (MFIs) began transforming themselves into regulated financial institutions during the third stage in microfinance history, the commercialization phase. Banco Sol in Bolivia began the transformation phase in 1992 and became the first commercial bank in the world with the sole purpose of providing microfinance services.[34] Despite the signs of change towards the end of the 1980s, the overwhelming majority of the MFIs operated as NGOs during the first two and half decades. This meant that their operations were not regulated or supervised by central banks. Moreover, although they were able to mobilize mandatory savings from their clients as a pre-condition for accessing loans, they were not licensed to mobilize deposits. The mandatory savings were not used for on-lending purposes. Most of the loan capital they used to run their operations was made up of donor grants.[35] Since 2000, the commercialization phase has become a dominant face of the microfinance industry.[36] A commercialized MFI is licensed and regulated by a central bank, meaning it has to meet all the necessary requirements, including, volume of capital, governance, competence, technology and infrastructure, which are much higher and more expensive than operating as an NGO MFI. There are different types of regulated entities: deposit-taking, loan and savings limited and commercial banks. Although the requirements vary for the three stages across different jurisdictions, they can all mobilize voluntary savings from the public that can be used for on-lending purposes. The other aspect of the commercialization phase relates to the conversion of MFIs into profit-making entities open for not only social investors but also private investors sharing dividends.[37]

Another development that occurred during the commercialization phase was the proliferation of microfinance investment ventures (MIVs) across Europe and America. The first MIV, ProFund, was established in 1995. By the end of 2009, more than 100 MIVs were in the business of lending (debt), investing (equity) or both, mostly in successful MFIs with a stronger appetite and capacity to absorb capital easily and quickly.[38] The capital need that was created by the expansion of the microfinance industry across the globe was partly met by these investment fund management entities and came at the time bilateral grant started dwindling.

Still another aspect of the commercialization phase relates to the mass interest and participation of commercial banks. For a long time, the commercial banks did not actively participate in the microfinance sector. In the early 1990s, mainstream financial institutions started realizing the potential of microfinance and becoming active players. Commercial banks have entered the microfinance market both as wholesale lenders and active direct service providers by initiating their own microfinance programmes. This level of interest and participation has come about partly as a result of the work done by MFIs to prove the "bankability" of the poor and partly because of developments in technology and scoring methodologies that enabled risk-modeling and mitigation.[39]

During this phase, microfinance came to be widely embraced as a powerful tool for poverty reduction. In 1997, the United Nations Secretary General published a report that led to the passing of a resolution recognizing the role of microfinance in development and poverty reduction. The report also encouraged all donors, governments, NGOs and UN agencies to actively engage in its implementation of microfinance in the respective member countries.[40] Microfinance was also perceived as a means of achieving the Millennium Development Goals (MDGs).[41] The popularity and international recognition of the microfinance industry reached its peak when the UN declared 2005 to be the year of microcredit and the Norwegian based Nobel Committee awarded the Grameen Bank and its founder, Professor Mohammad Yunus, the 2006 Nobel Peace Prize as joint recipients "for their efforts to create economic and social development from below".[42]

According to the report on the state of microfinance released by the Microcredit Summit in 2011,[43] there were over 190 million active clients by the end of December 2009 served by over 3500 MFIs. Of these over 128 million were among the poorest at the start of the microfinance programme. This means that about 640 million people were positively impacted by microfinance. In terms of geographic distribution over 91.4% of the reported poorest clients were in Asia. About 82% of the 190 million clients were women.[44]

THE TECHNOLOGY PHASE

When the best equipment available to most MFIs was an electric typewriter, microfinance operations were done largely on a manual basis during the first 20 or so years. The best practice advantages that come with computerized accounting, recording and database development were almost non-existent. Computers were rarely used and were more of a status and privilege mainly available to upper-level executives. Financial data and reports from branches and satellite offices were hand-carried, or sent by post or by fax or communicated verbally over the phone and accounting was done manually. As a result, inaccuracies, delays and incompleteness were common problems. This adversely affected the provision of accurate, complete and timely information needed for making informed decisions by boards of directors and managers. Moreover, loan officers had to carry cash for client disbursements as well as weekly and monthly loan repayments to deposit in the clients' MFI accounts. These were very unsafe practices and resulted in loss of money through fraud and theft. Transactions were costly, time consuming and frustrating to both clients and service providers. The only way of addressing transparency and delivery problems was by the MFIs expanding their physical presence and by establishing branch and satellite offices in multiple locations.

Outreach was also limited to physically accessible places. People in difficult-to-reach areas were not served at all. Those in poverty living in rural and remote areas were, therefore, at a huge disadvantage as they remained excluded from the benefits of microloans.

During the last 10 years, the technological revolution has changed industry mechanisms and accelerated the way business is done in the microfinance industry. Computer hardware and software were developed to enable MFIs to install computerized Management Information Systems (MIS). The use of computers by loan officers has become a common and accessible necessity. This has made the flow of transactions and information faster, more reliable and transparent.

Other sets of innovative technology include biometric cards, point of sale devices, ATMs, mobile banks and cell-phone banking. Categorized as "e-wallets," these technologies have made financial services accessible to people living in previously "unreachable" areas. The technology phase has allowed for a new wave of branchless banking which has become a solution to reaching impoverished individuals living in marginalized and previously unserved communities.

As a result of the technology revolution and increased connectivity, MFIs are partnering with telephone companies to deliver cheaper, safer and faster financial services, including transfers and insurance, in places where this type of technology was previously thought impossible. According to Roodman:

> Overall, as seen in Brazil and Kenya, technology is rearranging the economics of banking the poor, centralizing core banking functions while decentralizing the interface to the customer. The new approach splits retail from wholesale while lining via wires and radio signals. The retailers are local shopkeepers who provide the interface between paper and electronic money. They substitute for the loan officers of traditional MFIs, but they do not hold clients' money.... The digital interface of a card or a phone doesn't make the human interface obsolete; rather, as

with M-PESA, it provides a new way to delegate customer service to people who can do it more cheaply than brick-and-mortar banks can do.[45]

By the end of 2012, about 65% of Africa's population was estimated to be in possession of cell-phones.[46] In Kenya, where the greatest advancements have been made so far, there are currently about 28 million mobile phone subscribers. The phone-based money transfer system, M-PESA was launched by Safaricom in 2007 and is widely used by millions of Kenyans to transfer, borrow, buy insurance products and do other transactions using their mobile phones.

Another important change that the technological revolution has brought about relates to the introduction of a new way of global funding in the industry. The most notable practice is the provision of loans by people in the West to micro-entrepreneurs in developing countries via the internet facilitated by Kiva, which was established in 2005 in response to the need for working capital among entrepreneurs in East Africa. This is done through the posting of borrowers' stories so as to connect the lenders with their clients on a human level. Kiva in its turn uses local partners (MFIs) to manage the loans at the field level.[47] By March 2012, Kiva had distributed over $300 million in loans from about 745,000 lenders funding about 391,000 loans over the internet.[48]

THE MOVEMENT AND CAMPAIGN PHASE

One important development that happened in the history of microfinance relates to the formation of national, regional and global networks bringing practitioners in different parts of the world closer together to generate opportunities for the standardization of tools and practices, advocacy, transparency and accountability.

For a large part of the history of the microfinance industry, both international and local MFIs across the various regions operated in isolation with little mutual exchange of information, knowledge and experience. With the exception of workshops organized by donor agencies, CGAP and SEEP that occasionally brought representatives from MFIs, there were no global, regional or national structures to strategically and systematically facilitate mutual knowledge sharing in a co-ordinated way.[49] This changed radically after the Microcredit Summit of 1997 organized as a project of RESULTS under the leadership of Sam Daley-Harris.[50]

The Microcredit Summit brought together about 3000 delegates from 137 countries for the first time in the history of the industry. The Summit concluded with the following joint declaration:

> *Our purpose as an assembly is to launch a global movement to reach 100 million of the world's poorest families, especially the women of those families, with other financial and business services by the year 2005. We commit to the development of sustainable institutions which assist very poor women and their families to work their way out of poverty with dignity.*[51]

The Summit endorsed several activities that would need to be undertaken to achieve the stated goal. These included: building MFIs' institutional capacity in both developed and developing countries; developing, announcing, implementing and updating institutional action plans; promoting a learning agenda and the exchange of best practices; raising awareness by working with the media; and mobilizing funding.[52] This gave birth to the global Microcredit Summit Campaign.

To date, the Microcredit Summit Campaign Secretariat has been facilitating meetings to work towards the achievement of the global goal through a cohesive unity of purpose. The 2006 Summit Campaign in Halifax, Canada, formulated a new 2-fold goal of reaching 175 million of the poorest families with credit and other services as well as working to raise the income of 100 million families above the dollar a day threshold by 2015. The most recent summit, held in Valladoid, Spain in November 2011 aimed to alleviate poverty and reach the MDG goals.

Similar meetings have also been held at regional levels in Africa, Asia, Europe, Middle East, and Latin America.[53] Another outcome of the Summit was the proliferation of national and regional microfinance institutions, networks and coalitions with their respective secretariats and boards. These have been instrumental in enhancing the microcredit movement across the globe through campaigns, policy dialogues, advocacy/lobbying, awareness raising, training, knowledge sharing, and standardization undertaken at national and regional levels. By creating global goals and action plans including advocacy, the Microcredit Summit

Background History of Modern Microfinance

Campaign became the mother of all campaigns, shaping the microfinance industry as a global movement.[54]

Initiated by David Bussau, the co-Founder of Opportunity International, the Christian Microenterprise Development (CMED) Summit was held 1999 in Jomtien, Thailand. The Summit brought together 300 participants representing over 100 Christian development agencies, CMFIs, Christian foundations, mission agencies, and Churches interested in, or already, implementing micro-enterprise development programmes. The Summit resulted in the formation of what came to be known as the CMED Network. This was followed by another Summit in 2001 at the same venue. It was attended by 330 Christian delegates agreeing to share micro-enterprise tools, techniques and models. The second Summit resulted in the creation of the Christian Transformation Resource Centre (CTRC) as a service arm (secretariat) of the CMED Network. In 2003, three regional CMED conferences were organized in Romania (for Europe), Kenya (for Africa) and the Philippines (for Asia). Although the CMED Network never evolved as a coherent co-ordinating and lobbying body of the CMED institutions, CTRC now known as the Wholistic Transformational Resource Centre has continued with its role as a service arm.[55]

The Small Enterprise Education Program (SEEP), established by group of practitioners under the leadership of Elaine Edgcomb and Candace Nelson in 1985, was another early network that played a significant role in the making and strengthening of the industry into a global movement. SEEP's mission was to "connect microenterprise practitioners in a global learning community" with the belief that "sharing practical experiences within a trusting environment would result in improved microenterprise development practices. Currently, SEEP has 124 member organizations in more than 170 countries and organizes Annual Global Network Summits where representatives "share common challenges and solutions, learn about the most current issues facing associations and strengthen their institutional and service delivery capacity. It also supports Regional Network Summits, whereby associations gather to "discuss the specific topics and challenges that are most important to them as a region". During the last 14 years, 6 global and 9 regional Microcredit Summit Campaign meetings were organized.[56]

Although it represented the donor community, CGAP was another key player that emerged in the 1990s and contributed significantly to the shaping of the microfinance movement. Established in 1995 by nine leading donors and practitioners to "develop and share best practices, set standards, and develop technical tools and models", CGAP has played "a pivotal role in developing a common language for the microfinance industry catalyzing the movement toward good practice performance standards and building consensus."[57] Today, CGAP's membership has grown to 32 agencies including multilateral and bilateral development organizations, private foundations and international financial institutions. CGAP continues to provide various technical services relevant to the microfinance movement. In addition to the production of tools and standards, CGAP has also conducted market and impact studies and enhanced skills and knowledge through training and publications provided to both the donor and practitioner communities.[58]

Making Cents International (MCI) established in 1999 was yet another network that contributed significantly to the microfinance movement. As its mission, MCI "seeks to improve economic opportunities with a particular focus on youth, women, and vulnerable populations." Its products and services include: agribusiness and value chain development, entrepreneurship education, financial literacy, workforce development, MSME development, youth inclusive financial services, youth enterprise and livelihoods, curriculum design and capacity building, and knowledge management and sharing. During the last 12 years of its existence, MCI has partnered with more than 4000 local organizations in over 50 countries. It also organizes annual conferences on topical issues that are attended both by practitioners and donors and is making significant contributions towards the evolution of a youth inclusive microfinance movement.[59]

The Child and Youth Microfinance International (CYFI), established in 2010, is the youngest in the microfinance movement. It is "dedicated to making sure that every child in the world has a savings account when they graduate from primary school and has the financial knowledge and skills to be able to operate this account." CYFI held its first ever international summit on 2-4 April 2012 in Amsterdam which was attended by 346 participants from 83 countries as well as 70 children and youth coming from 40 countries. The participants represented the public, private, financial and civil society as well as academics, and other experts in the field. Summit participants made a commitment to work collaboratively to reach 100 million children in 100 countries by 2015. The summit brought together policy-makers from Central Banks and Ministries of Finance and Education who were in a position to ensure the inclusion of child and youth friendly financial products in regulatory frameworks and financial education in school curricula.[60] Since then several regional meetings and campaigns have been organized, giving rise to the global child and youth finance movement.

Microfinance clubs have been established in major financial centres – such as the Microfinance Clubs of New York, Paris and UK. These are voluntary groupings of practitioners, financiers, policy makers, academics and enthusiasts who meet together to share and learn from visiting speakers. The Clubs have played an important role in spreading awareness and acting as a forum for learning about and addressing some of the success and challenges in the microfinance sector.

Both donor and recipient governments have been involved in microfinance from its birth in various ways. On the positive side, almost all governments in developing countries have been actively involved in the promotion of microfinance as a poverty alleviation tool. This was partly as a result of the global, regional and national advocacy undertaken by MFIs following the Microcredit Summit of 1997 which was attended by many statesmen/women and partly because of the UN decision in 1998 to declare 2005 an International Year of Microcredit. Kofi Annan, the then UN Secretary General, made the following statement:

The great challenge before us is to address the constraints that exclude people from full participation in the financial sector. The International Year of Microcredit offers a pivotal opportunity to engage in a shared commitment to meet this challenge. Together, we can and must build inclusive financial sectors that help people improve their lives.[61]

As a result, recipient governments have created structures and funding to participate both as direct providers and wholesale funders providing funding to MFIs as grants and/or as loans at concessionary rates. Many governments have developed microfinance policies and standards to be followed by both NGO and regulated MFIs to streamline roles and control systems so as to ensure accountability and transparency. The central banks have created structures and related resources to regulate and supervise microfinance operations.

The general will is to create an enabling environment for the practitioners in recognition of the positive impact microfinance has on job creation, income generation, financial inclusion and poverty alleviation. On the negative side, many governments have gone into direct implementation (e.g. 3 of the largest MFIs in Ethiopia are implemented by the Government) creating distortions in the microfinance market. Some have also politicized their microfinance programmes/schemes for political gain particularly around and during election times with the tendency to discriminate between political supporters and opponents by regions and social groups. In a number of cases, they have wrongly or rightly waged negative campaigns against MFIs and resorted to closing down microfinance programmes (Andhra Pradesh in India), disseminated "no pay" populist campaigns (Nicaragua).[62]

Other key movements included the Social Performance Campaign (SPC), Smart Campaign, and Microfinance Transparency. The SPC resulted in the formation of the Social Performance Task Force (STPF) with the aim to "engage with microfinance stakeholders to develop, disseminate and promote standards and good practices for social performance management and reporting."[63] Social performance was defined as the "effective translation of a microfinance organization's mission into practice in line with commonly accepted social values."[64] The 11 Social Performance Indicators (SPIs) categories that started being measured under the leadership of MIX in 2009 included: mission and social goals, governance, range of products and services, social responsibility to clients, transparency of cost of services to clients, human resources and staff incentives, social responsibility to the environment, poverty outreach, client outreach by lending methodology, enterprises financed and employment creation and client retention rate.[65]

The Microfinance Transparency (MFT) movement was established in 2008[66] with the vision to be "the venue for the microfinance industry to publicly demonstrate its commitment to pricing, transparency, integrity and poverty alleviation." Specifically, it aims to create "a forum for the industry to report what actual interest rates are and why interest rates in competitive microfinance markets need to be higher than in commercial finance." To achieve this, MFT collects prices on all micro-loan products around the world and reports those prices through the use of a common, objective measurement system. MFT develops and disseminates education materials to better understand the concept and function of interest rate and product pricing, and advocates the importance of transparent pricing.[67]

The SMART campaign, also known as the Campaign for Client Protection in Microfinance, was launched in 2010 by a coalition of MFIs, networks, funders and practitioners. Housed at the Center for Financial Inclusion, ACCION International, the SMART campaign aims to "ensure that providers of financial services to low-income populations take concrete steps to protect their clients from potentially harmful financial products and ensure that they are treated fairly." The Campaign recognizes the critical importance of taking concerted and proactive actions by the industry to safeguard the interests of clients. Over the last several years the campaign reached consensus to endorse and apply seven Client Protection Principles including: avoidance of over-indebtedness, transparent pricing, appropriate collections practices, ethical staff behaviour, mechanisms for redress of grievances, privacy of client data, and mechanisms for complaint resolution. Currently, over 2000 MFIs, microfinance support organizations, investors, donors and individual professionals have pledged adherence to these principles developed in the spirit of putting the clients first.[68]

CONCLUSION

The provision of credit in small amounts for micro-activities undertaken by financially excluded impoverished individuals had been practiced throughout human history from biblical times. Modern microcredit or microfinance as we know it today started in the early 1970s. As in the past, contemporary microfinance was initiated by philanthropists with the aim to enable poor people to create jobs and generate income for themselves and their families by creating opportunities to access working capital that has been deprived by the mainstream financial market on the basis that they are "unbankable".

Pro-poor change agents, I will call them "microfinance revolutionaries", in different parts of the world, started microcredit schemes as a new way of tackling poverty in the developing world and thereby revolutionized the pro-poor credit system. With Grameen Bank at the helm of the new wave of change, innovative financial products, methodologies and tools were experimented and developed in the 70s and widely applied. They were successful in opening opportunities for accessing financial services by the poor, especially women, in ways and numbers that were never seen before and thereby brought about the microfinance revolution.

What exactly motivated these microfinance revolutionaries to do what they did? At least three possible reasons were behind the new revolution: (i) The failure of government-sponsored credit schemes to integrate and bring direct benefits to the poor, on the one hand, and make business sense, on the other: the donor-funded credit schemes of the 50s, 60s and 70s ended up being bad practice in that they benefited the "better off", especially politicians, with a high default rate and with increased marginalization of the poor, (ii) The recognition that poverty would not be addressed effectively without creating access to financial services that would liberate the poor from the usurious interest rates they were being charged by local loan sharks and the related injustice that kept them vulnerable and unproductive; (iii) The recognition that the poor possessed great potential and ability to fight poverty and change their destiny for the better provided that they were given the opportunity of accessing financial means and tools to engage productively.

For a large part of its history in the 20th century, microfinance focused on one of its core components: credit. The common belief was that the economically active poor were unable to grow their income-generating activities due to lack of access to credit and that the provision of working capital would enable them to generate more income and employment opportunities and thereby alleviate their poverty. Hence the focus was on microcredit. Moreover, although there were instances of microcredit *plus* approaches, most service providers applied a "minimalist" approach throughout the 70s, 80s and, in most cases, even in the first half of the 90s.

During the last 15 or so years, the scene has changed radically: a more comprehensive range of products and services consisting of loans, voluntary savings, money transfers, insurance and non-financial products have been offered. Hence the shift was made from microcredit to microfinance. It has also made a geographic shift by moving from its focus on urban areas to the difficult-to-reach rural areas. Socially, it has moved from focusing only on women to including men, youth, children, beggars, minorities, and people with HIV/AIDS and disabilities.

Some of the main features that distinguish the microcredit and microfinance phases of the industry include the following:

Commercialization: This created opportunities for many MFIs across the globe to operate as regulated banks and savings and loans institutions that enabled them to provide savings services and mobilize deposits unlike the time when MFIs operated only as NGOs in the first 25-30 years of the industry. While prior to commercialization, NGO MFIs mobilized only "mandatory" savings mainly for ensuring commitment and security, the industry has now entered an era in which more and more regulated MFIs are mobilizing voluntary savings used for on-lending purposes. This was also the phase when the industry learnt that the poor had more need for savings services than credit, the reason being that all had something to save and less were involved in business and hence there was less demand for credit. In Africa, for example, 802 MFIs in 33 countries reported 5.9 million active borrowers and 19.1 million depositors by 2011. In Eastern Europe and Central Asia, 465 MFIs in 20 countries reported 2.6 million borrowers and 7.6 million savers during the same period.[69]

Insurance provision: The provision of insurance services to poor people was hardly talked about in the first 25 years of the industry. The emergence of insurance companies offering insurance services to microfinance clients made during the last 20 or so years has changed the face of the industry in the 21st century. It created more security for both clients and service providers leading to an increased number of people participating in and benefiting from the industry.

Customer-driven approach: Microfinance has moved from being supply-driven to being client-driven: listening to clients and doing business in response to what they need and want rather than offering only what service providers are able to supply, including softening their requirements. Increased competition among MFIs and improved knowledge of the industry among clients empowered them to shop around and negotiate more favourable conditions and thereby influence the way MFIs behave in the market. The days when MFIs "imposed" what and how to offer services are gone. Consultation and not "imposition" has become the order of the day. Clients are increasingly exercising more power and influence. As a result of this shift, MFIs have begun to pay attention to the voices of their clients more than what they did in the 20th century. MFIs have also demonstrated an increased level of understanding of poverty and how to support poor people rather than constantly badger them for repayments.

Coalitions and networks: Following the 1997 Microcredit Summit, MFIs have created global, regional and national platforms and made more concerted efforts to advance the quality and performance of the industry and its impact on the lives of clients. Some of these global efforts include: industry standards and procedures, client protection, microfinance transparency and accountability, financial inclusion and social performance measurement indicators. The various joint campaigns have been and are being undertaken so as to ensure that clients are not adversely affected by usurious interest rate, multiple borrowing and hidden costs, on the one hand, and to keep the integrity of the industry, on the other. The coalitions and networks have also played a critical role in the production and dissemination of mutual learning and strengthening of joint advocacy and lobbying.

Technological advancement: The expansion of internet technology made it possible for MFIs to use new delivery channels that enabled them not only to reach previously unreachable areas, but also offer new products and services. Internet technology and mobile banking have enable MFIs to offer a more comprehensive range of products and services in relatively faster, cheaper and safer ways. This was particularly made possible following the commercialization drive that reached its peak in the 21st century.

Increased availability of funding: During most of the 20th century, microfinance relied on grants from both bilateral and multilateral sources for both innovation and loan capital. While this type of funding has diminished in the 21st century, the industry's funding base has been strengthened further through the mobilization of equity, borrowed capital, deposits, and internally generated incomes. Sponsorship programmes as well as online lending entities such Kiva have also created more room for mobilizing capital by linking groups and individuals in developed countries to individual and groups of micro-entrepreneurs seeking capital in the South.

Over the 4 decades of its existence, microfinance has emerged into a $70 billion industry and served a client population of about 200 million households, where the overwhelming majority are women, across the globe experiencing different degrees of positive impact. Thousands of strong and committed local organizations with ability to provide continued services on a sustainable basis have been established. The achievement made by microfinance was globally recognized through the award of the 2006 Nobel Peace Prize to Mohammad Yunus and Grameen Bank for spearheading the industry to success.

According to the report on the state of microfinance released by the Microcredit Summit Campaign in 2011,[70] there were over 190 million active clients by the end of December 2009 served by over 3500 MFIs. Of these over 128 million were among the poorest at the start of the microfinance programme. This means that about 640 million people were positively impacted In terms of geographic distribution over 91.4% of the reported poorest clients were in Asia. Of the 190 million clients, about 105 million or about 82% were women.[71] By September 2011, the microfinance industry in Africa alone recorded 23,000 service providers spread across 45 countries serving 71 million loan clients, 44 million deposit accounts and 18 million mobile banking service users.[72]

Despite all this, microfinance has been a target of medium to extreme criticisms thereby ending the "honeymoon" of unrivalled celebration and acclamation that it enjoyed in the 20th century. However, microfinance continues to touch millions of lives in more positive ways than any other pro-poor interventions and continues doing business as usual. Its good sides and strengths outweigh the "bad" sides and weaknesses the critics have amplified to discredit and undermine the industry. Part of the task of this book is to argue along these lines. Without denying the "bad" sides and weaknesses, facing microfinance, this book aims to argue, using the five cases of microfinance programmes implemented by five CMFIs, that it still works, does a great deal of good to the poor and is here to stay. I will return to the criticism of microfinance in the last chapter.

OPPORTUNITY INTERNATIONAL CASE STUDY
MAKONEN GETU AND GENZO YAMAMOTO

Genzo Yamamoto (Ph.D.) is the Director of Knowledge Management at Opportunity International and oversees the review, research, evaluation, and knowledge generation in relation to Opportunity's projects. Prior to joining Opportunity International, he taught modern international political and intellectual history at Boston University and at Wheaton College. Genzo has researched or evaluated development projects in South Sudan, the DRC, Uganda, Ghana, Malawi, and India, and has directed on-site research in Colombia, covering a wide range of topics including savings and dormancy, housing finance, youth apprenticeship programmes, agricultural finance, and micro-insurance.

Opportunity International's history shows its strong commitment to serve the working poor through microfinance. It was established in 1971 and has continued its service for 42 years. This chapter presents the organization's inception and development, its continuing vision and mission, its current products and services, its achievements and challenges throughout the years, and its desire to reflect Christ in every aspect of its work.

1 HISTORY

1.1 The formative years: 1971-1983

Opportunity International began as a joint collaboration between two Christian philanthropists, Al Whittaker and David Bussau. Early on, Whittaker and Bussau played separate, but key roles in reaching and supporting poor communities around the globe. Eventually, their common vision to serve the working poor would lead them to come together and form Opportunity International.

Al Whittaker faced a turning point in his career during his business travels to Colombia. In 1971, Whittaker found himself severely beset by the people he saw struggling and toiling to earn a living each day. Their inability to generate income and find employment made Whittaker ponder what could be done to alleviate the hopelessness and poverty of this situation. He strongly believed that capital in the form of credit could act as a means to support people trying to work their way out of poverty.

In areas without any formal banking systems, simply having the opportunity to access credit and other basic financial services would revolutionize their efforts. Whittaker desired to provide desperately needed capital to microbusinesses and entrepreneurs in the community that would give them momentum to grow, become self-sufficient, and sustainable. This desire led him away from his corporate career in the United States and to start something new. After he traveled back to the US, Whittaker listened to a talk explaining ways Christian businessmen were helping people affected by poverty through finance. He saw this moment as confirmation to pursue his vision and make it a reality. At this point, Whittaker was confident that this was the way God's promptings had been pushing him throughout his life. Inspired and resolute, Whittaker went to great lengths to take his desire to serve the poor and the idea of providing financial services and make it into something tangible. First, he left his position as President of Bristol-Myers US and moved into a small town house in Washington D.C. Then with his personal savings, Whittaker founded the Institute for International Development Incorporated (IIDI). Its purpose was to help the poor in Latin America to become entrepreneurs and to expand business through microcredit. IIDI went into active service in Latin American that year with its first loan given to a client named Carlos Moreno. Even with small beginnings, Whittaker began to bring hope and restoration to many in Colombia. Whittaker's ongoing work with IIDI created many other partnerships and laid the foundation for the establishment of Opportunity International.

David Bussau's life had a similar moment of transformation causing him to reorient his life in new ways as well. In 1976, Indonesia experienced a devastating earthquake (magnitude of 7.1) that demolished houses, temples, schools and hospitals. The earthquake left 5,000 casualties and many others homeless, hopeless, and abandoned. In the face of the tragedy, Bussau recognized great need and wanted to help those struggling to survive. Bussau worked as a successful business entrepreneur in Australia, but chose to become involved in the reconstruction efforts in Indonesia because of the desperate need. Because Bussau worked in the construction business in Australia, he found it easy to start by helping to rebuild houses, dams, and church buildings in the areas of Blimbingsari, Bali. He moved from village to village, using his skills and finances to reconstruct whatever he could, even organizing efforts to support others beyond his immediate reach. As Bussau worked side by side with the Indonesian people, he became increasingly concerned about the lack of employment and income opportunities that they had. Like Whittaker, Bussau desired to support the poor in their efforts to build a life for themselves and their families. He envisioned a solution that fostered job-creation rather than charity donations. Bussau wanted to lend money to individuals who could start their own businesses and create jobs in their community. Because of this vision, Bussau put his ideas into action and began giving out loans. Over time, this generous process scaled across many others. He eventually began to see the success of his efforts in giving entrepreneurs loans. Businesses developed and many began to repay the loans that Bussau had given out. Encouraged by the results, Bussau sold all his assets and businesses to found a new institution called Maranatha Trust (MT). The purpose of the institution was to raise funds and expand the lending program he started for Indonesia, channeling funds coming from Australia. With help of a local church, Bussau helped establish Kapal farm. Kapal farm operated as a loan institution. It grew rapidly, providing micro-loans and vocational training to the people in the area. The lending program emerged as a successful model of a business-led community development, garnering international attention.

Whittaker and Bussau shared a vision that led them to build organizations that would come together to serve those working their way out of poverty. IIDI and Maranatha Trust slowly began working together, partnering to reach people around the world through microfinance. This partnership would link their programs to form a worldwide network gradually developing into something more cohesive. IIDI's lending operation in Latin America grew and began developing lending programs for people and families in Indonesia living in poverty. In 1979, Bussau met with an IIDI representative in Indonesia named Hillary de Alwis who visited Kapal farm to learn about the micro-lending program and practices there. With a shared sense of respect for the work IIDI had been doing, Bussau scheduled a meeting with IIDI's CEO, Barry Harper. Both shared a vision and a desire to expand services in Indonesia. IIDI decided to bring on Bussau as project manager of IIDI's infrastructural projects (funded by USAID). Then in 1981, Bussau repositioned Maranatha

Trust into the small business lending component for community development in Indonesia working closely with IIDI. This move further enhanced the partnership and work between Maranatha Trust and IIDI, integrating their services to provide a more comprehensive effort to alleviate poverty in the area. Combining Whittaker's strategic framework and focus with Bussau's energy and innovation continued to drive further development in areas stricken by severe poverty. When IIDI expanded its program to the Philippines, Bussau was tasked with the responsibility of "transferring the lending methodologies from Indonesia" to the people living in the Philippines. The first local affiliate, Tulay Sa Pag-Unlad Inc. (TSPI) became operational in 1981, granting its first loan in 1982.

1.2 The expansion years: 1984-1997

Between 1984 and 1997, IIDI began fortifying its organizational structure to enhance its capacity to serve, establishing new goals and forming new partnerships around the world. Early in 1984, IIDI hosted its first international conference in hopes to collaborate with its partners, refocus its vision to serve the poor, and open new paths for the future. The conference was held in Sag Harbour, New York and brought together many field implementers, donors, and affiliates all into one place. The body of partners, all of which were created by Opportunity, proposed new goals to help to clarify their mission and enable IIDI to have a greater impact as it expanded. Their goals were to continue having close relationships with affiliates that IIDI supported by changing the term "affiliate" to "partner" or "partner agency" so as to more accurately represent the working relationship between organizations. Secondly, after learning about the unique challenges each regional division of IIDI, members decided to grant regional directors decision-making authority, creating a more bottom up approach to organizational implementation. Thirdly, IIDI wanted to promote a greater number of partnerships with organizations already working in the field, allowing these local partners to operate independently for three years before integrating with IIDI. The fifth goal for IIDI was to significantly strengthen its ability to provide on-site technical support, operating funds, and loan capital to partners in these expanding regions (goal of $300,000 USD).

IIDI took these goals into action between the years of 1984 and 1988. It was a period of expansion and strengthening for the entire organization ultimately resulting in a permanent partnership with Maranatha Trust.

IIDI grew, partnering with several new organizations in the Philippines, Pakistan, Sri Lanka, India and Indonesia. Also, Latin American partnerships continued to multiply as well, extending into Costa Rica, Peru, the Dominican Republic, Guatemala, Jamaica, El Salvador, Colombia and Honduras. By 1991, IIDI established 28 partners in 15 countries across South East Asia and South America. IIDI and its global partner Maranatha Trust began contemplating a new joint partnership that would significantly interconnect all of the work being done in Asia and Latin America. They contemplated how a single vision structured under one umbrella organization more readily fit the future goals of both organizations. As the two institutions reanalyzed the core business practices, visions, and future aspirations of their respective organizations, they saw a lot of overlap and created Opportunity International to work as one unified entity. IIDI changed its name to Opportunity International in the late 80s while Maranatha Trust took on the Opportunity name in the early 90s.

By 1996, Opportunity International expanded its partnerships and services into Africa and Eastern Europe, becoming fully global organization spanning across 4 continents. Opportunity International's Africa program started in Zimbabwe through the creation of Zambuko Trust, located in Harare, in 1992. Other local partners were established in South Africa (1993), Ghana (1994), Uganda (1994), Zambia (1996), and Malawi (1998). Simultaneously, Opportunity International recognized the need in struggling communities in Eastern Europe after the collapse of communism. They set up microenterprise development programs in post-Socialist countries such as Russia, Poland, Bulgaria, Romania, Serbia, Montenegro, Croatia and Albania to revitalize the struggling communities suffering from weakened economies. By the mid-1990s, the number of total partners grew from 26 to 53. The immense impact attracted additional partners from the UK (1992), Canada (1994), and Germany (1996). During this portion of Opportunity International's history, it established itself as a premiere institution that provided credible and responsible business options for micro-entrepreneurs, implementing microcredit practices in all the four regions of the two-third worlds (Africa, Asia, Eastern Europe and Latin America).

1.3 The commercialization and innovation years: 1997 to present

With notable global expansion, Opportunity International's growth demanded internal adjustments to its complex networks and channels of communication that would allow it to effectively support the field partners and providing effective service. Opportunity International looked inward and realized that its rapid growth and complex network created a lot of fragmentation and inefficiency from within. Network Design Council (NDC) was tasked to survey and analyze Opportunity International's structure and streamline it. They hoped to create a new organizational design that would increase successful impact inter-regionally and internationally. NDC conducted in-depth interviews, streamlined communication channels, and monitored global trends in the micro-enterprise development industry. After two years of research, NDC recommended the establishment of the Opportunity International Network division that could provide oversight to Opportunity International's operations and network structure, laying out plans for this change. This change would enhance Opportunity International's ability to collectively serve in more coordinated, efficient, and strategic ways.

In order to ratify this organizational change, Opportunity International hosted a global conference (in 1997) to instate these changes and resolutions. Additional changes were made regarding membership standards, accreditation of service centers, governance rules, and financial regulations. The proposed formalizations of practices were presented and accepted. The new membership structure along with the new Opportunity Network office changed the way Opportunity International oversaw and coordinated its global work.

After the restructuring, Opportunity International reevaluated its past goals in light of its new structure and capacity. It developed three new goals to actualize its new identity as a corporate entity: outreach, quality, and impact. At a meeting in February 1998, the Opportunity Network board outlined a five-year vision statement focusing on the following three goals:

- Outreach: to provide a cumulative total of 2 million USD in loans to families living in poverty, with an overall arrears rate of no more than 2% in the five-year period of 1998-2002.

- Quality: to create a world renowned network of business leaders working in the global microfinance community.
- Impact: to empower clients in such a manner that they become agents of transformation in their own communities.

These goals emphasized increased financial capacity, excellence in the microfinance industry, and actions centered around human development. A strong effort from Opportunity International aimed to establish commercial banks as a means of fulfilling the organizational goals. The establishment of banking systems would provide increased means to encourage the communities Opportunity International aimed to help.

The first regulated microfinance bank of Opportunity International was established in the Philippines in 2001. Many more were later set up in Eastern Europe, Africa and Latin America. Opportunity International currently has a network of 53 microfinance banking institutions around the globe: 6 in Latin America, 11 in Africa, 18 in India, 4 in Indonesia, 11 in the Philippines, and 3 in Eastern Europe. Many of these banks are still developing a full range of products and services in the developing areas that meet the needs specific to their respective communities. However, 11 of the banks already provide a full range of financial services: loans, savings accounts, bank transfers, investment options, and insurance products that meet the regulations and standards of the central bank in each country where they operate. Also, Opportunity International decided to provide micro-insurance services to existing clients. Partnering with the Micro Insurance Agency (MIA), Opportunity International decided to investigate new products that could service current more. Opportunity International and MIA assessed 10,000 of its clients and found a substantial demand for micro-insurance products. Life, funeral and property insurance packages that could meet their client needs were developed in 2002. A few years later, crop insurance was added to the range of packages that Opportunity International offered. This work and partnership with the MIA resulted in the MIA becoming a wholly owned subsidiary of Opportunity International in 2005. MIA operated with an independent board and set of management structures. However in 2008, MIA evolved into a new organization called MicroEnsure in order to "better reflect its new status in the market, innovation and aspirations to serve the poor throughout the developing world." Based in Cheltenham,

UK, MicroEnsure emerged as a world leader in the micro-insurance industry, serving about 3.6 million and operating in 10 countries across Asia and Africa.

The commercialization process shifted Opportunity International away from providing unregulated credit packages to a full suite of financial and non-financial services through regulated banks and microfinance institutions that included deposit based transactions from clients and investors. This development allowed finance institutions to give communities options that they never had before and train them to become economically self-sustaining in ways that they could not as a non-governmental agency.

As Opportunity International continued to expand, its influence spread to the organizations that worked in regions. Opportunity International formed a vast array of strategic partnerships to reach even more people than before. These partnerships proved microfinance had a place in all areas of the developing world. This became more evident as Opportunity began providing services to a diverse set of clients in various sectors of developing economies. Many partners included Compassion International, Habitat for Humanity, World Vision, Tearfund, and Millennium Village Project. Additionally, through the Women's Opportunity Fund (WOF), Opportunity International gained key insights on how to focus on developing the cutting edge products and valuable services for people who needed the most in their financial lives. WOF was created and part of Opportunity and developed the "Trust Group" lending methodology which became a powerful group lending tool. Through its involvement with Opportunity International, WOF was able to advance the gender agenda within the Network amplifying fundraising opportunities.

2 ORGANIZATIONAL STRUCTURE

By design, Opportunity International promotes a structure that maximizes the coordination between all of its partners around the globe. Opportunity International spans across multiple countries in each continental region and has various divisions that play key roles in its operation.

The Opportunity Network is now governed by three bodies: the Board, the Executive Council and Meetings of Members. The international board primarily functions to provide leadership and carry out governance duties for all associated parties within the Opportunity International Network. They uphold and sustain the mission and vision of the organization. They develop business plans, strategies, policies, standard operating procedures, and criteria for granting membership. Sometimes the international board participates in recruiting, accepting, appointing, and supervising the performance of officers and the GMO's CEO. The international board of directors is composed of 5 SM Directors, 5 IM Directors, 2 independent directors, and a chair of the Association.

The Opportunity International network of partners can be understood as a composition of two primary types of affiliates supporting members (SMs) and implementing members (IMs), as well as a tertiary type of member called "affiliate members". At the 2011 Global conference held in Chennai, India, the supporting and implementing partners worked together to clarify the roles they have historically played In essence, the Support Members exist to raise grants, debt and equity to support the development and growth of the Implementing Members who are either NGO MFIs or regulated MFIs. A third and final category of Members includes Affiliated Members, which corresponds to non-voting members of the association.

Operationally, the implementation of Opportunity International's programs is coordinated and managed by the International Network Service Office now called Global Microfinance Operations (GMO). The GMO is managed by a CEO who reports to the international board GMO divisions include: HR, Finance, MIS, Risks, Audit, Communications, and Transformation.

3 CLIENTS SERVED AND PRODUCTS OFFERED

3.1 Overview

Opportunity International serves 4 million clients in 23 different countries across Africa, Asia, Eastern Europe, and South America. There are over 1.2 million savings clients with a total of $114 million in savings deposits, having $99 as the average savings balance. There are 2.8 million loan clients with a gross loan portfolio of $542 million. A majority of these clients are women (93%). Insurance coverage is provided to about 4 million people. Opportunity also provides capacity-building services related to business management or personal development and has trained about 6 million clients. Targeted data on 1.5 million loan clients suggest an average loan size of $310 – a value that has been driven up by inflation rates in Africa – with 30-day PAR averaging 7.9%. Studies in 2006 and 2008 of different but significant samples of network clients showed that 90% and 60%, respectively, earned $1-2 a day. Operational sustainability across the network is currently at 94.5% and financial sustainability at 89.8%.

Targeted financial products have been constructed to meet the needs of the poor in specific economic sectors:

- Energy – work in various banks has begun to offer alternative energy products that can provide solar or biofuel energy to clients for their own use and potentially as microenterprise resources.
- Housing – in conjunction with partners such as Habitat for Humanity, we have provided housing microloans that help families build, expand, and renovate their homes in conjunction with financial literacy training and construction technical assistance.
- Agriculture – using a lending model that considers family and land profiles, agricultural finance seeks to address not only the production of smallholder farmers, but also the whole value chain in conjunction with extension service providers who provide agricultural training.
- Health – health insurance offers the possibility of being able to come through unforeseen medical difficulties in situations that would have otherwise led them to fall into a cycle of indebtedness and loss of income-bearing resources.
- Education – financial services are provided to social entrepreneurs serving the base of the pyramid, to schools, and to parents who seek to ensure education for their children.
- Trade and service – financial services given to clients who retail supplies and provide services needed.
- Cottage industry – financial and technical services given to clients who "manufacture", furniture, metal products, household utensils, basketry, wood work, clothing (e.g. school uniforms), shoes, agricultural implements, agro-processing, etc.

Opportunity also offers non-financial, capacity building and other services. Capacity building and skill development takes place externally with clients, and internally within the network. With clients, Opportunity International provides a wide range of training for clients: financial literacy training, responsible agricultural practice, apprenticeships for skill development, family planning and counseling, nutritional advice, professional training, professional medical services for HIV/AIDS, and many others often depending on the needs of a community. Within the Opportunity network, capacity building programs have included, among other things, management and leadership training, board training, staff on-boarding training, financial literacy training, MIS training, service delivery (mobile technology) training, product development training, and SPM training offered to board members, managers and staff as and when appropriate.

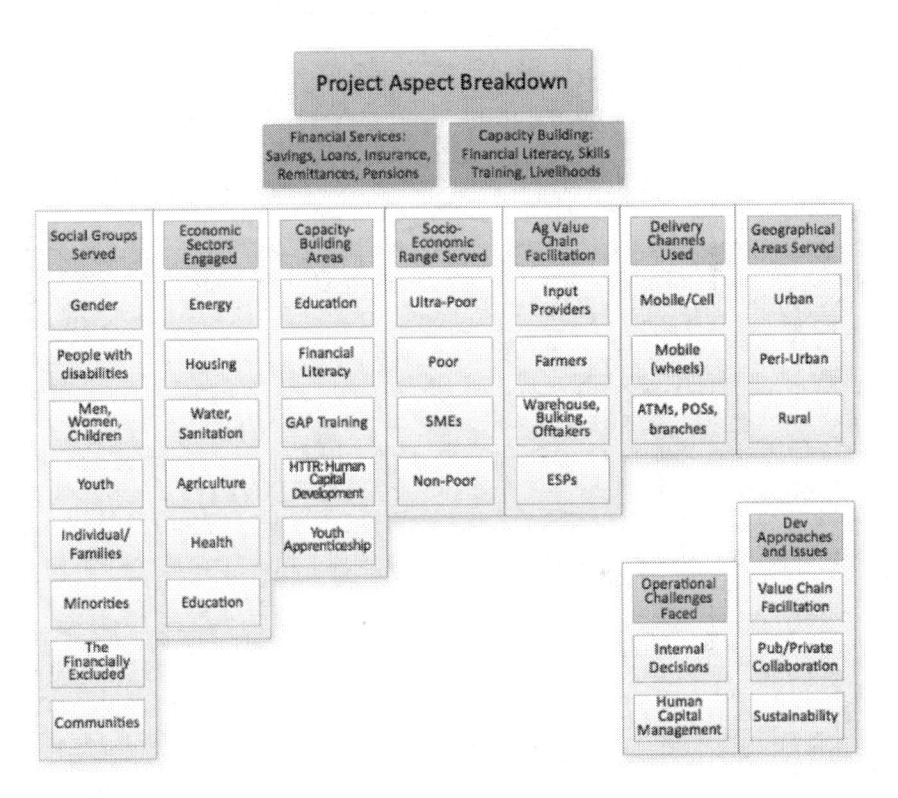

Project Aspect Breakdown

Financial Services: Savings, Loans, Insurance, Remittances, Pensions

Capacity Building: Financial Literacy, Skills Training, Livelihoods

Social Groups Served	Economic Sectors Engaged	Capacity-Building Areas	Socio-Economic Range Served	Ag Value Chain Facilitation	Delivery Channels Used	Geographical Areas Served
Gender	Energy	Education	Ultra-Poor	Input Providers	Mobile/Cell	Urban
People with disabilities	Housing	Financial Literacy	Poor	Farmers	Mobile (wheels)	Peri-Urban
Men, Women, Children	Water, Sanitation	GAP Training	SMEs	Warehouse, Bulking, Offtakers	ATMs, POSs, branches	Rural
Youth	Agriculture	HTTR: Human Capital Development	Non-Poor	ESPs		
Individual/ Families	Health	Youth Apprenticeship				Dev Approaches and Issues
Minorities	Education				Operational Challenges Faced	Value Chain Facilitation
The Financially Excluded					Internal Decisions	Pub/Private Collaboration
Communities					Human Capital Management	Sustainability

47

3.2 Financial Services

Savings

Recent studies show that savings practices and services mitigate some of the recurring and significant challenges for people living in poverty. However, only a small portion of the world's population living on less than two dollars a day has the opportunity to access any financial services at all (no more than 23%). This demographic has no safe means of saving or investing capital. Many simply do not have a secure place to keep their money or cannot find financial institutions that will bring services to them. Opportunity International brings financial services to these communities allowing individuals to put their capital in trusted institutions for the first time. These services aim to be convenient, secure, and interest-bearing savings accounts, slowly revitalizing poverty-stricken communities. Also, savings services helps people prepare building capital that they can draw upon in times of need. Without these savings opportunities, people are led to use insecure means of saving. Many might try to save by hiding money in their homes, give money over to collectors who promise safe keeping at a price, or purchasing items that do not depreciate significantly in value, such as livestock or jewelry. However, these options often result in a net loss of earnings, creating an ever present resistance in growth of their capital. Rather than restricting the utilization of personal earnings as the afore mentioned possibilities often do, microfinance institutions help many to provide for their immediate needs and open up the possibility for future investments and business opportunities of their own by providing fair and reasonable ways of saving.

While the basic concept of a savings product is fairly simple, Microfinance institutions must go through numerous steps before it can actually deliver savings products and services. In order to ensure that the proper client safe guards are in place, microfinance institutions (MFIs) must first become regulated banks to receive deposits. This is a lengthy application process that requires government oversight and reporting to obtain the status of becoming a regulated bank. Such regulation requires MFIs to have the capacity to provide for reserves, cash floats, loans, and other products before they can be authorized to take deposits for savings accounts.

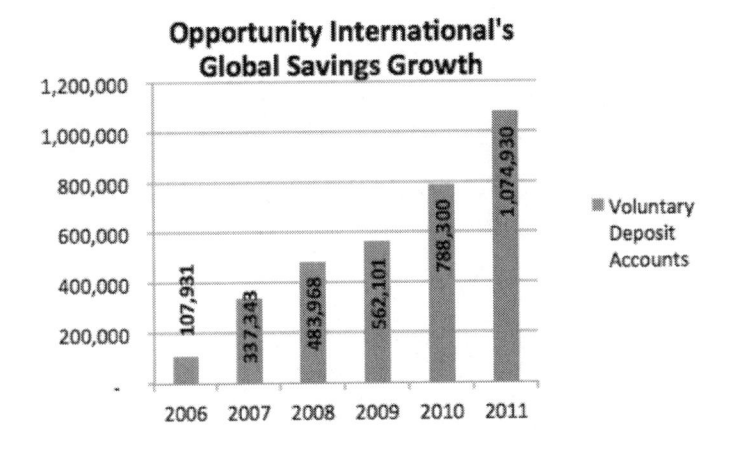

Opportunity International's Global Savings Growth

Year	Voluntary Deposit Accounts
2006	107,931
2007	337,343
2008	483,968
2009	562,101
2010	788,300
2011	1,074,930

There are also, many cultural challenges that inhibit the use of savings services. For clients that have little experience in formal banking, savings is a difficult product to sell due to limited financial literacy. They do not see the point nor the benefit of using them. Others may find it unfamiliar and distrust the bank altogether. Because, clients are unaware of formal savings products and their benefits, bank staff must be trained to incentivized and retain the use of savings products. Travel distances add to these deterring factors preventing people from actively saving over time. In order to overcome these challenges, Opportunity International follows a general methodology when approaching savings. It understands that financial literacy is crucial and ideally starts training staff to be able to communicate and market the bank's product and services. The training extends beyond presentations. Training actually engages staff through a variety of educational methodologies.

To make the products more attractive, Opportunity International continuously develops savings products to meet the needs of their clients, helping them to prepare for the most difficult of circumstances. Most Opportunity International banks initially start off with two basic savings products: ordinary savings accounts and fixed deposit accounts. While Opportunity's average savings balance is $99 USD, ordinary accounts have no specific minimum. In Malawi, Opportunity International requires 500 kwacha, or 3 USD (April 2012), as a starting balance, while Opportunity bank in Uganda requires no initial deposit. These policy choices reflect the consideration of unique regional elements in the implementation of effective services. For many of Opportunity International's savings accounts the interest rates fall between 5% and 7%. Other clients who can afford a fixed deposit savings account receive high interest rates averaging 10% to 11 %. In both cases, these can lead to increased income for the client. After banks get these initial products rolling, Opportunity utilizes upper management expertise, client feedback, and market research to customize the products and develop additional ones. Other products include term deposits, child savings accounts, agro-saving products that offer a mix of fixed deposit and ordinary savings.

Opportunity International has grown its savings portfolio considerably over the past 5 years, reaching over one million savings accounts and $106.5 million in savings deposits by 2011. In addition to a nearly 900% increase in savings accounts since 2006, Opportunity has experienced other positive results from its deposit-taking operations. In a study funded by the Bill and Melinda Gates Foundation in 2010, it was shown that Malawi farmers working with Opportunity were able to save six to seven times more post-harvest using term deposits. A separate study showed that groups of poor women in Kenya were able to receive a minimum 40% greater return on their business investments within four months of opening a savings account. Amongst the benefits are inherent risks that come with savings, such as overdrafts and account dormancy in addition to those already mentioned. However, Opportunity has sought to utilize innovative technology and best practices to overcome these challenges and replicate the positive results in all other regions of the globe. Current operations in Africa indicate that there is even greater potential to expand this service to at least 5 times its current status. Work is already being done to reach new clients in many countries in Africa.

Loans – Methodology

While Opportunity International offers a range of financial products, its roots are based in lending. Since the success of this initial project in Latin America in 1971, its loan portfolio has grown to over 2.7 million active loan clients across 23 countries. Through small business loans, clients have the opportunity to open their own businesses or expand pre-established ones. Opportunity International uses client-tailored microfinance lending methodologies and strategies–to empower the poor as they work their way out of poverty. Opportunity International's key lending methodologies consist of Trust Groups, Solidarity Groups, and Individual Lending.

Opportunity International's micro-lending has been successful because of its ability to minimizing risks, upholding key components such as convenient services, establishing simple application procedures, relying on character or other non-traditional collateral, building strong relationships between client, lender, and community, and immediate follow-up on overdue loans. Because of this, Opportunity International succeeds in mitigating much of the credit risk involved. To secure a first loan, clients typically first join a Trust Group to back one another's loans and collectively share risk. Trust Groups and the Trust Bank system have been designated as the principal lending methodology. This reaches large numbers of very poor entrepreneurs; and, in Opportunity's experience, it has proven to be extremely successful in encouraging holistic development, fostering well-being beyond increased income. Usually, assisted by a loan officer, 10 to 30 entrepreneurs (often women) come together in a self-selected Trust Group. They pick internal leaders and then undergo a mandatory four to eight weeks of training. They pledge to guarantee their jointly accessed loans and each other's businesses. This acts as an alternative to traditional requirements for monetary collateral. Mutual guarantees based on member trust in a self-selected group and peer pressure offer much greater security for small loans than individual guarantees.

Opportunity Trust Group loans range from $60-$500, with first loans averaging $142. Utilizing these first small loans, clients are able to build inventory, buy equipment, and diversify their businesses. Under the guidance of a loan officer, clients meet weekly to repay loans and receive transformative training and mentoring in groups, lowering operating costs and achieving sustainability. Indeed, the loan officer has proven to be an essential component as they educate clients, build capacity, encourage good business, and financial practices, and provide unique insights into the lives of the poor leading to better financial products (their insights have paved the path toward education loans in Africa, job skills programs for youth in Colombia, loans for latrine and water pumps in Malawi, etc.). As the loans are repaid and businesses grow, clients can access a wider mix of loan products and become eligible for larger loans. With repayments rates of 95%, money stays in circulation in the form of new loans for more poor entrepreneurs and demonstrates the Trust Groups' effectiveness in a grass-roots approach to poverty reduction. In empowering poor entrepreneurs, the groups foster self-reliance, local leadership and collective ownership to strengthen the community and local economy.

As entrepreneurs advance and businesses develop, clients can access Opportunity's second lending method, Solidarity Group loans. Based on the general principals of Trust Group lending, these are an advanced group of products with loans typically ranging from $200 to $1,500. Solidarity Groups are also smaller, with three to eight members. Often reaching out to those who are in need and have already achieved success from the initial Trust Group lending allows them to access larger loans to further grow their businesses.

At the most advanced level of lending, clients can access Opportunity International's Individual Lending program once their businesses have shown significant growth and capital absorption. These larger loans, ranging from $300 to $5,000 per person, must be guaranteed by traditional collateral or co-signers, at times requiring both, depending on the market and client. Through individual loans, these larger, growing businesses have the potential to create multiple jobs within the local economy.

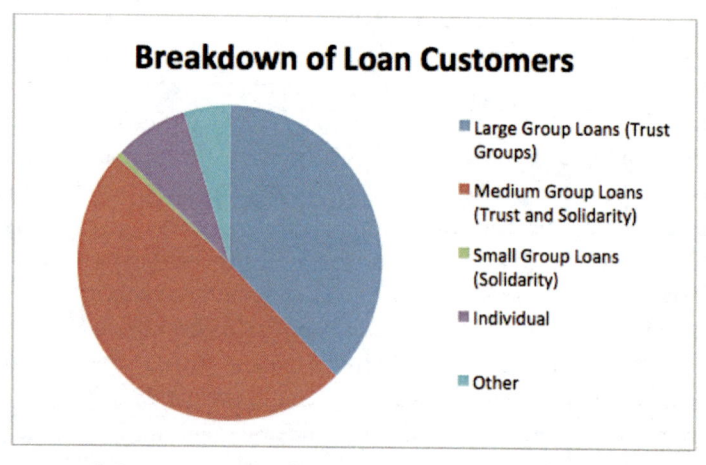

Breakdown of Loan Customers

- Large Group Loans (Trust Groups)
- Medium Group Loans (Trust and Solidarity)
- Small Group Loans (Solidarity)
- Individual
- Other

Other includes SME, non-business, and other loans

While these three methodologies provide the core foundation for Opportunity lending, they are dynamic strategies that evolve in response to market conditions and changing circumstances. Opportunity continues to work to offer all three lending methods and a range of loan products in its operating countries, conducting market research and tracking the effects and changes of these methodologies. For example, until 2010 Opportunity Tanzania Limited (OTL) only offered Trust Group loans. After listening to clients, OTL identified several disadvantages to this sole offering. One of the disadvantages revealed the fact that some potential clients found the 20 to 30 persons group size unattractive, and some preferred a more flexible payment plan over the weekly model. In response, OTL introduced in 2011 three new loan products: A modified Trust Group loan that reduced the group size to 10 to 20 members; the creation of a Solidarity Group loan that allowed smaller groups of four to eight members, bi-weekly repayments, and substantially larger loans. Throughout 2011, the number of OTL loan clients grew by 134% to 7,230 loan clients. OTL is currently working to launch Individual Lending and school fee loans in 2012 and additional new loan products in 2013.

A driving characteristic of all Opportunity lending methodologies is the commitment to serve the poor, especially women. Today, 93% of Opportunity's active loan clients are women. Several studies have shown that women have borne a disproportionate burden of the world's poor. This results in women typically having fewer options for earning a livelihood. However, women are much more likely to invest their resources in their children's well-being, which is why Opportunity International finds it so easy to invest in them.

Loans – Interest Rates

The challenge of microcredit is to make capital accessible for the poor at rates that are significantly lower than exploitative money-lenders, but offer rates that are high enough to allow significant yields. Standard commercial banks are often unwilling to serve the poor because of high costs and small profits. Opportunity International recognizes these costs, but uses solutions to make it possible provide services to the poor on a sustainable basis.

The main problem for many microfinance institutions is that cost of providing their products and services typically out paces the revenue gained from them in the long run. The amounts of money being managed and transferred are usually very small and fractions of the amount that US banks would work with on a daily basis. The sheer operating costs might simply be greater than the earnings, making operations less profitable and not sustainable compared to larger sized loans. These costs identified are comprised of four key components: Operating Expenses, Impairment Loss Allowance, Cost of Funds and Capitalization Rate.

- Operating Expenses. This item includes most recurring costs such as salaries, benefits, rent, utilities, and client training, which make up a proportionately large expense on small loans. Opportunity currently has an average loan size of $310, and incurs operating expenses that are 36% of the loan portfolio.
- Impairment Loss Allowance (Loan Loss Reserve). This component consists of the amount set aside for anticipated uncollectible loans. A rough proxy is the Loan Loss Rate that looks back to historical indicators. The average loan loss rate at Opportunity banks has historically been 2%-4%, but is currently about 6%-7% given the current economy.
- Cost of Capital. This includes the cost to borrow funds commercially as well as the cost of local inflation on equity. The cost of funds can range widely based on local factors, but this expense is around 2% of Opportunity International's global loan portfolio.
- Capitalization Rate that represents the capital that must be set aside for future growth. This varies significantly depending on bank financials.

Currently, established Opportunity International partners operate on 58 cents for every dollar loaned and hence average interest rates fall in that range. However, it is important to note the limitations of what averages could portray. Averages do not disaggregate by the contextual challenges of countries and so can provide only a vague sense of an organization's operations. For example, in 2008, while the global average was about 35%, the five countries with the highest industry-wide operating costs ranged from 50% to above 80% and Opportunity worked in four of the five countries.

On this, as in other areas, greater industry-wide transparency, the creation of flexible financial products that serve client needs, and the creation of a credit bureau would all further MFIs and keep the industry publicly accountable. As with the move toward Social Performance Measurement (discussed below), Opportunity has sought to increase the value proposition for the client even as it seeks to establish sustainable financial services.

Rural and Agricultural Finance

Opportunity International has been expanding its operations to rural Africa where financial services are traditionally inaccessible. As of 2010, Sub-Saharan Africa is widely recognized as the least banked region in the world, with no more than 12% of households actively holding financial services and products. In 2005, Opportunity International piloted a finance distribution program in Malawi directed at the agricultural sector. Malawi has 85% of its population living in rural areas often out of reach for and lacking access to banking services. The pilot program intentionally made services accessible to many rural farmers. The products were widely accepted leading to the success of the program. Now, the established banks provide a full range of financial services and training to smallholder farmers in Malawi, expanding to rural entrepreneurs in other countries such as: Ghana, Mozambique, Rwanda, and Uganda. Under its "Banking on Africa" campaign launched in 2008, Opportunity aims to reach five million new clients in Africa by 2015, enabling rural populations to foster growing economies and sustainable banking systems.

Rural and agricultural finance has a lot of unique challenges and hidden costs that are distinct from microfinance operations in urban areas. Everything from low population densities, lack of physical infrastructure, greater spatial dispersion, food insecurity, lack of financial literacy, beginning from a non-existent base and even less collateral than typical urban microfinance clients, all lead to high transaction and monitoring costs, hinder profitability and increase the chances of default on loans. In agricultural finance, these challenges are compounded by poor quality inputs and seeds, climatic risks, long loan periods with bullet repayments, a lack of established financial track record among small-scale farmers, poor credit culture, a need for savings to survive until the next harvest, and a variety of other problems. Past efforts by organizations have often failed due to inappropriate loan products, a lack of understanding for market influences, being unaware of farmers' and entrepreneurs' household pressures, and a failure to coordinate among key stakeholders. Successful implementation of banking services to rural, sparsely populated areas requires detailed analysis of client base and innovated strategies for delivery and implementation. In this context, Opportunity International has tailored a strategy designed to increase success rates for the farmer, other players along the agricultural value chain, and the banker.

When assessing a rural loan client, Opportunity begins with an evaluation of the farmer's commercial potential to move from subsistence farming to commercial production, including a detailed profile of the household. Using smart-phone and GPS technology, Opportunity International loan officers map a farmer's land to determine the size and location of the plot used for farming (the data often includes other factors such as altitude, water access, precipitation, etc.). Loan officers also conduct basic household questionnaires to identify client demographics. Family make-up, skill levels, and cash flow needs are some of the topics covered in the questionnaires. Another critical component of the assessment process involves understanding the farmer's crop portfolio. Before lending, agricultural loan officers research each crop to predict the direct and indirect costs of production, expected yield, demand, and market value. Opportunity International analyzes the information to determine how financial contributions and loans might help the farmer's farming plan to maximize his or her capacity to produce variety and quantity of food resulting in a profitable outcome. Although Opportunity International finds mapping analysis to be highly effective, some regions, such as Malawi, find it more cost effective to have its Extension Services Provider partners (ESPs) deliver some of the mapping and profiling services themselves. Extension service providers contribute technical support and market linkages to associations of 500 to 5,000 farmers, enabling increased crop yields and prices as well as income earned.

Opportunity International's agricultural finance strategy engages all stakeholders along the value chain. Opportunity International carefully monitors macro-level agricultural trends to better help the farmers succeed at the micro-level. Opportunity International's banks infuse capital into the value chains and facilitate its flow within the market, while partnering with local suppliers to provide better quality seeds and fertilizers. Opportunity International helps farms and the farming industry as it develops in rural areas, collaborating with NGOs and farmer groups to provide essential financial literacy training as well as training in good agricultural practices. Opportunity also helps arrange contractual agreements with agribusinesses to buy the crops, reducing price risk.

Nicaragua is a good example where Opportunity International gives loans and provides skill training to farmers to grow yucca and other cash crops such as hibiscus. Extension services and farm education as well as high-yield variety seeds and fertilizers are applied and regular monitoring undertaken. The farm products are then processed and packaged by the agro-processing plant set up by Opportunity in collaboration with the farmers and sold as finished products within and outside the country. The project has enabled the farmers to increase their yucca and hibiscus yields by 40% and 50% and related incomes by 28% and 30% respectively.

In the Philippines, Opportunity International partner ASKI (Alalay Sa Kaunlaran Incorporated) provides financial services to promote developing industries: water, energy, and agriculture. In terms of agriculture, 19,000 small-scale farmers participate in growing onions and cassava, which they used to supply to the local fast food chain Jolliebee Foods Corporation. That year, Jolliebee Foods Corporation reported sales of $1 billion during the year, enabling them to generate income and create food security for many. ASKI was awarded the 4th European Microfinance Award on November 16, 2012 "for its work serving people in rural areas with traditional financial services as well as community development efforts."

In order to provide services throughout the entire growing season, Opportunity International uses utilizes alternative delivery systems such as POS devices, ATMs, mobile vans, kiosks and container banks, and satellite branches where possible. These technologies reach clients in ways that traditional bank branches cannot, allowing Opportunity International to offer e-payments, money transfers and remittance services, and insurance products in rural areas. The method to delivering these products is an essential element in gaining client trust. In general, the more visible, regular, and secure the delivery channels are, the more likely it will earn the clients' trust. These elements help create great service that helps to attract and keep farmers from season to season.

THE RURAL MODEL

Coordinating with all stakeholders in the agricultural value chain is essential to the success of the farmer and Opportunity's agricultural finance initiative.

Strategic Links
● ● ● ● ● ● ● ● ● ● ● ● ● ●

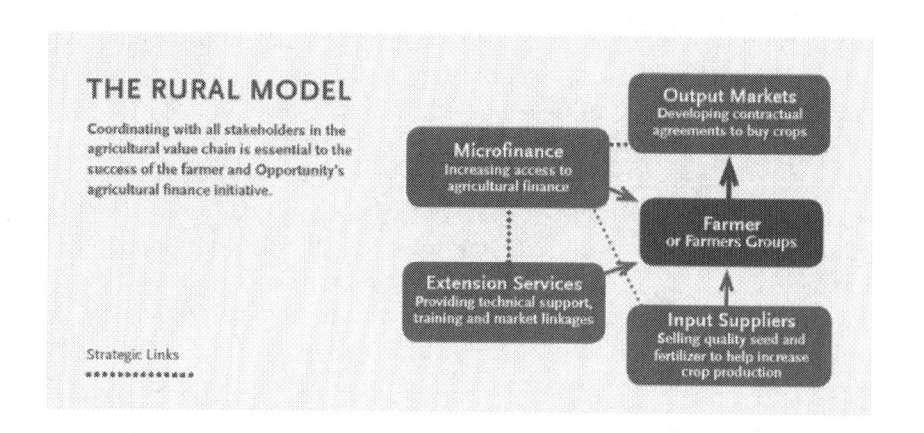

- **Microfinance**: Increasing access to agricultural finance
- **Output Markets**: Developing contractual agreements to buy crops
- **Farmer or Farmers Groups**
- **Extension Services**: Providing technical support, training and market linkages
- **Input Suppliers**: Selling quality seed and fertilizer to help increase crop production

The final step in Opportunity International's rural and agricultural strategy is to protect its banks' investments and work toward systems that are agriculturally sustainable. In addition to the methods mentioned before, it does so by using the low cost delivery channels like cell phone banking and those mentioned above and by securing credit guarantees, often in the form of mandatory savings of 10 to 15% of the loan amount. It also diversifies its portfolios among a variety of crops and regions, and to include non-agricultural borrowers and savers – Opportunity International's rule is to limit agricultural loan portfolios to less than 25% of a bank's total loan portfolio to spread risk.

Perhaps the most important lessons that Opportunity International has learned has been to continue to tailor its agricultural services to the needs of farmers in each country. While fundamentals may be transferable across borders, Opportunity International carefully customizes services, delivery methods and lending policies for each market. Before entering a new country, Opportunity International conducts thorough assessments of the economic and political environment created by both governments and donors as subsidies and well-intended yet problematic aid programs can deeply impact the agricultural market. It also assesses societal attitudes toward NGOs that impact financial behavior (historical backgrounds can such as communism, civil war, and failed NGOs can create a culture of distrust making it difficult to nurture group cohesion that requires trust) as well as the state of the infrastructure required such as roads, irrigation, power, and communication systems. Opportunity International must also ensure that its internal organization is equipped to move into rural finance, with proper recruitment and training of agricultural loan officers, have an agriculture team that understands both financial products and agriculture, robust systems to register and manage rural clients, agriculture-specific credit policies and procedures, systems to measure and mitigate agricultural risk and a committed, extensive outreach campaign.

In summary, Opportunity International is able to support groups of small-holder farmers and marginalized entrepreneurs, using highly detailed GIS mapped and profiled farm plans. Opportunity International ensures that banks and farmers will have access to inputs and the output markets, and financial services will extend to household safety nets with weather index insurance and credit insurance. Price risk mechanisms, such as contract production and extensive marketing, will be in place, and strong, strategic partnerships across the value chain will be created to support the target group of loan clients. In striving to meet these ideal conditions, Opportunity is extending its banking services to Africa's rural poor and proving successful in improving farm productivity, increasing food security and working towards alleviating rural poverty.

Micro-insurance

When living on the brink of poverty many people experience seemingly small events that have catastrophic repercussions on their financial security. Opportunity International offers microinsurance as another means to provide stability to people's lives and ensure economic development. Microloans and savings are not always enough to enable entrepreneurs and smallholder farmers to permanently escape poverty. Although the poor use these services to generate income, they are still vulnerable to crises that can cripple their businesses and drain their savings. A death in the family, precarious living conditions and volatile governments can put all that one has worked on in ruins. To protect against these risks, the developing world's poor has an immense need for insurance products. Of the potential 4 billion persons market, less than 2% currently have access to micro-insurance. In response to this massive undersupply, Opportunity International began offering micro-insurance in 2002 to provide the poor with a safety net for unexpected hardship or disaster. Since then, its business has grown to 2.3 million insurance policy-holders in eight countries across Africa, Asia and Latin America. Today, Opportunity International offers insurance products for the poor at risk through its subsidiary MicroEnsure, the world's first and largest micro-insurance broker. Created in 2005, MicroEnsure acts as the backbone and implementer for insurance services to Opportunity International's clients. As of July 2011, MicroEnsure served over 3 million people in poverty, reaching on average 200,000 new clients a month. Through MicroEnsure, Opportunity International is able to work with local insurance companies and other stakeholders to develop an increasingly wide range of insurance products designed to meet the ever changing needs of impoverished people.

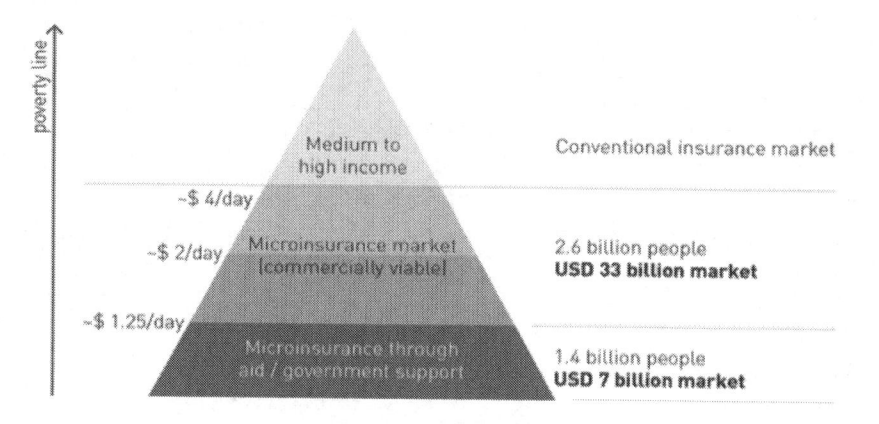

Source: Swiss Re 2010, Sigma No. 6/201 –
Micro-insurance – risk protection for 4 billion people

Term life insurance is one of the major micro-insurance products that Opportunity International is able to offer through MicroEnsure. With premiums averaging $1.50 per month for a family of five, it is one of the first affordable options for protecting family against the loss of primary income earners. Credit life insurance, a specific life insurance policy attached to a loan, protects a client's family and lenders from debilitating debt in the event of the loan client's death. Health insurance for the poor, including those with HIV/AIDs and other pre-existing illnesses, is another principal product. These policies, with premiums at $8 per year in some countries, can provide families with inpatient hospital treatment on a cashless basis in some countries and in others offer a fixed amount of daily cash and benefits to insure against hospitalization for certain ailments or surgery. For small-holder farmers, Opportunity International offers weather-indexed crop insurance that protects against the devastating effects of crop failure. Crop insurance can provide farmers with otherwise inaccessible loans for high quality seed and fertilizer, while mitigating banks' risk of default due to drought, flooding or other natural disasters. In addition to these main offerings, Opportunity and MicroEnsure have also designed policies covering funeral costs, property, political risk, livestock and warehouse receipts for farmers' stored stock.

MicroEnsure makes insurance available by providing the back end management and risk assessment measures. MicroEnsure performs as the entity coordinating with the risk carrier, educate clients, establishing necessary partnerships, designing products, training front office staff, keeping track of insurance clients, gathering market and client data, and processing claims. While Opportunity International may be able to generally calculate risk for the insurance products, most regulatory environments mandate that lenders outsource this risk to an institution with the dedicated capacity to professionally underwrite the risk. For this reason, MicroEnsure and other partners collaborate in providing insurance products for various regions, often utilizing the specialties of companies best suited for particular risk factors. Through this method, MicroEnsure can utilize carefully selected insurance companies' expertise and existing underwriting capital. MicroEnsure then partners with microfinance institutions (MFIs) such as Opportunity International, other NGOs, faith-based networks and telecommunication companies in order to provide broad access to clients. These organizations provide the client side, front end delivery of the insurance products. By filling the gap between organizations serving the poor and insurance companies, MicroEnsure helps to make micro-insurance accessible to the poor to help protect against unforeseen tragedies that make the poor especially vulnerable.

3.3 Non-Financial Services: Financial Literacy, Human Resource Development and Youth Program

Opportunity International recognizes the importance of improving the quality of life for its clients holistically. It offers services beyond just financial products. Alongside a full range of financial services, Opportunity

International focuses its efforts on developing people and providing training resources that enrich people's quality of life. These value-adding initiatives include financial literacy, human resource development, and youth programs. Opportunity International's educational and business training programs help to fully arm clients to make the most of financial products, but of their entire lives. Opportunity International truly sees that both the tools of finance, knowledge, and skills can completely transform families' and community's livelihoods.

Financial Literacy

In its 42 years of experience, Opportunity International strongly emphasized financial literacy programs in developing communities. Financial illiteracy is a widespread obstacle for the poor in the developing world (especially for women due to their exclusion and lack of opportunity). It has found that providing instruction in financial literacy, or the understanding of financial products and ability to make the most use of them, is just as crucial as offering access to financial services. In a 2009 Gallup survey of over 18,000 adults in 18 Sub-Saharan African countries, on average more than three in five Africans were not aware of microfinance institutions in their communities, and 18% had never heard of microfinance. Lack of awareness often leads to significantly low take-up and usage of financial products and increased vulnerability to exploitative services. In response, Opportunity International and its partners make it a top priority to increase clients' understanding of financial products, the importance of savings, wise borrowing and financial planning.

Financial education takes place on multiple levels of Opportunity International's financial inclusion initiatives. As noted above, a prerequisite for credit, loan clients must attend weekly or bi-weekly meetings to receive continuous training and financial education from loan officers. However, a large portion of the financial literacy target audience are not loan clients but rather current and potential savings clients, unobligated to attend training sessions. Audiences have varying levels of general education and experience with banks. Women often in rural areas have higher rates of illiteracy and lower levels of banking familiarity, requiring more intensive and dedicated training and education.

To reach potential and current clients, Opportunity International produces various educational resources. Opportunity International designs a variety of multimedia and print materials to reach its clients in powerful ways. The materials use colorful graphics and photos and include creative engaging story-lines that allow audiences to easily access and remember the principals involved. Media-based resources include financial training DVDs, television shows, radio broadcasts, board games, and comics.

Opportunity International strives to provide quality training and education, hosting a wide range of educational modules such as "Understanding How to Budget," "Multiple Borrowing and Bad Debt," "Why Save?" and "Your Financial Destination", "Understanding Crop Pricing," "Budgeting for Rural Families," and "Including Women in Financial Decisions." Through the wide range of resources, approaches and topics, Opportunity International aims to achieve change on three levels: cognitive change (enhancing knowledge), affective changing (adapting attitude and emotions), and behavioral change (altering behavior and habits). These changes will help clients, families, and communities to build a savings culture to plan for the future, responsible credit management and trusting relationships between consumers and financial services providers, all working toward sustainable financial inclusion.

Human Resource Development

Opportunity International aims to develop quality financial leaders within communities through their human resource development programs. Opportunity International uses both top-down and bottom-up approaches to develop people. The microfinance industry is growing, yet experienced leaders are in short supply. The lack of financial capacity and training is a major inhibitor in the growth and success of any organization working to improve the poor's access to and effective utilization of financial services. Loan officers are a crucial position that many lack the education for. Having 17,000 and expecting to hire nearly 7,000 new staff within the next five years, Opportunity International believes that enhancing Human Resource Development (HRD) is essential to scale up microfinance and reduce poverty. Therefore, it has adopted a two-tiered strategy to foster a Culture of Leadership and build a strong employee base through Hire Right, Train Right, Treat Right (HTTR).

The first half of the human resource development program, called the Culture of Leadership, aims to develop leaders within the Opportunity

International, training them to connect client expectations with employee outlook and performance. It is a top-down approach to organization-wide orientation. Targeting executive, senior and emerging leaders across the Opportunity network, it creates transformational environment for staff that transforms them and allows them to be an agent of transformation in their work with clients as well.

The Culture of Leadership program is a five step process of transformation. Anyone who goes through this is expected to have skills to become an effect leader in Opportunity International. Participants are taught about Opportunity International's identity, setting management goals, assigning program managers, conducting holistic transformation using training tools and feedback, and building a leadership pipeline through evaluation of current leaders and identification of new leaders. Developing the leadership pipeline involves pooling and training of high-potential candidates, often women, through the Emerging Leaders Program (ELP) NextGen initiative. Part of Goldman Sachs *10,000 Women Initiative,* ELP NextGen builds off the success of the ELP pilot. It is designed to support, retain and open doors for talented college graduates, loan officers and other high performers, increasing the quality and strength of the leadership pipeline.

The second part, HTTR is an in-branch bottom up approach to human development with the intent to create a participant led learning culture. It was first piloted in 2011 in Democratic Republic of the Congo. HTTR targets the service side of Opportunity International, working directly with the loan officers in this three stage program. Loan officers perform the client-facing duties in selling its banking services and serve as mentors with excellence. Playing such an active and critical role, Opportunity International expects its number of loan officers to increase by 400% by 2020.

HTTR has three phases, consisting of new concept education, experiential application, and testing and feedback under the supervision of an assigned performance. At each step this cycle is repeated to help reinforce the principles and lessons gained. Trainees are able to quickly learn new information with this approach, applying each newly learned skill and given feedback right away. HTTR aims to improve employee performance and thereby increasing client impact, reducing loan officer turnover, improving write-off ratios, and reducing operational risk. As an end result, this will lead to a transformed client-experience as officers will be more receptive to clients' needs and are better equipped to meet these needs. This method helps to establish and standardizing the loan officer training programme for all banks.

Youth Training

According to African Economic Outlook, the 15 – 25 year olds account for over 60% of Africa's population and 45% of its workforce. However, with limited work opportunities and a lack of income, these youth are more vulnerable to sliding into extreme poverty, participating in criminal activities and engaging in substance abuse. Sustaining growth happens by investing in future generations. To prepare future generations in the developing world to work their way out of poverty, business and financial training needs to also be directed at vulnerable youth. Despite improvements in education efforts, youth unemployment remains a widespread issue throughout the developing world.

In countries such as Ghana, youth in this age group typically cannot qualify for credit as they lack the capacity and resources to partake in income-generating activities. Opportunity International is involved in the solution and has developed two training program to help nurture youth's business acumen: the Sinapi Aba Trust Youth Apprenticeship Program and its youth entrepreneurial program in Colombia. The Youth Apprenticeship Program (YAP) is designed to improve the quality of life in Ghana through extensive training youth in a specific, employable career and, therefore, empowering them to become productive community developers on their own. Sinapi Aba Trust (SAT), a Ghanaian microfinance organization and member of the Opportunity International Network, is a three-year apprenticeship program that helps Ghana's most vulnerable unemployed youth. Upon graduation of the program, the youth will have essential vocational skills, health and business training, and access to capital to start their own businesses or take gainful employment in their field of training.

Under the five-year HIV/AIDS project funded by USAID covering Mozambique, Uganda and Zambia, Opportunity provided opportunities to over 1000 orphans and vulnerable children (14-20-year-olds), mainly female, to receive skills training in various trades as a result of which about 70% started their own business while others went into paid employment.

SAT YAP selects youth in need, recruiting them at local churches, gatherings, and radio advertisements. Once assessed for vulnerability level and potential to succeed and welcomed to the program, the youth participate in mandatory orientations and career counseling and workshops.

At the same time, master craftsmen and tradesmen are recruited based on qualities such as skill level, quality of work environment, training experience and commitment to the YAP program. Currently taught professions include carpentry, cooking and catering, dress making and tailoring, general electrical, information technology, photography, refrigeration, upholstery and welding. Apprentices and trades masters are then matched according to proximity and mutual interests, with typically two apprentices per trades master.

Through this relationship, both the student and the craftsmen mutually benefit – the youth gain knowledge and hands-on experience while the tradesmen benefit from additional workforce and access to Opportunity workshops. A project management committee oversees that apprentices' progress throughout the program, ensuring that they receive quality education in business as well as health issues such as HIV/AIDS and responsible reproductive health.

At the end of the three-year apprenticeship, a national proficiency exam is given for their trade. If successful in both passing the exam and completing the training with an 80% attendance rate, youth can then access a maximum GHS 500 (€220 euro) Opportunity start-up capital loan to assist them in beginning their careers. Since 2003, over 1,300 youth have or are currently participating in YAP, 77% of which are female. While the program experienced some challenges at the start, YAP has seen promising growth in recent years. YAP has nearly 300 students expected to graduate in 2012 and projects this number to reach 500 by the end of 2013.

Opportunity International Colombia and Compassion International partnered in early 2010 to develop a joint-pilot training program for children of some of Opportunity International's loan clients. Opportunity has been working with youth in Colombia since late 2009, and its largest project has been the youth entrepreneurship program, run in collaboration with Compassion International Colombia. While Compassion International provided youth with some business training, their program graduates often had difficulties accessing capital. The program acted as an extracurricular opportunity to explore business as a career or to generate income to cover further education. The program is a four-phase process where youth, ages 17-19, work in groups to develop business plans that could qualify them to receive capital to carry it out. Through this program many youth are able to use any profit gained to reinvest or put into a savings account. The goal is the help them learn about responsible business practices and financial products in a supervised environment.

The initial phase of the pilot project finished in late 2011, showing overall positive results. In the first phase, 440 youths participated in the first phase of the project, receiving training in entrepreneurship and business development, and nearly all had a brief hands-on business experience. This surpassed the original goal of 405 graduates. Of these 440 youths, 223 went onto the second phase of the program, receiving small loans and giving them the chance to generate a small one-time income. Currently, 143 graduates have continued into phase three, continuing to develop their own business activities. Opportunity International continues to oversee the program and hopes it continues into the future.

In 2006, Opportunity International researched savings accounts for children and their families that would help them pay for educational expenses. It developed the pilot project called *Opportunity Child Savings Account (OCSA)* which had three core components: children and their parents/guardian open an interest-bearing savings account positioned as a long-term investment with opportunities to use the funds for secondary school education, (ii) provision of matched money by Opportunity as incentive, and (iii) provision of financial education to children, parents/guardians and teachers. At the beginning of 2012, Opportunity launched another youth-inclusive microfinance program in Malawi in partnership with UNCDF focusing on 12-17 and 18-24-year-olds. This is a four-year project and aims to develop and deliver the following:

- Savings accounts for at least 41, 612 youths age 18-24
- Startup and working capital loans to 7,036 youths age 18-24

- Micro-insurance coverage, such as credit life and business property to 7,036 youths
- Artisan (vocational) and entrepreneurial training to 500 youths age 18-24
- Financial literacy and life skills training to at least 50,594 youths age 12-24
- Development of strategic partnerships with local and international Youth Services Organizations to link with youth and engage in capacity-building

Housing, health and education

Recognizing the importance of improving community infrastructure, Opportunity International provides financial support for technical construction groups that provide home and infrastructure improvement services. Opportunity International partners with Habitat for Humanity International in various countries, helping them to build infrastructure. During the period of 2004-2010, Opportunity helped orphans and vulnerable children as well as their care-givers by building and improving basic shelters in Mozambique, Uganda and Tanzania. About 10,000 orphans and vulnerable children were provided with safe and healthy housing as well as renovated and newly built homes and over 1000 were trained in housing construction and maintenance.In Ghana and India, short-term loans and construction technical assistance (CTA) were provided to help improve homes. Some projects helped to add an extra room to create more space and reduce overcrowding caused by large family size. Other projects include installing utilities such as electricity, water, toilets, kitchens; completing existing buildings (roofing, painting, plastering, flooring, door and window frames; and in some cases building incrementally. In the process, people, particularly community artisans, improve their awareness and skills in construction and maintenance. The program in Ghana has included services helping home owners to survey and map their properties resulting in certified "property folios" as a way helping them to create better documentation that are likely to contribute towards obtaining land title. Despite the challenges faced these projects have proved to make significant impact of the improvement of the quality of life including children's education.

Opportunity has also made substantial efforts to provide health services for its clients in different ways particularly through education during regular client meetings. The six-year program in Mozambique, Uganda and Zambia referred to above for example, 49,000 vulnerable families and peer educators were trained in HIV/AIDS.

Opportunity has, since 2006, piloted three different initiatives with the aim not only to create education opportunities and offer increased access to marginalized and poor communities, but also deliver quality education by strengthening small and low cost private schools to complement public efforts. Not only has Opportunity given education fee loans to parents to enable them meet their children's educational needs, it has also given loans to such schools to expand and improve educational facilities and create favorable learning environment; provided training to proprietors in human and financial management and to teachers in child friendly/child empowering teaching methods.

Overall, these interventions have contributed to improvements in access, quality of education and academic performance among the poor. Some of the countries that have benefitted from the strategic educational initiatives undertaken by Opportunity include Ghana, Uganda, Malawi, Rwanda, India, Dominican Republic and Nicaragua. In Nicaragua, Opportunity has launched its own school in collaboration with local communities and authorities, a technical school, whereby children are taught both academic and ecotourism/agricultural skills.

4 TECHNOLOGY

Introduction

In first world countries like the United States, many industries benefit from the pre-existence of basic infrastructure. Paved roads, smart power grids, social identification, and readily available access to branch banks and ATMs make it relatively easy for banks to set up their services for people to access them. Infrastructure like that rarely exists for people living in rural communities. Technologies are used to circumvent these barriers and provide the tools to allow Opportunity International to deliver the finance services even in the midst of these challenges to those with no access. In order to deliver professional services that are cost effective, Opportunity International uses cutting edge banking software and delivery tools. By doing this, Opportunity International circumvents a lot of the practical challenges of reaching people and granting them access to secure banking services in rural communities. These technology-enabled delivery channels include low-cost satellite branches and kiosks, ATMs and POS devices, mobile vans, and cell-phone banking.

Commercial banks knowingly steer away from rural and peri-urban poor because of the challenges. They often do not see such operations as having the necessary profit margins they would like. Opportunity International tries to overcome these challenges through technologies. As a bank, Opportunity International actually tries to bring its services to clients through mobile banking. Instead of building a branch that many people wouldn't be able to access, Opportunity International drives mobile banking vans to the people. Instead of social security numbers, Opportunity International offers biometric scanning technology to confirm identity and secure access to bank accounts. Also, Opportunity International manages its banking software using commercial grade banking software. These solutions aim to maintain Opportunity International as a banking institution that provides quality services and continues to grow in the future.

In response, Opportunity International has invested $20 million over the last ten years to go towards electronic and mobile technologies that ensure strong solutions to the challenges it faces. Opportunity International uses various technologies to reduce the high operational and transaction costs that typify the industry and overcome barriers such as geographic isolation, illiteracy, and transportation expenses. This commitment to technological advancement has provided efficient, creative solutions in the form of foundational information and communication technology (ICT) components and innovative delivery channels. Combined, they form the infrastructure and delivery channels needed to providing clients with closer, safer, and cheaper access to banking services.

Foundational Manage Information Systems Components

In terms of distribution, one of the largest barriers is the challenge of providing wide, reliable distribution systems that can reach the rural poor. Banks want clients to come to them. When that cannot happen because of undeveloped infrastructure in a region, Opportunity International chooses to find ways to go to them. Microfinance institutions in such regions are

Opportunity International Case Study

increasingly transitioning to "branchless banking" (i.e. cell-phone banking) to actually deliver services to rural communities. The delivery channels require different tools than a branch office would. Several ICT components serve as the foundation for Opportunity International's mobile operations and delivery channels.

In particular, Opportunity International uses biometric identification systems, electronic funds transfer (EFT) switches, and remote banking stations to deliver cost-efficient solutions to the challenging demands of microfinance. The EFT switch enables remote client identification through biometric identification technology. Opportunity International does offer traditional card-based identification, though many do not use it. For countries without a national switch and card option, Opportunity developed **BIDS** (Biometric Identification System), an alternative biometric system. Identifying a client this way allows for more convenient and secure access to clients who do not have any other forms of identification. It also enables clients who cannot read and write to still use these services, the system recognizing them by a physical aspect of who they are. To make this happen, clients are enrolled into the database by an employee at an outreach center who scans finger prints, available identification documents, and a profile photo. Mozambique and Rwanda use BIDS to store client fingerprint data at the bank and remotely authenticate with a biometric reader.

While a number of African nations have instituted national switches, they can be unreliable and costly to use. In some cases, Opportunity International has chosen to install switches that will meet its needs and provide the infrastructure to support its services. The electronic funds transfer (EFT) switch is the next essential component in bringing banking solutions to remote clients. EFT switches are necessary to operate Opportunity International's cell phone banking operation, ATMs, and point-of-sale (POS) devices enabling these delivery channels to interface with the host system, Temenos 24. This switch enables the remote and core devices to send electronic messages, answer account balance inquiries, and authorize and record transactions remotely.

Temenos 24 (T24) is Opportunity International's core banking software platform. The platform fully integrates with front end lending, savings, and insurance products, while providing back—end portfolio management, system transactions record keeping, and other financial

71

calculations. Additionally, it also performs treasury, accounting, financial reporting and other functions. Through providing banks with real-time client data, T24 is essential to carrying out all day to day activities.

New Delivery Channels

Since, these traditional brick-and-mortar branches have large initial costs Opportunity International prefers other methods to reach the most remote and provide widespread coverage marginalized populations. Satellite branches and kiosks offer a more affordable method of providing a full-range of financial products outside of urban communities. Satellite branches, although generally still made of bricks and mortar, are smaller in size and lower in cost to construct. They typically have five to ten loan officers and five to 20 tellers. Kiosks, sometimes referred to as mini-satellites, are made from shipping containers or other low-cost materials and are a quick upgrade from mobile vans in areas of increasing demand.

ATMs and point-of-sale (POS) devices in rural markets are another method of enabling clients to withdraw cash and make transactions without needing to travel to a full-service bank or branch, saving both time and money. In many markets, ATMs and POS, are the only safe transaction option. Opportunity can offer its services through an ATM or POS device at trusted outlets such as retail shops or post offices, mobile vans and bank branches. Opportunity integrates its biometric technology into its operations, offering secure access without the need for a formal identity card.

Mobile vans, Opportunity International's "branches on wheels," deliver banking services and brining financial services to people in rural areas for the first time. Opportunity International invested in a fleet of armored vans equipped with computers, ATMs and POS devices, notebooks and loan officers that can connect to the main server and enable real-time online transactions. Vans have four to eight call points where it stops on a given route to reach people in a region. They travel the routes once or twice a week. The vans tailor their services to the rural poor and can adjust to observed demand by adding or pulling call points on the route. They have been highly successful results across the five implementing countries of Ghana, Malawi, Mozambique, Rwanda and Uganda. As of April 2012, Opportunity deployed 22 mobile banks in the five countries, serving 89 stops. The initiative has most successfully taken hold in

Malawi, where 12 mobile units serve 45 stops. In some regions of the country, mobile banking has widely been accepted, with savings clients increasing 480% (22,082) in the Southern region. In Malawi, clients and Opportunity International banks are mutually benefiting from the presence of mobile banking. Remote clients are receiving more frequent and accessible banking services, allowing them to cut down transportation costs and providing much safer savings storage. For Opportunity International, vans ultimately help test new markets for prospective branches while growing client bases grow not only by increasing their market access but also through doubling as rolling billboards.

Although very successful, these rural outreach efforts do have some disadvantages. Initially cheaper than brick-and-mortar branches, mobile banks accumulate steep costs at roughly $240,000 per unit (plus operating costs of $40,000). Country variables such as transportation infrastructure, terrain, and climate only add to the amount of money needed to maintain each vehicle. Furthermore, the more rural a community is the harder it is to reach and many people in these areas do not have an innate interest in banking services. Without a large client base, it can be hard to continue offering financial services. Opportunity International hopes to develop these new markets, making sure to minimize costs as much as possible. Large inputs are needed to gain confidence in mobile banks. In some areas, mobile banks will expand. In others, it may need to be replaced by low-cost satellite offices. Where routes may be reduced, mobile vans can still be used for off-site branch support and deployed to non-regular events such as football games, market days, and conferences.

Although the discussed technologies are effective, cell phone banking has significantly changed the way financial services are able to reach those without access. Cell-phone banking, also called mobile or m-banking, uses mobile phones as a delivery channel for financial information and services. It is particularly effective in developing countries in comparison to other technologies because cell phone usage is already relatively widespread and is experiencing high growth rates. Between 2000 and 2010, cell-phone subscriptions in the developing world per 100 inhabitants have increased from nearly zero to 70.1. In these countries, cell-phone banking works through SMS format or other text media, rarely utilizing internet-based systems as they are often unreliable. Through texts, clients are able to conveniently and securely perform a variety of tasks including balance inquiries, loan repayments, bill payments, fund transfers, receipt of salary or government payments and airtime purchases.

Opportunity International utilizes two different types of cell-phone banking: bank-led solutions and telco-led solutions. Bank-led solutions are initiated by an Opportunity International bank or a related institution, and often enable all its customers to access their accounts through their cell-phones. Contrarily, in telco-led solutions, the bank partners with a telecommunications company, or telco. Through this, bank customers who are subscribers of that phone service can conduct transactions through their cell-phone. There are also different types of cell-phone banking services. Electronic money services, currently used by Opportunity banks in Ghana, allow clients to use their cell-phones as their main access to their bank account. Mobile money services, or electronic money, are stored in a customer's digital wallet through a mobile network operator's server. Customers load mobile money into their digital wallet and withdraw it as cash at participating retail agents, transfer it via SMS, pay bills or make purchases.

In many areas, cell-phone banking has been widely accepted, receiving extremely positive feedback. Opportunity International's banks in Malawi and Kenya currently boast over 46,000 m-banking clients. Opportunity International Bank of Malawi's bank-led service accounts for approximately 42,000 of the subscribers, which is particularly impressive when compared to 5,850 users as of December 2010. In Kenya M-PESA, a mobile money service, offered by Safaricom and utilized by over 4,000 Opportunity clients, has amounted to over 14 million customers since launching in 2007. In surveying M-PESA users, 90 percent stated they trust that their money is safe with M-PESA and 92% said they would be worse off without the service.

Mobile banking is the most complicated of new delivery channels as it requires special partnerships with telecommunication and other technology companies. Only together these companies create the innovative cell-phone banking solutions. Some of the complexities in Ghana, involve using a mixed model with both bank-led and telco-led solutions. The In Uganda, Opportunity International plans to launch a telco-led cell-phone banking service, subscribing to Interswitch's MobilePay service, while continuing discussions with MTN, a South African-based telecommunications group. In Rwanda, Opportunity

International had originally planned to implement a telco-led solution, but experienced large delays that resulted in the inability to pursue mobile banking in the region.

5 FUNDING

Opportunity International receives funding from bilateral and multilateral organizations: donor agencies, foundations, corporations, churches, individuals, charity organizations, social investors, commercial entities, depositors (savings), and from borrowers (interest and fees), on the other. All of these means for funding are as either grants or non-grants.

Grants

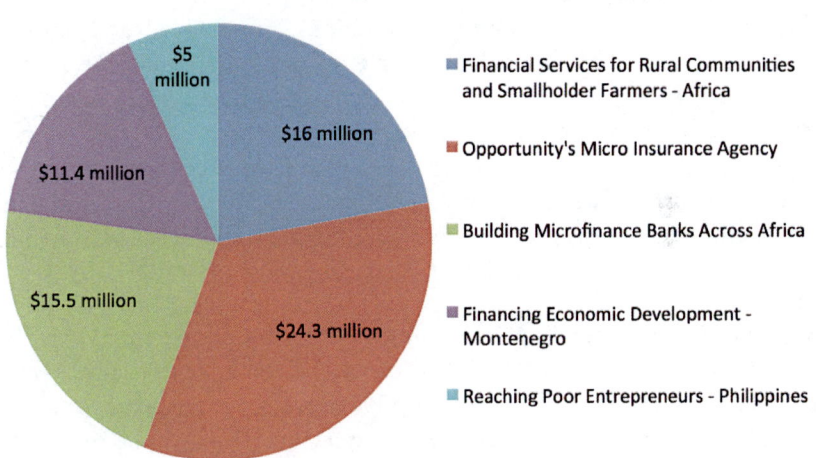

Example of Grants Utilization

- Financial Services for Rural Communities and Smallholder Farmers - Africa: $16 million
- Opportunity's Micro Insurance Agency: $24.3 million
- Building Microfinance Banks Across Africa: $15.5 million
- Financing Economic Development - Montenegro: $11.4 million
- Reaching Poor Entrepreneurs - Philippines: $5 million

Like most NGOs, Opportunity International began by receiving grants to start its services and programs. During the early years of operation, Opportunity International acted as a non-regulated NGO and heavily relied on funding from government organizations. During the last 15 years, the scene has changed dramatically. Opportunity International has appealed to the private sector and receives funding from many new sources: corporations and foundations. Opportunity also receives gifts from technical parties and donors as a sole recipient and/or in partnership with other players in the capacity of a prime- or sub-contractor. Churches, charity organizations and individual citizens have also given small and large amounts in support of both general and specific program activities. In most cases, substantial proportions of the grants mobilized are utilized for the purposes of technology, product development, innovative initiatives, piloting, research and development, and institutional capacity building in managing large-scale projects. The diagram above sheds some light.

Non-grants
Opportunity International utilizes non-grant resources as well. These funds consist of equity, debt, deposits and earnings that are retained to expand its reach to a growing base of clients.

Commercial borrowing
This relates to capital borrowed from various international and domestic commercial sources by Opportunity banks for on-lending purposes. At the time grants are increasingly becoming difficult to access partly because of changes in donor policies and practices, and partly because of the economic downturn, commercial borrowing or debt financing has become an important source of capital in the microfinance market. Commercial banks and Microfinance Investment Ventures are the main sources of borrowing.

Equity
With the exception of one MFI where two other NGOs together own 50%, Opportunity is a majority or 100% owner of stakes in its operations in Africa. One MIV owns an overage of 11% in two entities and another 2.6% in one. Most of the other equity investors are NGOs who have been involved prior to conversion and or acquisition.

Deposits
These constitute voluntary savings made by clients most of whom would never had chance to open bank accounts partly because they have no access to banks and partly because the amounts being saved are too small for any profit-oriented financial institution to be interested in offering such services.

Internally generated income

All the above sources are external. However, Opportunity Banks also generate income internally through their respective operations. These include incomes from interests and fees incurred from loans given to clients. As Opportunity doesn't practice dividend sharing to investors, whatever profit is made is ploughed back into the banks' business thereby boosting the capital base. This is the most critical income source as it determines the extent to which the IMs are operationally and financially sustainable.

6. IMPACT

One of the more rigorous studies that have been done of Opportunity's work has been in Malawi where research sought to measure the impact of financial services on the lives of poor people among the clients of Opportunity International Bank of Malawi (OIBM), and compare it with changes in the lives of non-clients living in the same communities. In 2010, an MBA graduate student at the Northwestern University Kellogg School of Management led the research team of 10 independent, native and bilingual Malawians to administer surveys in Malawi's Northern and Southern regions. The third-party group comparison study showed that clients were more likely than non-clients to report improvement in the growth of their businesses and in their ability to provide for their families over the last 12 months. And clients were more likely than non-clients to show greater changes on each of the business performance indicators – average weekly sales income, net income, family expenditures, and savings – suggesting that Opportunity clients earn more, spend more on their families, and also save more than their peers who have never received a loan from a microfinance organization. The following paragraph highlights some specific findings:

> *Clients of Opportunity International Bank of Malawi (Opportunity Malawi) who receive microfinance business loans are more likely to report improvement over the last 12 months compared to a similar comparison group of non-clients in various business and personal areas such as sales income (24% more likely), net income (20%), money saved (22%), number of customers (17%), ability to pay suppliers (17%), overall quality of life (15%), comfort of one's home (17%), amount of assets (18%), and children's education (17%). These differences are seen even when controlling for other possible explanatory factors such as current income, age, gender, industry type, business age, and education and are statistically significant at very high levels of confidence often in excess of 99%.*[73]

In order to assess more accurately the impact that its work is having on clients, Opportunity is now moving to implement Social Performance Measurement (SPM) and the Progress out of Poverty Index (PPI) across the network. When implemented, this will gather on a network-wide basis, measurements on indicators touching on governance and staff commitment to social goals, client protection, products and services that meet client needs, social responsibility to staff, client monitoring, and responsible financial performance.

The following table shows a dashboard of social indicators developed for Opportunity's SPM system.

Categories	Indicators
Client outreach – reporting on who we are reaching	- Income levels (moderately poor <$5pd, poor <$2pd, extreme poor <$1.25 pd) - Gender – % female clients - Targeted minority – % of clients from excluded groups) - Rural/urban – % of rural clients - Excluded (unserved) clients – % of clients who had never had access to formal financial services
Range of services – reporting on what services are offered	- # of distinct financial services offered to clients on a substantial basis - % of clients receiving financial education - # of distinct non-financial services offered to clients on a substantial basis
Client protection – reporting on how we are delivering services	- Responsible pricing of loan products – partner pricing relative to the country average +/-% - Client retention (%) - Staff retention (%)
Client satisfaction – reporting on how we meet clients' needs	Clients' satisfaction mechanisms Client satisfaction measure
Client transformation – reporting on how we are transforming lives	- Economic (change in income levels) - No. of jobs created - Personal (accesses to appropriate health services, access to sanitation facilities, decreased vulnerability) - Social (access to education for their children, participation in key household and community decisions)

	- Spiritual (increased love for God and neighbor – client reported)
External reporting – partners' commitment to external reporting	- Number of external reports submitted from a defined list (Mixed Market, SPTF, MF Transparency, National Social Performance Publication, Published Social Ratings/Social Audits)

SPM implementation	- Self-assessed rating on the 17 standards covering each of the key sections in the - Universal Standards for SPM (USSPM)
	   - Social goals are defined and monitored
	   - Board, Management and Employees demonstrate commitment to Social Performance
	   - Clients are treated responsibly
	   - Products, Services, Delivery Models and Channels are designed that meet clients' needs and preferences
	   - Employees are treated responsibly

Social Performance Management for Opportunity Network: A Dashboard of Social Indicators

Given Opportunity's mission to facilitate the transformation of the lives of poor people, there is a clear need to be seeking to monitor the impact of its work on their lives. This has not been without challenges. For microfinance banks seeking to become sustainable, the additional costs involved in studying impact can seem a luxury. The level of client data that need to be collected in order to provide a robust study can be prohibitive for the loan/savings officer to gather in the ordinary course of her/his work processes. Under such circumstances, assessments can end up relying on the capability of the organization to find funding for studies.

In addition, the Opportunity structure that has provided significant levels of autonomy to country partners to implement policies that are particular to their respective contexts can prove difficult when it comes to network-wide agreement on the importance of client studies to say nothing of indicators.

Despite these challenges, however, Opportunity has seen some progress on these issues. Private donors, philanthropic foundations, technical donors, supporting network partners, and implementing network partners have all begun to move toward a common position that acknowledges that a deeper understanding of the impact that

Opportunity's work has on the lives of individuals, families, institutions, and the community is essential. New methods and technologies such as a customer relationship management system and an input system that would allow the gathering of client data more possible at scale are being pursued. And the ongoing efforts and discussions of SPM have begun to move toward a network-wide acknowledgement of key indicators that the whole network can be following together. All of these demonstrate that Opportunity will be able to produce a more comprehensive and vigorous impact study in the years to come.

CHRISTIAN DISTINCTIVES

Opportunity International has explicit Christian motivations and biblical foundations for its work. These are listed in its vision, mission, core values, and motivations. Opportunity aims to follow the call of Jesus to reach the poor and participates in the mission of the church in some of the poorest regions of the world. Trying to be holistic in its approach, Opportunity International builds relationships that lead to moments of Christ defining impact in their communities as a microfinance institution.

Mission

Opportunity International's mission is "to empower people to work their way out of chronic poverty, transforming their lives, their children's futures and their communities." Opportunity International is not only committed to help people increase income and prosper materially but also to become better in terms of character, accountability, responsibility and integrity. Opportunity International's commitment to transformation emanates from the Biblical principle that men shall not live by bread alone but also by the word that proceeds from the mouth of God.

Core values

The core values of Opportunity International include: commitment to the poor, respect, integrity, stewardship, humility and transformation.

Motivation

Opportunity International is motivated by the call of Jesus Christ to love and serve the poor through microfinance services tailored to meet the needs and potential of the poor. For Opportunity, serving the poor is a vocation in response to God's calling:

> *Calling* is the key to our motivation. We do not do what we do merely to meet personal needs, to be compassionate, or to improve local economies. We serve because in doing so we are fulfilling a unique calling from someone whom we serve – our Creator. It is part of what we were meant to do. God does not need us in any sense that suggests his inadequacy to accomplish all that He will without us. We are called to the privilege of participation in what He is doing in the world.[74]

Opportunity International believes that serving the poor is an act of obedience and tantamount to serving God. This is based on the words of Jesus, written in Matthew 25: 35-46. "In as much as you did it to the least of these my brethren, you do it to me." It accepts its clients as bearers of God's image and treats them with the dignity and respect they deserve. Every interaction with clients is viewed as an opportunity to reflect God's love.

Non-financial services

In addition to the financial services provided by every other MFI, Opportunity offers non-financial services including financial literacy, life skills, leadership skills and character formation based on Biblical principles and values. Its services are open to all people regardless of religion, gender and creed. Although not a requirement, some of Opportunity's staff, particularly Loan Officers, pray for their clients and visit them when they suffer from illnesses or go through other difficulties.

Family focus

Opportunity International believes that the wellbeing of its clients, their families and their communities is inextricably intertwined: The well-being of clients depends on the well-being of their families and communities of which they are a vital part. As a result, Opportunity's relationships with its clients' families and communities are characterized by the same respect that characterizes its relationships with its clients.

Moreover, the majority of Opportunity International's clients are women. In contexts where women are not traditionally allowed to work outside the home, women entrepreneurs become empowered through increased knowledge and exposure they receive their peers and loan officers in group settings. When they earn their own money, they tend to become less dependent on their husbands as they exercise independence. Husbands tend to be threatened. On the other hand, when their businesses go wrong, they may get into trouble with their husbands as quarrels over the utilization and control of money as the latter often tend to control and misuse of household income. Both scenarios have potential for creating family frictions and conflicts leading, in some cases, to domestic violence and even divorce. This is destructive to family life and brings adverse consequences on children. Opportunity International believes the family is core to society and works to enhance love and harmony between husbands, wives and children. Clients are, therefore, trained and counseled in the principles of ethical living.

Impact measurement
Many MFIs tend to focus more on measuring their institutional profitability and portfolio quality and less at the changes experienced by their clients. When clients were considered, measurement tended to focus on economic changes related to employment and income generation and more on quantitative than qualitative indicators. As pointed out in chapter 2, for example, the 11 social performance indicators jointly formulated in 2009 by MIX and the Social Performance Task Force (SPTF) focused on measuring the social performance of MFIs and didn't seem to directly deal with client impact. They were rather meant to be used for collecting social performance data from MFIs around the world and providing a platform for benchmarking and analysis."

As one of the leading standard-setting MFIs, Opportunity International does look at institutional profitability and portfolio quality is committed to the implementation of the social performance indicator. However, it also looks at other factors described in the previous sections such as holistic client impact, employing a more comprehensive definition that looks at indicators that go beyond monetary.

8 CURRENT CHALLENGES
Opportunity International continues and will continue to face challenges as it branches into new regions of the world. The four main challenges include the ongoing challenge to understand and engage clients' needs, the challenge of optimizing human resources and management internally, the challenge of

network standardization and consolidation, the challenge of strategic expansion, the challenge of measuring impact, and the challenge of adapting to the ever changing external factors within the region. Opportunity International understands that the challenges noted below are often challenges common the industry as a whole. They are listed here to note how these challenges in particular are among the key challenges that have required Opportunity International to establish strategies and initiatives to explicitly address them. The points begin with internal operations and move toward larger, more macro-level, challenges.

The ongoing challenge of understanding and engaging client needs ever more deeply

Opportunity has sought to produce services that meet client needs and potential. However, there is greater awareness that more can, and must, be done to deepen the Network's understanding of this search further. That such understandings should lead to better products and services needs no mention. But it has hitherto been too easy to have this to happen unsystematically. A process that systematically gathers and analyzes client realities, and then uses this for product development must be operationalized throughout the Opportunity network and rigorized to produce reflections on services provided across the network. In this regard, Opportunity has welcomed developments in the microfinance industry to make the implementation of social performance measurement (SPM) an industry standard; and, Opportunity hopes to have this implemented across Africa this year, and in other areas the following year.

But the implementation of SPM is crucial because of what such process signifies. The implementation has required a network-wide review of the transformational mission of the organization, a revived discussion of how the organization as a whole can make these objectives of transformational development core to Opportunity's values, products, and services, and involved discussion of the indicators that will be jointly followed. Implementation of SPM processes, then, has signified for us a step toward further making the vision of transformation a part of the organization's DNA. One could argue that the significance of this outweighs even the implementation of SPM processes, though no less essential to making the organization ever more connected to client needs.

The challenge of optimizing human resource management internally

One of the key challenges Opportunity is facing involves the finding of key personnel for its operations. The creation of commercial banks that can handle all the necessary requirements for upholding professional and industry standards of client protection and reporting to central banks requires personnel with high levels of expertise. At the same time, the mission of Opportunity to serve the poor does not easily allow for salaries capable of retaining its best officers. Indeed, Opportunity has faced a considerable amount of poaching from other MFIs and banks – being seen in some regards as a useful training ground that produces highly capable and qualified officers.

For these reasons, in Africa, Opportunity has implemented employee on-boarding and internal leadership training programs that establish a career development pipeline. The former invites ownership of the organization's mission, objectives, and accomplishments across the organization across all ranks. The latter seeks to nurture internally, within the organization, a trained cadre of highly capable officers that would allow Opportunity to use the talents of their personnel more nimbly across the organization.

The challenge of network standardization and consolidation

The speed with which network partners have expanded their work, the project innovations that are posing new operational, financial, and system challenges, and the expanding global reach of the organization as a whole, have resulted in a pace of expansion that is more rapid than some current systems and processes could follow. Although, as one might expect, Opportunity has network-wide processes in place, a recent review has made clear how there needs to be even more standardization across the organization in various systems and processes. This would not only provide for better understanding and strategic development throughout the organization as a whole, it would also more efficiently and effectively bring the resources (whether in knowledge, skills, technology) to bear on operations in various countries – something that has been pinpointed as a key component of driving down operational costs across the countries.

In a sense, the two areas noted above can be seen as part of the process of standardizing data collection and operational processes. The current

SPM and human resource development initiatives underway both seek to provide greater understanding and operational efficiencies across the organization as a whole instead of having each country tackling these in isolation. While no doubt each country will have its unique contexts requiring customization, such processes can potentially provide intra-organizational insights to bear on various aspects such as client needs, product development, organizational development, human resource development, delivery channel innovations, technology innovations, and greater understanding of what brings about transformational development to name a few.

The challenge of measuring transformation

As discussed in the impact section above, vigorously measuring the impact of microfinance on the lives of clients is complex and costly. Developing agreed definitions of concepts, frameworks and indicators has been found difficult. As a result, very few "scientific" impact studies with good quantitative and qualitative outcomes have been undertaken throughout the history of the microfinance industry making it difficult for the industry to support its claim of positive impact with evidence.

While it shares this general industry challenge, Opportunity is also faced with a further challenge of its own. As a Christian MFI, Opportunity is not only interested in measuring material and social impacts. It is also interested in measuring the impact of its programs on the overall transformation of the lives of its clients. Despite the continued and varied efforts made since 1976, Opportunity has not found developing agreed definition and measurable indicators of transformation easy. The challenge remains and the search continues.

The challenge of external factors

While the above are internal challenges, Opportunity also faces external challenges that are common to all MFIs. Some of these include: weak and unfavorable economic environment and regulatory practices, politically motivated microfinance initiatives causing market biases, political interventions, conflicts, natural disasters, multiple borrowing, and money sharks. These and other external factors that Opportunity cannot influence adversely affect the success of microfinance programs. To cite some examples: The politico-economic environment in Zimbabwe during the last decade led to the total collapse of Opportunity's largest program in Africa early 2000s. The program in Nicaragua was affected by the "no pay" campaign of 2008/2009. Opportunity program in India and Indonesia were affected the Tsunami of 2004. The hurricane in 1998 affected the programs in Central America. Another external challenge is the increasing indebtedness of clients as a result of multiple borrowing that weakens Opportunity's goal of prospering the poor.

These are some of the many challenges facing Opportunity as it seeks to move forward – no doubt challenges that are common to many such organizations. Despite challenges related to engaging clients in deeper ways, Opportunity takes these challenges as a set of opportunities to grow more and serve better in the following ways:

Applying a client-centric approach

The application of this approach means that Opportunity is a client-led MFI and is increasingly allowed itself to become a listener, attentive and responsive to the voices of its clients. As a result of this approach, Opportunity has increasingly allowed itself to become a listener, attentive and responsive to the voices of its clients. The various customer satisfaction surveys and studies have been key tools for the listening process of and building relationships with clients. As a result, Opportunity has been able to design and offer client-tailored products and services. It has also been able to practice flexibility to a certain degree by changing frequencies of client meetings and repayment schedules as per contextually appropriate and possible.

Diversifying products and services

In response to client-expressed needs and potential, Opportunity has diversified its products and services from serving only existing businesses to serving value-added ones, including housing, health, education, water and sanitation, energy, and value chains; and (ii) adult clients to serving children and youth (12-24 year-olds), small landholders, people with disabilities and people living with HIV/AIDS; Of these the agricultural/value chain and education finance products constitute the most important components. In the case of agriculture finance, Opportunity helps smallholder farmers to develop their subsistence farming to a commercial level through the provision of appropriate loan sizes needed for the right types of inputs, village mapping and profiling, extension services, linkages with commercial service providers, mechanization, financing of warehouses, and support to agriculture value chain businesses. In terms of education finance, Opportunity provides loans to small school proprietors for expanding and improving educational infrastructures, including water and sanitation, thereby enabling children in poor and marginalized areas, school fee loans to enable parents pay for all their children's education, savings accounts to ensure that children do not discontinue their education when a parent or a care-giver dies, and basic business and management training to school proprietors and teachers' training. The main goal here is to enable poor children to have access to quality education in conducive, safe and child-friendly environments in which teachers, parents and students are satisfied and academic standards are improved.

Investing in innovation and technology

Opportunity recognizes the importance of innovation and technology for bringing services closer to where people are, reaching out to more poor and marginalized people and villages, and delivering in the most secure ways possible ways. To realize this, Opportunity has continuously invested in research and development in cutting-edge products and revolutionized its distribution model. Some of these delivery channels include:, mobile vans equipped with tellers and ATMs, cellphone banking, ATMs, POS devices, smart-cards with biometric IDs, as well as brick and mortar branches, satellites and ATM kiosks. These innovations have been and are being made with the view to enhance efficiency and keep transaction costs in order to lessen the costs (interest rates) borne by clients and increase their income while striving to ensure institutional sustainability. The other creative innovations included the different lending methodologies developed to meet different client needs and potential. It has also invested in financial education to tackle the various socio-cultural barriers that have hindered the poor from accessing financial services.

Investing in organizational development and capacity building

Recognizing the key role played by effective organization in leadership in the success of its program, Opportunity has sought to ensure professional excellence not only by recruiting people with state-of-the-art competence, but also by making sure the number of staff is adequate and continuous skills and leadership training are offered. The 17,600 staff of which 9,800 are loan officers, serving globally are part of the success made. The GMO with its various specialized divisions and regional offices manned with professionals of high caliber provides the needed technical assistance to the IMs implementing Opportunity program across the globe.

Investing in MIS
Opportunity recognizes the importance of accurate, complete and timely information gathering and data collection for effective policy- and decision-making processes, and for proper accounting and reporting. It has, therefore, from very early on, taken actions to set up a globally operating MIS that is developed, monitored and maintained by global, regional and national teams.

Evaluating its programs and producing knowledge
Being a learning organization, Opportunity has sought to continuously conduct evaluation and research into its operations so as to draw lessons and develop tools for improving performance and efficiency.

Partnering with other service providers
Given that microfinance is its core niche, Opportunity has sought to implement several of its value-added interventions such as housing, education and health through strategic partnerships with other service providers with the right specializations.

Building good relationships with donors and host governments
Opportunity recognizes the importance of having mutual understanding and good relationships with donors and national authorities. It has therefore continuously sought to engage its donors and local governments through workshops, conferences, insight trips and regular reporting which have been instrumental in promoting donor education and mutual trust.

9 CONCLUSIONS
Opportunity always has been and continues to be a community of trailblazers seeking to bring hope and life to the people in the world that need it most. From its inception, Opportunity International transforms lives by providing dignity and love specifically to those stuck in poverty. Decades

ago, Al Whittaker and David Bussau followed their call to boldly organize, collaborate, and include those who wanted to bring about the economic and personal transformation for areas of the world that needed it most. They had faith that they could alleviate areas of scarcity and poverty and elevate them to become areas of flourishing. At its core, Opportunity International believes that every human being deserves the opportunity to create and maintain a secure life and that it can make a difference in the world by walking side by side and serving those in need.

Opportunity shares this desire with everyone it works with, bringing together client and service provider into a mutual, life-giving relationship. This is significant because the two form a powerful relationship that fuels Opportunity's outreach and heart level impact. This is reason Opportunity International finds both sides so eager to work with one another. What connects them so well is a shared hope, optimism, and desire for people everywhere to have dignity and well-being. Both are trailblazers and opportunists dedicated toward a work outside and greater than themselves. Both live with faith and determination to change their lives and the lives of their communities every day, forging new paths when necessary and seizing opportunities when they arise. There is a growth and meaning shared across continents and between people. Because of this, clients, partners, and service providers become natural allies, all working of the sake of transforming lives. By working together, Opportunity does what no individual can do on their own strength. It provides a network of resources, people, and services that enables a world of opportunity.

Today, Opportunity International continues to be deeply immersed in the lives of people living in poverty, providing opportunity for communities to break the perpetual cycle of poverty, turning it into a sustainable cycle of success. Opportunity tries to continue enhancing its capacity to do so in holistic ways. One of the main ways that opportunity continues to do this is to listen and receive consumer insights on the ever changing needs and challenges that people have as they strive for a better life. As Opportunity International continues to provide sustainable financial services to poverty stricken areas across the globe, it remains vigilant, drawing upon past successes and achievements to maintain its quality service.

VISION FUND INTERNATIONAL CASE STUDY
NATHAN BROWN AND RICHARD REYNOLDS

Nathan Brown currently serves as VFI's Christian Commitments and Client Education Manager, ensuring the appropriate expression of its Christian identity across diverse contexts, as well as promoting dialogue-based educational products for group clients of its MFIs. He is also an adjunct professor at Eastern University, teaching courses on microfinance and market development for its MBA programme in International Economic Development.

Richard Reynolds (Ph.D.) has been serving as the COO of VisionFund International (VFI) for the past 4 years. He is currently the Director for Global Operations for VFI, managing the day-to-day operations in the regions and global VFI initiatives. He currently resides in California with his wife and children.

HISTORY

World Vision was founded in 1950 by Dr. Robert Pierce ("Bob"), a young American evangelist, who had first been sent to China and South Korea in 1947 by the Youth for Christ missionary organization. On Pierce's trip he was inspired by the poverty of one little girl to pledge a monthly amount to the girl's local church to ensure her care. This generated the idea of child sponsorship and World Vision.

The first area that World Vision focused on was orphans and other children in need, beginning in South Korea, and then expanding throughout Asia. The programme soon spread throughout Latin America, Eastern Europe, Africa, and the Middle East. In the 1960s, World Vision started providing food, clothing, and medical care to citizens of impoverished countries after natural disasters by soliciting donations from major corporations. Resources from child sponsorship assisted poor children with food, education, healthcare and vocational training.

In the 1970s, World Vision embraced a broader community development model and established an emergency relief division. It attempted to address the causes of poverty by focusing on community needs such as water, sanitation, education, health, leadership training and income generation.

World Vision began the 21st century by strengthening its advocacy efforts, particularly on issues related to child survival and poverty alleviation. It became more active in working with governments, businesses and other organizations in addressing issues such as child labour, children in armed conflict and the sexual exploitation of women and children.

World Vision has become a leading humanitarian organization. Some 44,000 staff members (including part-time and temporary staff and employees of microfinance institutions) implement programmes of community development, emergency relief and promotion of justice in 97 countries.

VisionFund International (VFI) is the 100% owned subsidiary of World Vision that manages and or owns all the microfinance institutions for World Vision. As part of a child focused organization, VFI seeks the sustained well-being of children and fulfilment of their rights within families and communities. Having experimented with various community-owned revolving loan funds in the 1980s, World Vision first started supporting microfinance institutions (MFI's) in the early 1990s. By the early 2000s, the size and complexity of the microfinance organizations operated in over 35 countries required the creation of a specialist organization to manage them. VFI became that organization and has since been staffed to own and manage microfinance institutions supported by World Vision. VisionFund does not require a specific organizational structure, believing that this should be driven by the local context and needs. As a result, organizations are both regulated and unregulated and non-profit and for profit organizations. However, from a VFI perspective, all are treated the same with an expectation to be both able to cover all their costs (operationally sustainable) and to be mission focused.

These microfinance institutions have largely been credit focused organizations but beginning in 2009, VFI began to explore the provision of savings and insurance services for its clients. Most loans are for businesses since VFI believes it is essential that clients have the capacity to repay loans but there has also been increased lending for housing loans (approximately 10%) and social products (e.g. school fee loans) where clients can demonstrate an ability to repay and there is a clear impact on the lives of children. The financial performance of each MFI is tracked monthly through financial reports, as well as VFI staff at a global level working with each organization. The social performance or mission focus is tracked quarterly. CEO performance includes both areas and decisions on investments and lending.

What distinguishes VFI's microfinance work as well as creating a challenge is that it is part of a wider development organization. The majority of World Vision's work is in marginal communities and, in particular, rural communities. The development challenges in such communities are enormous and poverty is compounded by markets that are very imperfect and, in some cases, not even working. For example, former command economies in Eastern Europe have dampened the entrepreneurial spirit among older generations. Lead firms often abuse their positions of power, preventing those at the lowest levels in value chains reaching their full potential. Access to financial services is necessary, therefore, but not sufficient for development to happen. For example, to increase their incomes, farmers in Tanzania not only need capital to invest in fertilizer, but also they need markets to sell produce and new knowledge and farming/ conservation practices. VFI seeks to promote its microfinance work in areas where World Vision works by a process of integration. This involves working at both a national level (strategy and planning) down to each Area Development Programme (ADP) where more detailed plans are developed.

ADPs are a comprehensive way to tackle poverty across extensive areas, usually including several communities. Skilled national staff members work with local people to plan and implement a programme that will last for up to 15 years. World Vision gives priority to helping communities to work together to find ways to improve their future, and especially focuses on the needs of children. Microfinance is necessary, therefore, but not sufficient for change. As a result, VFI seeks to be both more rural focused and more integrated with World Vision in its provision of microfinance services. Area Development Programmes (ADPs) are:

- **Child-focused:** Children are included as agents of change in the communities.
- **Community-based:** ADP design and implementation is based on community needs and priorities.

- **Empowering:** World Vision helps to build the capacity of the people themselves and empower them to carry out their community development processes.
- **Long-term:** World Vision commits to long-term funding and involvement with communities – from 10 to 15 years.
- **Multi-sectoral:** Interventions address the multiple causes of poverty and injustice.
- **Funded by multiple sources:** Funding comes from a combination of child sponsorship and public and private funds – as appropriate and where possible.
- **Sustainable:** Empowered communities are able to sustain improved livelihoods.

WV's Development Programme Approach has four main aspects: Contributing towards child well-being, working with communities and partners, equipping local level staff, and basic programme parameters. The following programme effectiveness standards are organized according to these four aspects of the approach. These standards are the basic principles of WV's development programmes and are the basis for the programme self-review and quality assurance. They are intended to be applied flexibly according to context.

Contributing to the well-being of children within families and communities, especially the most vulnerable

1. The programme contributes to the sustained well-being of children, especially the most vulnerable.
2. The programme vision and priorities are developed with and owned by the community and local partners.
3. The programme integrates lines of ministry, sectors and themes, reflecting the national office strategy and the local vision and context.
4. Programme design, monitoring, evaluation and reporting clearly reflect the programme's contributions to child well-being outcomes.
5. In programmes with sponsorship, sponsorship minimum programming standards are applied through programming that contributes to the sustained well-being of children, including

registered children and enables meaningful engagement with sponsors.

Working effectively with communities and partners
6. World Vision's preferred local role is to serve as a catalyst and builder of the capacity of local partners and partnerships for child well-being. In areas where children face critical needs demanding immediate action, WV works with local authorities to plan its direct operational role in addressing these issues while strengthening the capacity of partners to assume the role over time.
7. Programme staff support communities and local partners in advocacy with government and other authorities.

Equipping local level staff
8. Key programme staff members are committed to incarnational living among the people they serve.
9. Programme staff members have the core competencies required to fulfil their roles.
10. Programme staff members have access to the technical resources and support that they need.
11. Programme staff members engage in regular, intentional reflection and learning that leads to improved practice.

Basic programme parameters
12. The geographic size of the programme is manageable and corresponds to existing local government boundaries.
13. Adequate resources are available to achieve the programme outcomes and meet organizational requirements.[75]

VISION, MISSION AND CORE VALUES
World Vision has what are referred to as "core documents," which include its vision and mission statement. These core documents are central to how the organization operates and firmly establish the identity of the international partnership at the highest level. VFI has adopted World Vision's vision as its own: *Our vision for every child, life in all its fullness; Our prayer for every heart, the will to make it so.* It is inspired by and based on a verse from the Bible 'I have come in order that you might have life, life in all

its fullness.'[76] As a child-focused organization, everything that World Vision does seeks fullness of life for all children. World Vision believes that it communicates God's love to clients and their children through its work in microfinance. World Vision and VFI do relief[77] and development work, including microfinance, in order to express God's love and bear witness to God's Kingdom.

World Vision's primary purpose is to promote human transformation, seek justice and bear witness. As a part of World Vision's larger mission, the specific work that is done in VFI also promotes transformation, seeks justice and bears witness to God's Kingdom. VFI's mission is guided by World Vision's overall mission but VFI's mission identifies how it will live out the shared vision in terms of its particular work in microfinance:

We improve the lives of children living in poverty. Our services in the developing world unlock the potential for small businesses to grow. This enables children to grow up with improved health and education giving them the foundations to build a positive future.

We empower poor women and their families with small loans and other financial services. We help create real and lasting change by giving our clients, women and men, the training and support to run successful businesses that will provide a sustainable income.

We unlock the potential for communities to thrive. VisionFund is part of World Vision, a Christian relief, development and advocacy organization. Applying the principles of our Christian ministry we work together to provide the foundations for local economies to flourish in healthy and safe communities.[78]

ORGANIZATIONAL STRUCTURE

VisionFund International is the microfinance subsidiary of World Vision International (World Vision). VFI is mandated by World Vision to:

1. Provide governance, risk management control and specialty advice/support to all of its MFIs whether owned or controlled by VisionFund or World Vision.
2. Manage the funding of all MFIs including donations and debt financing from VFI and third parties directly to the MFIs.

At its September 2003 meeting, the World Vision international board authorized the creation of VisionFund International (VFI) as a controlled

Vision Fund International Case Study

subsidiary of WVI, for the purpose of housing a global capital fund to support and strengthen WV's microfinance operations throughout the partnership.[79]

VFI operates as a federated network, meaning that each MFI has its own board of directors, its own CEO, and functions fairly autonomously. However, all MFIs share the same vision statement, which is also World Vision's. Furthermore, regional directors and other VFI and WV staff serve on the MFI boards. Standard operating policies, uniform loan applications, and consolidated reporting all contribute to VFI's identity as a unified network.

There are currently 36 MFIs in the VisionFund network. All MFIs are majority owned by either VFI or World Vision. Not all MFIs are 100% owned because in some countries a second or third shareholder is required. There is an ongoing initiative to transfer all MFIs to VFI ownership. There are currently 11 MFIs that are fully owned by VFI. The others are still in process. VFI generally refers to each MFI in the network as a VisionFund affiliated MFI.

The organizational chart in Figure 1 (which provides a representative sample) demonstrates how each MFI fits into the bigger picture of VFI and integrates with the corresponding World Vision national office to contribute to the broader work of the World Vision Partnership:

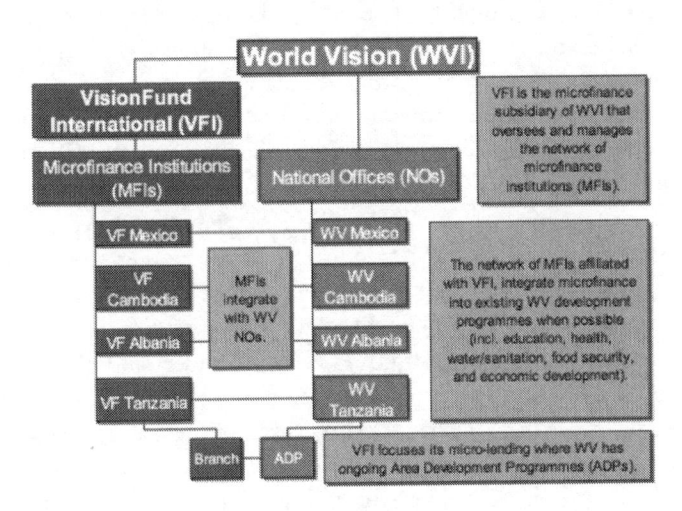

Figure 1

At the highest level, the World Vision International President/CEO, COO and CFO all serve on VFI's board.[80] This ensures that the work of WV and VFI is closely integrated as a holistic package. In fact, this holistic ministry is VFI's unique strength as a provider of microfinance.

At the national level, WV's ongoing work, especially in development, helps communities provide such things as education, health, water/sanitation, food security, and economic development. VisionFund affiliated MFIs collaborate with WV national directors to ensure co-operation and a unified strategy in each country.

VFI focuses most of its micro-lending, along with support and training, in local communities where WV has ongoing area development programmes (ADPs). The development work done by WV creates the framework where micro-enterprise can flourish. Then, in essence, VFI provides the microfinance engine that helps these communities and families develop their economic well-being through enhanced livelihoods which in turn enables those families to better provide for their children's health, nutrition, education etc. At this level, MFI branch managers and credit officers collaborate with WV ADP managers and staff. This integration can take the form of complementary strategies, targeting, co-ordination, and reporting, etc.

For VFI, integration is viewed from three main perspectives:

- **Strategic Alignment.** The WV national office and the MFI develop and implement complementary strategies with interlinking goals and impact indicators that contribute to child well-being, including measurement and reporting of child well-being targets.
- **Organizational Integration.** VFI coordinates with WV at regional and national levels in terms of strategic planning and local governance (e.g., local WV senior staff members serve on the board of each MFI). In addition, MFIs must target a proportion of clients within WV target areas (e.g. ADPs), with the target % to be agreed as part of the annual planning process.
- **Programmatic Integration.** The MFI Branch and WV ADP staff must be jointly involved in the planning process, from design and implementation through to evaluation and re-design of programmes. This includes involvement in assessments (where possible), joint development of log-frames (where the community

Vision Fund International Case Study

identifies microfinance as a priority), as well as budgets, MOUs, detailed implementation plans, impact measures, and evaluation studies.[81]

TYPES OF CLIENTS SERVED AND PRODUCTS OFFERED

VFI is primarily a microcredit provider, although it is increasingly exploring savings and insurance services. At the end of September 2012, it had just over 686,000 active borrowers. Of these, 68% are women and 83% are within WV ADPs lending to a variety of activities:

Type of loan	Description	# Active Borrowers	Average Loan Size
Agriculture/Animals	Input supplies for smallholder farmers	352,000	$514
Commerce/Trade	Retail, grocery	214,445	$402
Service	Hair salons, restaurants	45,740	$941
Production/Industry	Hardware, woodworking, etc.	15,880	$667
Housing	Home improvements	13,924	$1,241
Consumption	School supplies, goods purchases, etc.	44,347	$411
Total		686,336	$579

Figure 2

As is evident, average loan sizes vary by country and region, but the overall average loan size across the VisionFund network is $579 USD:

Region	# Active Borrowers	Average Loan Size
Middle East/Eastern Europe	182,459	$1,230
Latin America/Caribbean	119,734	$642
Asia Pacific	223,786	$309
Africa	160,357	$291
Total	686,336	$579

Figure 3

VFI does not have a fixed way of lending, but adopts a mix of individual, community bank and solidarity lending methodologies, based on the local context, competition and environment. It does, however, encourage group and solidarity lending as the preferred methodology.

These have the potential to link more effectively with World Vision savings groups that already have the group mentality and dynamics. Figure 4 demonstrates the breakdown of % of clients in each lending methodology:

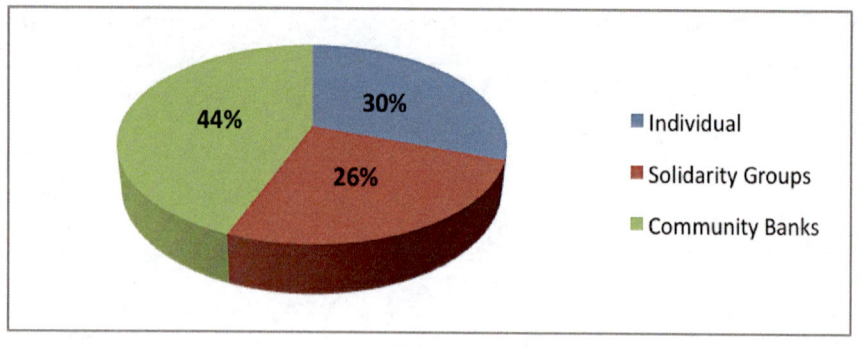

Figure 4

Pie chart:
- Individual: 30%
- Solidarity Groups: 26%
- Community Banks: 44%

VisionFund is exploring savings and has just over 252,000 savers at present. Interest is generally paid on savings accounts annually, unless local regulation requires it to be more frequent.

VFI interest in savings is primarily as a means to improve the coping mechanisms of the poor. By providing safe and accessible means of saving, it is hoped this will increase the potential for the poor to manage crises and ensure that the impact on the children or on the productive resources in a business are minimized when faced with crises such as sickness in the family.

There are two types of savings products, compulsory savings and voluntary savings:

- **Compulsory Savings**. Compulsory savings are taken by the MFI from clients as collateral for loans and held in a segregated account to which the client has no access. Where local market conditions, regulations and MFI sustainability permit, the MFIs pay interest on compulsory savings.

    Each VisionFund affiliated MFI must be permitted under local regulations before it can take compulsory savings, and must abide by all legal and regulatory requirements related to taking and intermediating compulsory savings.

Compulsory savings must be returned to the client when the client exits from the MFI if the loan has been fully repaid. Alternatively, the funds may be moved to the client's voluntary savings account. Compulsory savings may also be used to cover any unpaid loan amount as permitted by local laws.
- **Voluntary Savings.** Voluntary savings are funds deposited by clients for safe-keeping by the MFI, and are available for withdrawal in full or in part, according to conditions set out in the contract between the client and the MFI.

Because the development of voluntary savings products and services can be very complex and expensive, and because mobilizing savings changes the risk profile of the MFI, VFI maintains very strict monitoring of savings and transformation projects and expects MFIs to engage VFI at the very earliest stage of planning to offer savings products and services.[82]

Employees of VisionFund affiliated MFIs are encouraged to open voluntary savings accounts, and VisionFund encourages each MFI to consider designing a product specifically for employees and employees' immediate relatives.

One of the potential side benefits of voluntary savings to the MFI is that savings can be a source of local currency funding for the expansion of the MFI's loan portfolio, thereby improving the sustainability of the institution.

4.1 Insurance

VFI has at present very little development in the insurance area outside of life insurance (loan insurance in case of death). However, it has started to explore the possibilities of offering crop insurance and health insurance to its clients through partnerships with insurance companies.

The following policies guide VisionFund MFI's as they explore insurance products:

Guidelines
- Guid.9.1: MFI's **should** seek to provide clients with insurance to protect the loan in cases of client death, and to self-insure unless this is not allowed by local regulation.

- Guid.9.2: All other Micro-insurance services **should** be provided through partner (non-WVI/VFI entities) agencies **unless approved** in writing by VFI for the MFI to operate an insurance company or activity.
- Guid.9.4: MFIs **may** charge a loan insurance fee based on best practices and context

Requirements
- Req.9.1: MFIs **must** ensure proper agreements are in place, reviewed by local legal counsel, VFI Product Director and the NO prior to engaging in micro-insurance activities with a partner agency.
- Req.9.2: Transparent and competitive bidding should be in place in selecting the insurance company and should include price, product capability and benefits, customer service, reputation and financial solvency.

(from VisionFund Microfinance Operating Policies v2.0)

4.2 Non-financial products and services

Non-financial services that empower the poor are encouraged in all VisionFund MFIs with the following guidelines:
- In general, non-financial services (e.g. market linkages, sector training) are carried out by the WV office rather than by the MFI.
- MFIs are encouraged to work with the WV National Office (NO) on emergency relief programmes when they happen. Where agreed with the NO or Humanitarian & Emergency Affairs (HEA), relief funds may be used to support existing clients to move to new industries, or recover from emergencies, and to lend to new clients where agreed with the NO/HEA.
- Non-Financial Services should only be provided by the MFI (e.g. business training) where it is able to generate revenues or donations sufficient to fully cover the related costs.[83]

The primary non-financial product that VFI promotes in its MFIs is client education.

Client Education

In order to contribute to the well-being of its clients' children, VisionFund is increasingly providing a series of adult education modules to community bank and solidarity group clients of its MFIs. Utilizing materials developed by Freedom from Hunger[84] and others, clients engage in dialogue and problem-solving on selected topics that respond to real needs in their daily lives. Topics include financial literacy, business, health, agriculture, HIV & AIDS, etc. They are covered in 7-10 sessions lasting approximately 30 minutes and are accessible to illiterate clients. Each session is delivered weekly or bi-weekly by a field agent (usually credit officers) during regular repayment meetings.

Client education particularly benefits child-bearing women living in poor areas and suffering from chronic hunger. Effecting behaviour changes for the women positively impacts the quality of life of the whole family, primarily the children. By providing women with life skills and knowledge, the programme builds the mothers' capacities to provide better care for their children increasing their health, well-being and potential in life. Studies have shown the positive impact of providing education sessions to women on breast-feeding, immunizations, child nutrition, etc.[85]

The client education model addresses the fact that microfinance services are not sufficient to lift the poor out of poverty alone. It can be an effective platform for achieving closer integration between VisionFund MFIs and World Vision programmes through a hybrid model of education. For example, credit officers could provide training on financial literacy topics to World Vision savings group members, while World Vision staff could facilitate education on health topics like malaria, nutrition and HIV & AIDS to MFI clients. A pilot to test this integrated approach is planned for FY13.

To date, 5 VisionFund affiliated MFIs have begun implementation of client education and an additional 12 have received training with plans to implement in the near future. VisionFund Tanzania is also developing a series of client education videos to be played in branch offices or on mobile devices.

Technology Applied

As an organization with a rural focus, VFI views technology as having the potential in the future to dramatically change how it is able to deliver services at a low cost to clients in remote rural areas. Each MFI has its own MIS, utilizing everything from simple spreadsheets to sophisticated multi-faceted systems. At present, in countries such as Kenya and Uganda, mobile payments are increasingly being used to make payments and pilots are being worked on in Tanzania and Cambodia for collection of data using mobile devices that will allow for the quicker processing of loans.

Interest Rates and Fees Charged

VFI seeks to charge market rates for its products. Both locally and globally, VFI compares interest rates to the local market. It is important to understand that rates are not uniform and will differ from country to country depending on loan size. Likewise, pricing varies based on different products that reflect the relative risk of each product (for example, agricultural loans are generally priced higher than other less risky loans). In general, however, interest rates reflect local market rates, cost of capital, and the MFI's ability to cover costs based on VFI standards and client protection principles.

In most cases, when comparing prices and loan sizes by product, VisionFund MFI's are either at or below the market price. For those cases where rates are above the market, VFI is working with the MFI to see how it can reduce its price to bring it in alignment with the market.

21 VisionFund MFIs submitted data to MIX (in 2011 or 2012), and 7 MFIs received Social Reporting awards from MIX in 2011.[86] VisionFund is also supportive of MFTransparency and their efforts to gather and publish rates (13 MFIs report to MFT, where possible).

Methodology

Loans made by VisionFund affiliated MFI's are handled by the following three methods:
- **Community Banks** are VisionFund's preferred lending methodology. These loan circles create an opportunity for the poorest entrepreneurs to obtain credit. Self-selected groups of 15-30 borrowers (typically women) from the same community form a lending group and elect their own leaders. It is important that groups self-select responsible members whom they trust, because

the entire group acts as a guarantor for every member's loan. The members are then trained in effective loan management and leadership skills and they agree to cross-guarantee each other's loans.

Because credit officers work with groups rather than individuals in training and handling loans, the costs of community banking are low. This methodology also enables cost-effective provision of loans as small as $50. The MFI lends money to the community bank, which in turn, lends money to each member. Members must save a specified amount before they receive a loan.

One loan and one contract are made out to the entire loan group. Arrears by one member impact the whole group, since it is one contract and, therefore, the whole loan and entire group is late if one member is late. This is done because members do not have existing capital or collateral to guarantee outstanding loans. The group screens potential borrowers and tracks each repayment, building their leadership and sense of pride along the way.

Weekly or bi-weekly meetings ensure loans are tracked and repaid as well as offering clients encouragement, accountability and support. These meetings can also include educational sessions in financial literacy/business skills or other topics such as health and agriculture to help build clients' skills.

Ultimately, community bank members improve their entrepreneurial skills, incomes, and businesses. As members repay their loans, they become eligible for larger loans. Eventually, enterprising members with a good repayment record are allowed to form smaller solidarity groups and receive more sizable loans. Community bank loans typically range from US $50-500 (the average loan size is $311).

- **Solidarity Groups** are designed for more experienced entrepreneurs with larger enterprises. Solidarity groups have fewer members than community banks, with an average of three to six people who guarantee each other's loans. Borrowers guarantee to the MFI that each member of the group will repay, and if they do not, other members will be personally held responsible for the outstanding debt. Members who make repayments on time become eligible for larger individual loans. Solidarity group loan sizes range from US $300-800 (average loan size is $413).

- **Individual loans** are geared toward clients who have either grown their businesses successfully through a solidarity group or have medium-sized businesses that qualify for individual loans ranging from US $500-5000 (average loan size is $1,111). Loans typically require either two guarantors or collateral. Borrowers often create a multi-year business plan in consultation with their loan officer.

FUNDING

VFI is funded from a range of sources including donations, third-party lending and retained earnings. One of the pioneering initiatives is in partnership with WV offering loans through World Vision Micro in the U.S.[87] This is a website that allows for donors to donate for a specific client to fund their loan. The loan has been pre-funded by the MFI and the funds allow for the loan to be financed. The donor then receives information on the loan at the mid-point and the end of the loan using social performance information collected by the staff of the MFI on that client. This fundraising initiative is still in the early stages of development but it is promising. Micro currently features entrepreneurs from Armenia, Cambodia, Ethiopia, Indonesia, Kenya, Philippines, Mexico and Rwanda.

SOCIAL PERFORMANCE – IMPACT

VFI's approach to social performance, or translating mission into practice, is best described by the diagram below. This shows how VFI's mission to serve children is reflected throughout the process from targeting to outcomes. In targeting, VFI seeks to focus on working where World Vision works (i.e. the *rural* areas where WV works). By focusing on women VFI seeks to increase the direct impact on women[88] and by using tools like the Progress out of Poverty Index (PPI).[89] The PPI is a poverty scorecard that uses non-financial indicators to measure poverty levels of MFI clients. It was developed by the Grameen Foundation based on an approach developed by Mark Schreiner of Microfinance Risk Management, L.L.C. The PPI estimates the likelihood of clients who fall below various poverty lines. Each PPI is country specific and utilizes that country's income and expenditure household survey.

The PPI uses ten simple indicators that field workers can quickly collect and verify.[90] Scores can be computed by hand on paper in real time. With 90% confidence, estimates of the groups' overall poverty rates are accurate to within +/-2% points. Using the PPI, MFIs can target clients below the poverty line and track changes in poverty levels over time. 25 VisionFund MFIs are currently in the process of implementing the use of the PPI.

This is then complemented at the product level by increasing focus on developing products that will intentionally contribute to child well-being outcomes[91] and by policies and procedures that ensure that clients are treated fairly. VFI is also seeking to ensure that the risk of over-indebtedness is minimized by promoting improved analysis of loans and client education. Wherever possible, MFI's use the local credit bureaus to avoid clients taking on too much debt and by complementing this with increased focus on smaller loans. By doing so, it is believed that the risk of over-indebtedness can be minimized.

VF'S SOCIAL PERFORMANCE APPROACH

Mission: Impacting children

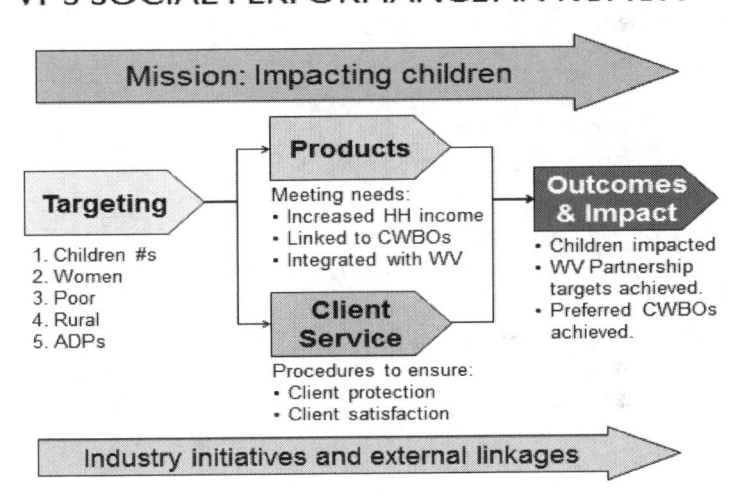

Targeting
1. Children #s
2. Women
3. Poor
4. Rural
5. ADPs

Products
Meeting needs:
- Increased HH income
- Linked to CWBOs
- Integrated with WV

Client Service
Procedures to ensure:
- Client protection
- Client satisfaction

Outcomes & Impact
- Children impacted
- WV Partnership targets achieved.
- Preferred CWBOs achieved.

Industry initiatives and external linkages

Figure 5

VFI's approach to social performance starts with its Christian identity and mission of impacting children. Under the governance of committed leadership, these are translated into practice by:
1. targeting primarily poor women with dependent children in the areas where WV works
2. providing impact-focused and integrated products
3. ensuring client protection and satisfaction
4. collaborating with and contributing to the broader industry
5. measuring outcomes and impact, with the primary focus on child well-being

The sustained well-being of children within families, especially the most vulnerable, is the over-arching goal of all VisionFund products and services. World Vision's Child Well-being Aspirations and Outcomes (Figure 6) provide a practical definition of World Vision's understanding of well-being for children. World Vision views the well-being of children in holistic terms: healthy individual development (involving physical and mental health, social and spiritual dimensions), positive relationships and a context that provides safety, social justice, and participation in civil society.[92]

Based on Luke 2:52: "Jesus grew in stature, wisdom and grace with God and with others," the 4 child well-being aspirations are the following:
- Girls and boys enjoy good health.
- Girls and boys are educated for life.
- Girls and boys experience love of God and their neighbours.
- Girls and boys are cared for, protected and participating.

The four aspirations are divided into 15 child well-being outcomes (see Figure 6). They describe the developmental outcomes for children that contribute to these aspirations. Because child development is based on holistic and interrelated factors, the child well-being outcomes are interdependent. Effective programming can affect multiple outcomes at the same time.

GOAL	Sustained well-being of children within families and communities, especially the most vulnerable			
ASPIRATIONS	Girls & Boys:			
	Enjoy good health	Are educated for life	Experience love of God and their neighbours	Are cared for, protected and participating
OUTCOMES	Children well nourished	Children read, write, and use numeracy skills	Children grow in their awareness and experience of God's love in an environment that recognises their freedom	Children cared for in a loving, safe, family and community environment with safe places to play
	Children protected from infection, disease, and injury	Children make good judgments, can protect themselves, manage emotions, and communicate ideas	Children enjoy positive relationships with peers, family, and community members	Parents or caregivers provide well for their children
	Children and their caregivers access essential health services	Adolescents ready for economic opportunity	Children value and care for others and their environment	Children celebrated and registered at birth
		Children access and complete basic education	Children have hope and vision for the future	Children are respected participants in decisions that affect their lives
FOUNDATIONAL PRINCIPLES	Children are citizens and their rights and dignity are upheld (including girls and boys of all religions and ethnicities, any HIV status, and those with disabilities)			

Figure 6

Growth in terms of portfolio size, profitability and child well-being are not the only measures of success for VisionFund. Tim Dearborn, World Vision's former partnership leader for Christian Commitments, comments: "Stop here and we sell ourselves, our donors, our mission and the poor short.

VisionFund MFIs fulfill the same mission as World Vision. VFI promotes human transformation: The flourishing of those in poverty depends on more than money. VFI seeks justice: Businesses exist to contribute to making life right. And VFI bears witness to the kingdom: Activities that express the love of power, rather than the power of love, that reinforce individual gain at the cost of community well-being, that encourage reliance on human effort and resources without regard to God, and that irreparably damage creation, are contrary to the will and ways of God."[93]

VFI, along with the rest of the microfinance industry, has focused on loan size and numbers of clients (and in the case of World Vision the number of children) as proxies for impact indicators. Now, as the wider microfinance industry has become more evidence-based, VFI is seeking to work with WV to measure the outcomes of all of its work in the ADPs where World Vision works. This is still in the early stages, but by focusing on the outcomes at a child level VFI hopes to be able to measure its contribution in more concrete ways. While anecdotal evidence is not enough to "prove" VisionFund's impact, the following are a few examples of client success stories from VisionFund MFIs:

Jacqueline
Jacqueline saved for years to buy a sewing machine. Then a $400 loan from VisionFund changed her life. She bought another sewing machine and then another. Now she has 24 sewing machines and employees to run them, designing and producing school uniforms in her African village. Her children are well provided for and enjoying school – her daughter has plans to become a doctor.

Isidro, Purificacion, Luis and Juan
After receiving training in agriculture from World Vision, a VisionFund loan enabled these four Honduran farmers to form a co-operative and grow sweet potatoes. An additional loan then helped them switch to more profitable plantains. Access to credit meant that they could farm on a scale that generates enough profit to increase their living standards, send their children to school, improve their homes and buy medicine.

Top
A Cambodian mother of four, Top, joined other women to apply for an agricultural group loan to increase the productivity of their farms. They borrowed $25 for fertilizer to grow rice, $100 to buy cows (which produced 3 calves) and $125 to buy land and irrigation equipment to grow rice. Since then, Top's annual income has almost doubled and she has diversified into growing watermelons. Her children are thriving with better food and education. Her daughter wants to study to become a teacher.

Hayk

Hayk, an Armenian farmer, used to work on a collective farm when Armenia was part of the former Soviet Union. He now owns his own farm and, with the help of loans from VisionFund, he has increased the range of crops he cultivates, leased additional land, built storage for farm produce and hired 4 full-time and 2 seasonal employees. His increased income covers school fees for his three children and medicine for his elderly parents. In the future, he hopes to expand the family home and hire additional farm workers.

Sophat

Sophat lost his left leg to a landmine during Cambodia's civil war in 1985 when he was a 20 year-old soldier in the government's army. He met Socheat, whose limbs were deformed from birth. They married in 2001, three years after the country's UN-administered first democratic election agreed upon by fighting factions.

Sophat and Socheat then started to sell boiled potatoes and snacks to primary school students near their parents' house, 300 meters from the section of the national road in Tram Kok district, approximately 10 kilometres from the provincial town of Takeo.

In 2002, Sophat learned from an NGO how to repair motorbikes and bicycles while receiving a government allowance as a disabled veteran. Following the vocational training, lack of capital prevented him from using his newly acquired skill to increase his household income. The couple continued with their boiled potato and snack business for three more years, with a daily income of US$ 1.25.

Sophat finally managed to put his skill into practice when he received his first loan of US$ 150 from VisionFund (Cambodia) in 2006 to buy the necessary equipment to repair bicycles and motorbikes. Socheat stopped selling the potatoes and snacks to help Sophat's more profitable job.

Since then, the couple has been living in a makeshift wooden hut they built on a plot of idle land with agreement from the property owner. They built their home on the national road, which they believe will expose them to more business opportunities. With subsequent similar loans and growing income over the past years, this hard-working couple has expanded their business to selling coffee, gasoline and snacks in addition to the bicycle and motorbike repair service.

Now with three children, 7-year-old Karat in grade 1, 5-year-old Kiri in kindergarten, and 2-year-old Ratha, they have seen household income rise 10 fold, improving their living conditions and social relations as well as inspiring hope for the future. "Since borrowing from the organization, our minimum daily income is US$ 12.50. There is a huge difference in income from US$ 1.25 to US$ 12.50," Sophat says. "My family has experienced progress. For now, we have money to buy food and we are happy."

"With our previous business, we were unwilling to buy desserts or fruits to eat. Now we are willing to buy them for our children," Socheat adds. "For our relationships with our neighbours, most of them appreciate our business and like to help by buying goods, having their motorbikes or bicycles repaired, and buying gasoline at our shop," Sophat says. They thank VisionFund Cambodia for providing Sophat with loans requiring no collateral and charging lower interest rates than local private lenders.

CHRISTIAN DISTINCTIVES

As the microfinance subsidiary of World Vision, VisionFund carries the "branding" of one of the most well-known and respected Christian organizations in the world. However, that does not necessarily mean that VFI operates any differently from other secular MFIs. In order to distinguish itself, VisionFund has developed definitions of Christian MFIs (10.1), created preferences for targeting the poorest entrepreneurs (10.2), developed policies rejecting discrimination and proselytism (10.3), and produced materials describing VFI's integrated, holistic approach to development (10.4).

VFI's Definition of Christian MFIs

The following lists describe how VFI views its affiliated MFIs. These are not exhaustive lists, but they provide characteristics of what VFI believes a Christian MFI is – and is not.

As a Christian MFI we:
- seek to follow Jesus in all that we do
- are from diverse Christian traditions – Catholic, Orthodox and Protestant
- incorporate Christian witness in our operations
- support the spiritual development of our staff

- view our products and services as one piece of holistic development
- establish God-honouring relationships
- seek to provide hope to clients with our products
- understand and value a diversity of beliefs and faith traditions
- encourage and incorporate prayer in the lives of staff
- are complementary to the church

As a Christian MFI we *are not*:
- a missionary agency
- denominationally affiliated
- discriminatory in our practices
- an organization that proselytises (i.e., using financial services to coerce conversion)

(from VFI's Defining Christian MFIs and Christian Witness)

Focus on the poorest of the economically active

VFI targets clients based on its mission and double bottom-line approach to microfinance (that is, ensuring sustainability while making a social impact). VFI's mission is to empower the enterprising poor to liberate themselves and their families from poverty. The financial bottom-line of sustainable microfinance operations requires that VFI lend only to credit-worthy clients. If a client, of whatever faith, does not meet the lending criteria, that client will not qualify for a loan. The social bottom-line of affecting children in areas where World Vision works, however, means that VFI intentionally targets poor and vulnerable entrepreneurs. VFI's microfinance management policies state that VFI-affiliated MFIs preferentially target:[94]

- clients within World Vision programme areas, primarily area development programmes (ADPs) where applicable
- female clients, who, based on numerous studies, use their income for the well-being of their children more than men
- the poorest micro-entrepreneurs (established by PPI and other poverty score-cards) within the local context
- micro-entrepreneurs (including irregular and informal self-employment) with business experience

These policies further define the poorest, or most vulnerable entrepreneurs, as including the poor and very poor, women, under-served rural areas, and excluded groups such as disabled persons, people living with HIV and AIDS, and youth.

Rejection of Discrimination and Proselytism

Despite its preferential targets, VFI does not discriminate amongst clients with regard to ethnicity, political affiliation, or religion, amongst other things. Financial services are available without regard to religion, meaning that loans are available to all credit-worthy clients whether they are Christians, Buddhists, Muslims, or followers of any other faith. VFI's microfinance management policies are abundantly clear about VFI's stance on discrimination:

> *Microfinance services are available to the poor regardless of ethnicity, religion, gender, caste, race, political affiliation, disability, or health status.*[95]

Furthermore, VisionFund does not prioritize Christians in its provision of financial services, using faith as a 'dividing line' in the communities in which it works. For example, VisionFund affiliated MFIs do not provide better loan terms or larger loan sizes based on their clients' faith. Likewise, VFI does not provide financial services to Christians before providing them to people of other faiths.

Proselytism occurs whenever assistance or influence is offered on the condition that people listen to a religious message or as an incentive to change religious beliefs. VFI's rejection of this kind of unethical witness is unequivocal:

> *Rejection of Proselytism. We do not use financial services, power and influence as incentives to conversion. We believe this is unethical and dishonouring to people as well as to God. (from VF Guiding Principles on Witness to Jesus Christ)*

VFI does not offer financial services on the condition that people listen to the message of the Christian gospel. VisionFund's engagement in microfinance is not a means to gain converts but a concrete expression of witness to the good news of Jesus Christ. VisionFund staff members are motivated by God's love to provide financial services that empower poor entrepreneurs to liberate themselves from poverty. VFI does not attach the promise of financial services to an acceptance of the Christian faith. VFI does not use microfinance as a means to promote Christianity. This means that VFI-affiliated MFIs do not have clients engage in mandatory Bible studies, devotions, prayers, and so forth.

Related to proselytism is the concept of pre-evangelism. In this approach to development, microfinance is seen as a precursor to mission or as a 'foot-in-the-door' in order to evangelize clients. This view sees salvation of souls as the primary goal and microfinance as a means to achieving that goal. While other Christian organizations may espouse this approach, which implies that the MFI's role is preparing people for evangelism, VFI rejects it. VFI does not define success based on whether or not people are converting to Christianity as a result of its work. Again, VFI's engagement in microfinance is not a means to an end but an expression of witness to the good news of Jesus Christ. As opposed to an evangelistic organization that seeks converts, VisionFund/World Vision "hopes that all we do will bear witness to God's unconditional love and contribute to people experiencing fullness of life as followers of Jesus Christ in an environment that respects their rights and freedom."[96]

Clear policies, organizational motivation, and an organizational culture that respects people of any faith background all underscore VFI's explicit rejection of discrimination and unethical forms of witness.

Integrated/Holistic Approach

Some development organizations have historically defined poverty as simply a lack of material things and have focused on providing a solution that provides basic necessities. Other faith-based organizations have minimized the economic aspect of poverty, focusing solely on the spiritual facets.

In contrast to these narrow approaches, World Vision recognizes that poverty is not just material deficiency, but rather a multi-faceted issue with social, economic, political and spiritual aspects. World Vision's understanding of poverty takes into account the multiple factors that work together to bring about the condition of poverty, such as lack of income, poor health, inadequate education, powerlessness, food insecurity, and hopelessness.

In the same way, World Vision's core documents embody a multi-faceted approach to combating poverty that includes relief, development and advocacy. VFI is one of the primary development programmes within World Vision that addresses economic issues affecting community members. Nearly 6,000 MFI staff members comprise over 13% of all

World Vision staff worldwide. It is one of the reasons why VFI-affiliated MFIs target clients within geographical areas where World Vision is operating.

By combining loans with relief, advocacy and other development initiatives, VFI and World Vision provide a holistic, comprehensive approach to tackling poverty. In fact, this holistic ministry is VFI's unique strength as a provider of microfinance. As you can see by Figure 7, VisionFund's work complements the work of WV to help people pull themselves up and out of poverty.

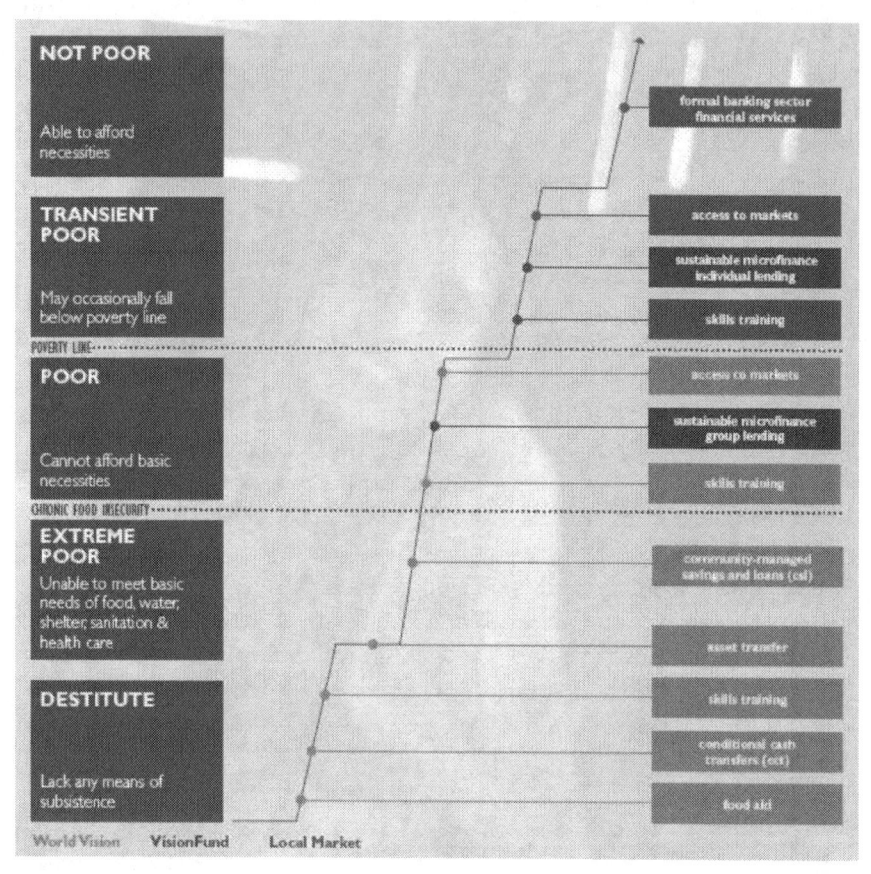

Figure 7

World Vision and VFI seek to provide appropriate interventions at each level of need. As the "ladder" progresses, people have more capability and they are expected to do more for themselves. VFI's work meets needs that other types of World Vision work cannot meet (expanding income and jobs so that clients can provide for themselves and their children), and World Vision's other work meets needs that cannot be met by VisionFund (such as healthcare and education). Finally, clients are equipped to enter local markets and compete for themselves.

CHALLENGES OF BEING A CHRISTIAN MFI

Some of the challenges that VisionFund faces are cultivating a diverse staff from many faith backgrounds (11.1), maintaining its Christian identity amidst a diversity of opinions (11.2), and reducing the potential for fraud (11.3).

Multi-faith Staff

The VFI network includes several MFIs which are not in predominantly Christian contexts. In fact, nearly half of VisionFund affiliated MFIs are in environments where a faith other than Christianity is the majority religion. Since VFI is committed to hiring indigenous staff, staff members in many MFIs are followers of another faith.

VisionFund respects and values staff from other faith backgrounds and their significant contribution to its work. VisionFund believes that all people, not just Christians, are created and loved by God. In VFI, diversity goes beyond simply tolerating one another. Rather, VFI respects all staff members as made in God's image, regardless of their faith tradition, and celebrates the richness of diversity amongst staff by creating a participative environment that values all opinions and contributions and by supporting the development of all staff members. Though it is not VFI's role to provide for the spiritual needs of staff of other faiths, VFI understands the importance of demonstrating religious and cultural sensitivity:

> *Staff members are not pressured to engage in practices that go against the central tenets of their faith. At the same time, they are expected to show understanding and reasonable support for World Vision's Christian identity and ethos of which*

they were made aware when they were hired' (from World Vision's Ministry Policy on Interfaith Relations)

While respect is demonstrated to staff of all faiths, VFI is committed to hiring Christians in senior leadership positions to ensure the integrity of each MFI's identity: "Managers and senior leaders (CEOs, CFOs and COOs) evidence professional competence and spiritual maturity, reflecting Christ-like values in life and work. We affirm rare exceptions to the appointment of Christians to leadership positions."[97]

Striking a balance between extremes

Core documents (vision, mission, core values, etc.) and several related policies describe World Vision's identity and work as falling on a spectrum somewhere between a secular humanitarian organization at one end and a Christian evangelism organization at the other. As World Vision and VisionFund have grown rapidly during this past decade, they have added over 20,000 new staff, not all of whom have fully understood the position of the organization between these two poles.

While the majority of staff members are in alignment, there are differing opinions on how VFI should appropriately express its Christian identity. On one side, some individual staff members would like VFI to expunge its Christian identity entirely, while others on the opposite extreme would sanction proselytism. Embracing this 'middle' position is full of complexity and nuance, but vital to the sustainability of the organization.

In 2011, orientation modules were created for staff to avoid confusing the purpose of VisionFund with a church or mission organization, without abandoning its Christian identity. These materials, which were made available in twenty-two languages represented among MFI staff, clarified and defined *appropriate* Christian witness for staff worldwide. A questionnaire with several key statements related to Christian identity and approach to witness was used to evaluate the effectiveness of these modules. The results demonstrated that the majority of statements (60%) demonstrated positive movement toward increased alignment with the organizational position (with 34% substantial positive change).[98]

Questionnaire Statements:
Change from baseline to post-orientation

- Substantial Positive change (12/35): 34%
- Positive change (9/35): 26%
- No change (11/35): 31%
- Negative change (2/35): 6%
- Substantial Negative change (1/35): 3%

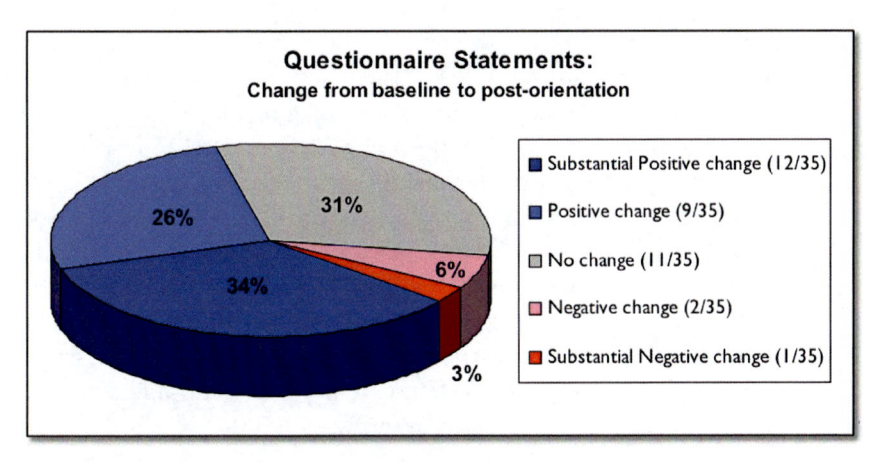

Figure 8

While there has been significant progress toward increased alignment, living in the tension between the extremes continues to be an ongoing endeavor within VisionFund and World Vision. Uncomfortable, but ultimately healthy, discussions are helping VisionFund to maintain a balance of remaining secure in its Christian identity, while being sensitive to the diverse contexts in which it operates.

Potential for Fraud

VisionFund MFIs depend on the integrity of staff just as much as on the integrity of clients. If staff cannot be trusted to maintain their integrity, then the whole system breaks down. Christian MFIs are no more immune to fraud than secular MFIs. If anything, they can be more susceptible because of the potential to abuse the Christian principles of grace, love, integrity and trust.

VFI employs two key tools to combat the potential for fraud in its MFIs:

- An Integrity and Risk Reporting (IRR) policy is available for staff to use. The purpose of this policy is to maintain the highest standards of integrity for the organization. The policy does this by making it possible for people to report issues in a confidential and, if necessary, anonymous way, through an international hotline.

These reports are followed up in a professional manner that protects the person who initiates the report.
- While an MFI cannot tolerate a lack of integrity from its staff, it needs to acknowledge that the temptations do exist. It can help preserve good staff by providing space for staff to talk about temptations they may face and what sort of systems and controls can help to encourage and reward integrity. In 2011, VFI published a series of devotional topics, authored by Larry Reed, that handle difficult questions and challenges that MFI staff face on a daily basis.[99] Two of these topics deal with stealing and fraud, providing practical solutions that can help staff confront, avoid and report financial temptations or transgressions.

CONCLUSION

VFI's mission and vision seek fullness of life for its clients and their children. What distinguishes VFI's work is that it is part of a wider development organization. VFI works closely with World Vision in strategic and programmatic ways, and it focuses its work in the geographic areas where WV is working. Through integrated products and services, VFI helps transform the lives of the people it serves.

A diverse array of lending activities is funded through different methodologies, but community banks and solidarity lending are the preferred lending methods. Particular emphasis is placed on social performance, by targeting primarily women with dependent children, providing impact-focused and integrated products, ensuring client protection and satisfaction, and placing primary focus on child well-being.

The work of VFI is motivated by God's love and the understanding that all people are created in God's image. It is VisionFund's hope that people would experience fullness of life as followers of Christ, but has developed clear policies rejecting proselytism and discrimination. Ultimately, VFI's engagement in microfinance is not a means to witness but a concrete expression of witness to the good news of Jesus Christ.

Some of the challenges that VisionFund faces are managing a diverse staff from many faith backgrounds, maintaining its Christian identity amidst a diversity of opinions, and reducing the potential for fraud.

FIVE TALENTS CASE STUDY
TOM SANDERSON

Tom Sanderson is the UK Director of Five Talents. He read economics at Cambridge and did his Masters in Economics at University College London before working as a Government Economic Advisor in the Ministry of Agriculture in London. He spent five years as a community development worker in Uganda with the Church Mission Society where he was involved in many types of development interventions, mainly grant-based. He also helped to establish the first Five Talents microfinance programme in Uganda seeing it grow to serve thousands of local entrepreneurs.

Five Talents is a Christian microfinance NGO established by the worldwide Anglican church in 1998. This chapter traces the origins of Five Talents, its activities and rapid growth. It outlines Five Talents' distinctive approach to delivering microfinance in partnership with the local Church and their strong focus on reaching marginalised communities with business training and promotion of savings as well as credit. The charity draws its name from Jesus' Parable of the Talents and is an inspiring example of the Christian faith in action.

HISTORY

It started with a friendship. Gladys Chiwanga needed some winter clothes to cope with the cold winter in the USA. She was studying at Virginia Theological Seminary in the USA. Angela knew Gladys from a previous trip to Tanzania and kindly bought her some warm cardigans and a coat.

Gladys' husband, Bishop Simon Chiwanga, was coming over to visit Gladys in 1998 and the two couples, Bishop Simon and Gladys plus Angela and her husband Rev. Martyn Minns, soon became close friends.

Learning about the struggles and hardships of the communities in Tanzania really fascinated and troubled Martyn and Angela. Both Simon and Martyn recognised their equivalent Christian calling and similar Church ministry, but the context of their service and leadership could not be further apart. Martyn was leading Truro Church, a vibrant Anglican Church parish in Fairfax, Northern Virginia, just outside Washington D.C. – the neighbourhood of the political classes and America's elite.

Bishop Simon was bishop of Mpwapwa Diocese in Northern Tanzania, home to some of the poorest and most remote communities on the planet, where families are not able to adequately feed or educate their children.

Simon was also serving as chairman of the Anglican Consultative Council, one of the so-called "instruments" of the worldwide Anglican Communion. His role included preparing for the forthcoming 1998 Lambeth Conference, held every 10 years, where all Anglican Bishops from around the world are invited to attend a three weeks' conference in Canterbury, England.

In discussing the conference and the contrasts in their personal stories, the two couples felt called by God to explore a practical response. "It is good to pray for one another, but God also wants us to act and do something practical" – was their strong sentiment.

Diane Knippers was working at the Institute on Religion and Democracy in Washington D.C. She was appalled by the desperate stories of deprivation that Simon and Gladys were sharing at her home church in Truro – particularly the burden on families, women and children in Tanzania. She conducted some research into development interventions and identified Micro-Enterprise Development (MED) as a practical, grassroots method of enabling the poor to earn a living and thereby sustain and improve family livelihoods.

Diane identified David Bussau from Australia, co-founder of Opportunity International, as a key resource person to help develop the conversation. Martyn knew Rev. Dr. Vinay Samuel from England as another informed expert with a background in MED. The idea of an Anglican-wide initiative to focus on MED was forming and the name "Five Talents" – taken from the Parable of the Talents in Matthew's Gospel, chapter 25, began to crystallise.

When the Lambeth Conference took place in Canterbury in England in 1998, Simon Chiwanga hosted a reception for Bishops and their wives to consider the practical means of helping those around the Anglican Communion to address long-term poverty. The turnout was overwhelming. The method of developing micro-enterprises and using microfinance was presented. The name "Five Talents" was suggested. The Archbishop of Wales, Dr. Rowan Williams, supported the initiative, commenting on the similar needs in deprived communities in Wales for solutions which empowered the poor and brought dignity to their lives.

Five Talents Case Study

The then Archbishop of Canterbury, George Carey, presented a cheque for £1,000 to Bishop Simon to start the Five Talents programme (pictured).

A resolution was passed in the Conference proceedings (Resolution V.2f):

> *Noting that revolving micro-credit projects – such as those managed by Opportunity International, Grameen Bank, ECLOF and others – equip the poor with the credit needed to start small businesses and create jobs with dignity, [the Conference] commends the efforts of these various development agencies. It further welcomes new initiatives such as the Five Talents project, a micro-credit development initiative designed to combat world poverty, and commends it for its implementation.*[100]

Perhaps most significant, was the short conversation at the end of the conference when one of the Bishop's wives said to Martyn with conviction – "please, you must make this happen". Martyn recalls the eye-to-eye contact and the imperative in her voice, not in a haunting or threatening way, but a compelling, urgent and vibrant imperative to make this vision a reality. Maybe she had attended previous conferences and other such meetings full of good intentions and seen little or no fruit. Five Talents was too important and too significant to be left on the shelf.

Returning home after the Lambeth Conference, the Five Talents initiative was still in its infancy. Martyn spoke about it in his local parish church. They did some fund-raising and gathered $5,000. With Diane's help they registered Five Talents in the USA as a non-profit organisation. In faith, they hired the first chief executive, Craig Cole, in 1999 who refers to those early days as having six staff members – "Me, Myself and I, plus the Father, Son and Holy Spirit."

An office was established and, in 2000, the first micro-enterprise partnership was made with the Church in the Central Philippines and a national NGO called the Centre for Community Transformation (CCT).[101] A Memorandum of Understanding was signed and Five Talents injected some loan capital and operational funds to CCT's existing microfinance programme enabling a new branch to be opened in the slums around Manila.

The three-way partnership was no accident. Craig, with the help of David Bussau and others, researched the situation and made the connections. The Episcopal Diocese of the Central Philippines was active in preaching the Gospel but keen to demonstrate the Good News in practical assistance to their local communities. CCT was already running a microfinance programme with a Christian staff and vision and was looking for ways to reach new areas and co-operate with local churches to build credibility and a strong foundation. Five Talents was perfectly placed to bring these two parties together, initiating the conversation to identify a shared vision and helping to stimulate action by providing financial resources. The transformational impact of Christian micro-enterprise development was quickly observed and the stories coming back to the Five Talents supporters in the USA were a tremendous encouragement to carry on.

VISION, MISSION AND CORE VALUES

From these early beginnings, Five Talents' vision has always been to focus on helping the poorest and empowering them in practical ways to bring them hope. The micro-enterprise approach has an innate dignity about it. People can choose and develop their own business from which, with hard work, they accrue their own profit to benefit their own families and employees. This self-governing attribute avoids most of the pitfalls of top-down, sometimes patronising, development interventions and it values the intrinsic talents of the people themselves. The economic incentives to work hard, make profits and enjoy the fruits of one's labour are strong and with MED those incentives are clearly aligned.

The Parable of the Talents in Matthew 25 (verses 14-30) is of course a remarkable inspiration for the Five Talents NGO. The parable is amongst a set of three parables pointing to the sudden return of the "Master"; the "Bridegroom" and the "King". All three highlight the need for a practical response to the imminent return. For the ten virgins (verses 1-13), they had to be ready with oil in their lamps or they would miss the bridegroom and be excluded from the banquet. For the people referred to as "sheep and goats" (verses 31-46), they were expected to feed the hungry, be hospitable to strangers, clothe the naked, care for the sick and visit those in prison.

Similarly, the three servants in the Parable of the Talents were expected to make a return on their master's loan capital at least as much as the low-risk interest from a bank deposit account. The penalty for not doing so was severe – like in the other parables – and in this case, going to the place of "wailing and gnashing of teeth" (verse 30).

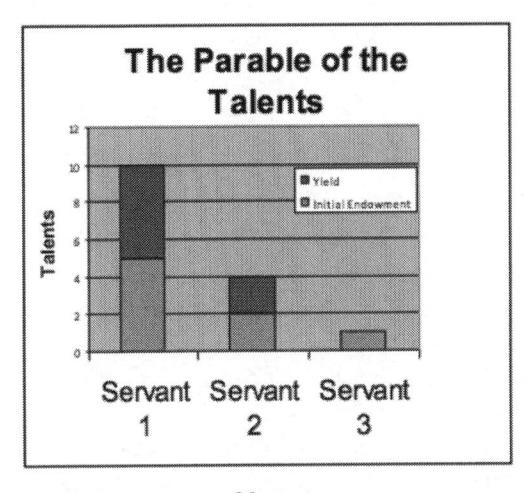

Chart 1

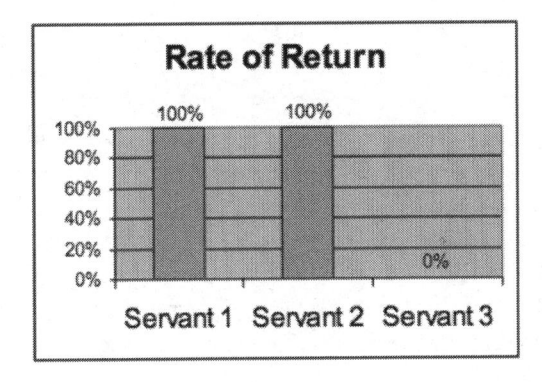

Chart 2

A talent in Biblical times was the largest measurement of money. It was actually a measurement of weight – around 60kg – and it did not have a constant value. A talent of gold, for example, would be worth a lot more than a talent of bronze. While commentators differ somewhat over the approximate value of a talent in today's economy, all would agree that it was a very large amount of money, equivalent to around 20 years' wages for a manual labourer.

With this interpretation of the main message of the parable, Five Talents' values are drawn from this and other particular aspects of the story. The charts above help to unpack some of the details in economic terms.

Chart 1 highlights the initial endowments and yields in a static and absolute way. Chart 2 calculates the rate of return for each servant, showing the dynamic position. From here one can clearly see the underperformance of the third servant and the joint top performers (and hence equal endorsement) of servants one and two. Other points to note, carried forward in Five Talents' training and core values,[102] are as follows:

1. Everyone is entrusted with "talents" – generous initial endowments. God loves each of us so much that He has entrusted large amounts of "talent" in us.
2. Each according to his/her ability – we have different abilities and rather than jealously observing others' talents, we should concentrate on earning 100% rate of return on those talents that we have been endowed with.
3. We are expected to use those talents and multiply them – two of the servants in the parable generated a 100% rate of return – doubling their portfolio in the time available. The third servant simply buried the talent and was severely reprimanded.
4. Hard work is good for you – the first two servants "went at once and traded". Elsewhere in the Bible, work is commended and laziness despised.
5. Risk, initiative, creativity and enterprise are expected – how else were the servants meant to multiply their endowment? Of course wise investment choices and careful due diligence are needed to do so.
6. We are all called to account – transparency, integrity and accountability are strong themes. You cannot hide from your creditor or indeed the loan officer or taxman. You need to repay

the loan in full. You know the right thing to do and you should do it.
7. Affirmation and commendation – "well done good and faithful servant" their wonderful phrase rings out from the Scripture. The reward for faithfulness is immense joy.
8. Progressive inheritance – since you have "been faithful with a few things, I will put you in charge of many things." Trust can be demonstrated, earned and rewarded.

Another core value, stemming from Five Talents' foundation, is the desire to serve the Church and to help the local Church to be the "hope of the world".[103] The Archbishop of Canterbury, the Rev. Dr. Rowan Williams, referred to Five Talents as a "gift to the Anglican communion"[104] in a missional sense, saying "The Church has a distinct advantage in delivering microfinance services through its local presence, credibility and network. Microfinance has a broad impact on communities and livelihoods, helping the poor while preserving their dignity."[105] This is not just for the Church to help its own members, but to be a practical agent for social care and improvements in and amongst the whole community irrespective of faith or tribe or gender.

The Church is an incredibly valuable ally in the fight against poverty for a number of reasons. Firstly, the Christian Church in low-income countries is an important civil society organisation. The Anglican Church itself has a global membership of around 85 million people,[106] with the largest concentration in Africa. It has a well established network and structure that has withstood conflict, disaster and political unrest for well over 100 years. Secondly, as Belshaw et al. note in their book "Faith in Development":[107]

Christian institutions are rooted in their communities. They have developed a credible leadership familiar with the needs of the poor, familiar with cultures, histories and contexts of its people. Religious communities approach their development work from a unique perspective that reinforces the moral and ethical values systems of these communities.

This implies that Church-based organisations have the benefit of understanding the local context more than foreign organizations whereby 'experts' go to 'do development' in developing countries.

Thirdly, the Church is largely stable and trusted – with both its membership and leadership drawn from members of the local community. It is respected as a credible institution by both Christians and, in many cases, non-Christians alike. It promotes a non-corruption culture with good accountability structures (although worst case scenarios can always be found). Finally, the Church has a biblical mandate to care for the poor, meaning that its members understand 'caring for the poor' as a core value in the out-working of their faith; in fact it is sometimes said that the Church is "the only society that exists for the benefit of those who are not its members."[108] All in all, these factors contribute to the Church being a powerful partner in development.

Five Talents' partnership with the local Anglican Church builds on these strengths to reach out to all needy people in a community, irrespective of faith. The Church leaders can also help overcome some of the information asymmetries[109] and moral hazards[110] associated with lending money to people and groups who have no previous known credit history. They can also help in the recruitment of loan officers, local staff and board members who have skills and integrity. Five Talents has also benefited greatly from the infrastructure that the Church can provide in terms of office space and community meeting spaces.

The Mission of Five Talents is presently articulated as:

Fighting poverty, creating jobs and transforming lives by empowering the poor in developing countries through innovative savings and microcredit programmes, business training and holistic development.

Five Talents has a strong emphasis on savings and business training and not just micro-credit. There is a clear focus on reaching the poorest groups and communities that other microfinance providers are not reaching. For example, in India, the Five Talents' programme supports the *Dalit* community; in Tanzania, the programme is focussed on women only; and, in places like South Sudan and Northern Uganda, the Five Talents' programmes are working in post-conflict communities.

As Peter, one of the loan officers in the Peru programme, said: "we accompany people on their journey out of poverty" and "we provide transformational microfinance, not just cold transactional services". Five Talents seeks to treat people as whole persons, recognising the competing claims to their scarce resources and helping them to plan and invest wisely.

But there is also a very strong message of "tough love" in line with the parable. Five Talents has adopted a phrase referring to its loan officers; that they have "the heart of a pastor and the mind of a banker". Of course that is not to say that pastors do not have good minds, or bankers, good hearts (!) It simply emphasises both the relational and professional nature of the services that are offered and which will be described more fully later in this chapter.

ORGANISATIONAL STRUCTURE

At the time of writing, Five Talents has grown to have two main fundraising and reporting offices: one based in the USA, near Washington D.C. and one in the UK, near London. Each office is self-sustaining from donated income with its own paid staff and volunteer board. There is also an international board of Five Talents that comprises volunteer board members from the two main offices, plus experts in their own fields from around the world. The international board meets quarterly and provides the forum for joint reporting to ensure consistency with the mission and industry best practice and also for planning future partnerships and expansion. All three entities – Five Talents USA; Five Talents UK and Five Talents International – are registered as NGOs (charities, not-for-profit). It is hoped that more offices will be opened in the future.

Country	Field Partner
Philippines	Center for Community Transformation
Uganda	Five Talents Uganda
Kenya	Thika & Embu Community Development Trusts
Tanzania	Mama Bahati Foundation
S.Sudan	Mothers' Union of Sudan and World Concern
Burundi	Mothers' Union of Burundi
Peru	Ecumenical Church Loan Fund (ECLOF), Peru
Bolivia	Semillas de Bendicion (Seeds of Blessing)
India	Diocese of Madras, Church of South India
Indonesia	GERHATI
Myanmar	Mothers' Union of Myanmar (Burma)

Table 1 Five Talents Field Partners

The programme partnerships are made with local microfinance field partners that are each registered in their own jurisdictions as NGOs and appropriately registered with the national ministry of finance and central bank. At the time of writing, Five Talents has 11 field partners named above.

These microfinance field partners are selected according to the following principles:

1. A shared Christian vision and motivation to reach the poorest groups and communities with appropriate microfinance services – irrespective of faith (not just serving the Christians);
2. Strong governance, local leadership and capability to run an effective microfinance scheme;
3. A business plan and operational processes to demonstrate that capability;
4. Links with and support from the local Anglican Church leadership.

Generally, Five Talents is approached by local institutions that are looking for a partnership. There is an application process that also considers such issues as the relative need, funding and geography, as part of the due diligence process before Five Talents enters into a partnership. Over the years, many applications have been received, and some have been accepted and are currently active while others have completed their partnership phase and are no longer active.

Five Talents' mode of operation is to provide grants from the US or UK offices to each of the field partners according to annual and quarterly performance targets. These grants remain in the country concerned and are used in the local currency for operational costs or loan capital. Where a local microfinance institution becomes operationally self-sustainable, that is, earning enough interest from outstanding loans to cover operational costs, subsequent grants to that partner diminish over time or get allocated towards new branches or more challenging locations.

Five Talents has not invested capital with its partners on a commercial basis for a return. Instead, Five Talents has focussed on helping smaller microfinance institutions (MFIs) to professionalise and reach self-sustainability, at which point the MFI can seek investment finance from alternative sources. As such, Five Talents has partnered with brand new or relatively young MFIs needing capital for growth and technical assistance to strengthen governance and improve operations.

As the microfinance sector develops in each country, Five Talents tries to focus its resources on providing "smaller loans to poorer people in more risky places"[111] than other microfinance providers. The Five Talents' savings-led programme in Burundi, which is currently serving 13,500 members, reaches some very rural and remote villages where members are saving a fraction of a dollar per month, and loans are in the region of $5 to $15 per person. There are no commercial providers serving such clientele for obvious reasons. As a Christian NGO, Five Talents tries not to displace or distort other economic activity. Instead it seeks to be a catalyst – inspiring, enabling and accelerating micro-enterprise development where it would otherwise be sluggish or held back. This requires a regular review of the programmes and resource allocation.

Microfinance exemplifies, promotes and works through the principle of subsidiarity – delegating responsibility to the level where decisions affect and are felt by the decision-makers themselves, rather than being imposed from outside. This helps people to feel in control and responsible for their destiny. This is part of the "micro" in microfinance, where each client owns his or her own business and is responsible for decision-making in that business, especially around how to plan, grow and invest. Microfinance is built from this "micro" level, upwards into groups of individual business-owners; and then clusters of groups; whole programmes and national offices. Taken as a whole, the impact can be huge. For example, in Kenya, some members from the local Trust Group in Ithanga are forming a chicken co-operative so they can supply restaurants and supermarkets with frozen chicken. Adding value along these market linkages is creating more jobs and developing the local economy.

Five Talents has tried to design its governance structure so that local operations are trusted and responsible to their local oversight board, with lighter touch monitoring from international boards. We believe this model emulates the microfinance approach and is effective and scalable.

However, getting the governance right has been a tricky balance over the years, as rising needs and standards in impact monitoring have necessitated very close information flows. There is also the increasing need for financial accountability as the magnitude of funds in circulation has grown. The emphasis on Christian values and identifying people of skill and integrity at all levels of leadership have helped Five Talents overcome these challenges. This has been complemented by the requirement for external audits across all partners and the Five Talents offices, with standard reporting procedures and new initiatives to share learning and experience across the different programmes. Currently, the Five Talents UK office oversees the programmes in Kenya, Uganda and Tanzania, while the Five Talents USA office oversees the rest. There is close co-operation and joint funding which requires careful co-ordination.

PRODUCTS AND SERVICES

Five Talents is uniquely focussed on micro-enterprise development, principally through business training and microfinance. All of the programmes use the group model for training and delivery of services. This is cost-effective and builds solidarity. Groups in some programmes comprise 5 people (e.g. Uganda). In other programmes the groups can comprise 15 people (India, Chennai) or 100 people (Kenya).

Some groups meet to save, borrow and repay weekly; others fortnightly and others monthly. Five Talents is sensitive to avoid a "one-size-fits-all" approach and instead tries to build on existing customs and practices. There are many lessons to learn from each of the different programmes, although standard measurement criteria and definitions are adopted across all of the programme partners to aid in monitoring and reporting. These follow industry standard definitions, the main ones being portfolio at risk, repayment rates and self-sustainability. The main products and services are summarised below.

Financial Literacy

Through the partnership with the Mothers' Union in Burundi, Sudan and Myanmar, Five Talents has recognised the importance of financial literacy for its particular target group. The Mothers' Union,[112] which is an Anglican agency with a presence in almost every developing country, has pioneered programmes covering Family Life, Literacy and Education. Now with Five Talents' help, this has extended to include financial literacy in the countries listed above.

This involves helping people (not just women) to handle money, count money, count change, make a household budget, and calculate whether they are making a profit. These are vital skills in business and personal finance, and help to prevent abuse, corruption and theft.

Business Training

Together with the Five Talents programme in Uganda and assistance from the Chalmers Center for Economic Development,[113] Five Talents has developed pre-loan business training that is given to new members. The curriculum covers 4 main topics:
1. choosing your business
2. business planning
3. marketing
4. record-keeping

The course is usually delivered in modular style by the local loan officers over 4 separate group training sessions. Each session takes two hours, with full participation. Ongoing training and mentoring is provided at group meetings by visiting loan officers and for mature groups by peer trainers.

Occasionally small teams of 4-8 people from the USA or UK visit the programme sites and participate in group or cluster training sessions. This is a wonderful opportunity for experienced business professionals from the West to share their skills. This unique "Business as Mission" programme has helped engage influential business professionals as financial supporters and volunteers. However, enthusiasm is often tempered by highlighting the risks of traditional development aid and a patronising "we know-it-all" approach. Equally, the local staff members encourage the local members (trainees) not to take everything for granted but to challenge and weigh up the advice that the visitors bring. On such trips, a fun stand-up dialogue is often conducted early on in the training course to break down the barriers and illustrate this point. The dialogue involves asking the following questions (overleaf) to one of the expatriate visitors and to one of the local residents.

Although this is a humorous game, it is effective in quickly shifting the power in the training session and highlighting to the participants (and the visitor) that high academic prowess is no substitute for local knowledge in running a successful local business.

Question (for example in Tanzania)	Usual answer from the business professional from the West	Usual answer from the business owner from local programme location
1. Did you complete primary schooling?	Yes	Yes / No
2. Did you complete secondary education?	Yes	No
3. Did you attend University?	Yes	No
4. What is the name of the President of this nation?	Umm?	President Kikwete
5. What is the name of the local MP here?	Umm?!	Mr. Msigwa MP
6. How much is a litre of kerosene here?	Umm?!	2,300 Tz shillings
7. What is the daily wage rate for a labourer?	Umm? Guess	5,000 Tz shillings
8. How much is a kilo of sugar?	Umm? Guess	2,500 Tz shillings

Table 2 *A fun illustration of knowledge relevance*

Savings Groups

Five Talents views savings and loans as important means for people to do four key things:

1. To smooth income and expenditure profiles over time and thereby avoid expensive loan sharks or the temptation for inappropriate over-consumption.
2. To take advantage of investment opportunities that arise.
3. To meet emergency needs such as sickness, crop failure, disaster etc.
4. To meet life-cycle needs such as birth, baptism, education, marriage and death.

This is explained by Stuart Rutherford[114] who also observes that people in low-income countries have a strong desire and need for convenient, affordable and safe savings products.

In every Five Talents programme there is a savings component, be it compulsory (as a condition of group membership or entitlement to a loan) or voluntary. The local partners are not generally registered as deposit-taking institutions, and, therefore, such savings cannot be mobilised and leveraged as a loan portfolio. Instead, the savings are kept intact as security against individual and group loans and for the benefit of the members. Registration as a deposit-taking institution usually means a significant step up in regulatory burdens and fees which most of the Five Talents' partners are not ready or willing to take. Indeed, in most situations where Five Talents works, the scale of operations and the target group being addressed does not warrant such an advanced model. Five Talents is rather seen as formalising and professionalising smaller microfinance NGOs to help them reach or move towards operational sustainability. As the local institution matures, the local leadership may decide to convert to a formal regulated financial institution. Five Talents would help them, but with careful attention to its core mission of microfinance for the marginalised and the costs and benefits of doing so, relative to other supported partnerships.

Depending on the particular programme, savings can be a fixed amount every period (e.g. weekly or monthly) or a flexible amount. The amounts saved range from 5 pence per month in Burundi to around £5 per month for some clients in Kenya. Withdrawals are usually allowed only once an outstanding group loan has been cleared, although some programmes operate initially as a savings scheme and then transform into a microcredit scheme as the operation matures.

In addition to accumulating personal savings, some groups have agreed amongst themselves to contribute to a welfare or emergency fund to cover unexpected events of their members. Catarina (pictured) in Burundi was a beneficiary of her groups' emergency fund after she fell off a bicycle, lost her front teeth and needed medical attention.

Small Loans
"Small" in Five Talents terms means a starting loan of the equivalent of £15 up to a maximum of around £500. The range varies from programme to programme and the average outstanding loan amount hovers around £70 per person. Five Talents monitors this average and checks that it is not creeping upwards over time which might indicate ever larger loans to existing clients. Instead, Five Talents follows its mission of helping existing clients to establish their business and thereafter reaching new clients with first-time

loans. In this way, the portfolio is constantly "churning" – serving new clients with very small loans and saying goodbye to "mature" clients who might have benefited from a series of 4 or 5 loans. A good example of this is Lydia (pictured) in Uganda whose tailoring business has grown over 5 years, helped by a series of five microfinance loans from Five Talents Uganda. She is now training other seamstresses and is graduating off the loans programme herself and becoming a role model for new clients, sharing her skills and experience.

Five Talents encourages members to invest their loan into a productive business that will generate a profit for the family sufficient to repay the loan with interest, while also providing a surplus for livelihood improvements. Clients most often invest their profits in their children's education, paying for school fees. Other examples include better nutrition, healthcare and housing. Five Talents reports that one client, when asked what impact the loan had made on their family life, replied that they can now have two meals per day, implying they had previously only eaten one meal per day.

This emphasis on productive activity forms part of the pre-loan training and is further enforced by the group dynamics. There is a formal loan application procedure and loan agreement – sometimes signed by a thumbprint for those who are illiterate and advised by their fellow group members and loan officer.

The small loans are group-based. Group members are the best judge of each others' character and commitment. Occasionally a member will divert his or her share of the loan to an "unauthorised" activity. This may be an emergency need, in which case the members might choose to help their colleague with the next repayment instalment. Or it might be an ill-advised impulse buy, in which case the members may have stern words and there can be a strain on group dynamics. These issues are best avoided by thorough pre-loan group formation and group training. But in rare cases (usually in the first cycle), the groups break down and they sometimes forfeit their savings or get barred from future applications.

Insurance

Some of the Five Talents programmes have linked up with local insurance providers to insure the loans in the event of death or serious injury. The usual fee is around 1% of the loan value and where offered, most clients

Five Talents Case Study

choose to take up this policy covering credit-life and critical illness. Our partners have had a handful of claims over recent years and clients and relatives have appreciated the services and co-operation with the insurance companies who provide expert services in addressing the moral hazards and asymmetries of information associated with insurance products. Micro-insurance is an expanding market and more sophisticated products may become available and affordable in due course.

In some of Five Talents' savings programmes, groups have sometimes chosen to establish a special "pot" of pooled savings as an "emergency fund" which can pay-out to cover medical or other emergency needs. This group-based self-insurance is becoming popular in the savings-led schemes, as it allows more discretion and flexibility than formal insurance cover. It relies upon clear criteria and transparent decision-making to maintain credibility within the groups.

METHODOLOGY

As outlined above, Five Talents has several methodologies adapted to the local circumstances. However, our programmes fall into two main categories.

Savings-led Microfinance

This is where groups of people save collectively and regularly in groups. The accumulated savings can then be rotated as small loans to individual group members. Loan recipients negotiate the terms of the loan (term and interest rate) with the group. The amount is usually a multiple of personally accumulated savings and entitlement to a loan is only normally granted after a period of regular saving. For example, a person may have saved £4 per month regularly for 5 months, and accumulated £20. Depending on the rules of the group, that person may be entitled to 3 times his or her savings, namely a loan of £60. In the Five Talents programme in Kenya, such a loan would be repaid over 6 months with 1% interest charged per month on a flat rate basis. The repayment schedule would look as follows (overleaf).

Although the monthly interest fee is 1% per month, the Annual Percentage Rate (APR) of this loan is actually 20% pa.[115] This compares with the central bank base rate in Kenya of 18% pa at the time of writing and the inter-bank rate of 22% pa. Inflation in Kenya, at the time of writing, is running at 18% pa.[116] So an APR on a microfinance loan of 20% pa is comparatively cheap, especially considering that a client with no credit score or physical assets for collateral would not normally be eligible for a bank loan and a local money-lender in Kenya might frequently charge 500% APR depending on the amount, duration and risks.

Principal £60	Repayment	Interest (1% flat rate)	Total repayment
Month 1	£10	£0.60	£10.60
Month 2	£10	£0.60	£10.60
Month 3	£10	£0.60	£10.60
Month 4	£10	£0.60	£10.60
Month 5	£10	£0.60	£10.60
Month 6	£10	£0.60	£10.60
Total	£60	£3.60	£63.60

Table 3 Repayment schedule at 1% per month flat rate

In such a savings-led scheme, the interest accumulates to the group and is dispersed to the group members once a year as a kind of shared dividend. This is the first time that most people have ever earned interest on their savings and serves to attract more savings customers. This method is sometimes known as the Accumulated Savings and Credit Association model (ASCA) or the Village Savings and Loan Association model (VSLA).

The Five Talents partner in Kenya has adopted this kind of model on a parish basis, and the Diocese of Thika now has 43 parish groups with a total membership of 4,500 people who have collectively saved a total of $780,000 over a period of 7 years. This is equivalent to an average saving rate of $2 per person per month for 7 years. It is astonishing how quickly a large sum of money has accumulated and the opportunity provided for members to borrow from their groups.

Obviously there are risks associated with handling money in rural areas, and, therefore, all groups deposit their pooled savings in their linked retail bank in the nearest town. Travelling with cash is risky and the groups have developed mechanisms for safely distributing and delivering the money to mitigate those risks (e.g. 3 people travelling to or from the bank but only person actually carrying the money, while others act as decoys or bodyguards). The development of mobile telephone money

Five Talents Case Study

transfers is helping alleviate these risks, as well as improving security and saving time.

In two of the villages where Five Talents operates, the local partner has recently helped the groups to transform into Financial Services Associations (FSAs). In this model, the group opens a shop-front community bank, where non-members can also deposit savings and apply for small loans. This opens access to the whole community and increases the volume of transactions. A relationship is established with the retail bank in the nearest town, and the community bank has become an "agent" of the retail bank, offering basic services on the same terms as the retail bank. Revenues are generated from fees and loan interest, and expenses incurred on office costs and personnel. Over a three-year period, the margins are expected to be sufficient to pay a bank teller, manager and security guard on a sustainable basis.[117]

The key features of the Five Talents' savings-led microfinance model are as follows:

1. It is self-governing and, therefore, can be sustained long after the initial establishment and training by Five Talents.
2. It is well-suited to remote, rural or post-conflict areas, where the costs of routinely sending loan officers would be high.
3. It encourages a culture of savings which are often referred to as "hot-money" in contrast to "cold-money" that comes from outside the community.
4. Repayment rates are usually extremely high for such "hot-money" since people know that the money belongs to the community.

Credit-led Microfinance

This is "traditional group-style" micro-lending where the loan capital comes from donated funds channelled through Five Talents. Members are required to form solidarity groups. The Five Talents partner trains those groups and handles all loan applications, monitoring and loan repayments.

This is generally a higher cost approach than the savings-led model above, since the programme requires several paid employees (including loan officers, an accountant and a manager). The loan officers travel out to the groups on a regular basis for training, business mentoring, and to observe the record-keeping and repayment process.

In a mature microfinance programme of this type, a sufficient number of members (usually more than 3,000) are borrowing and repaying loans with interest which is sufficient to recoup the operational costs (including the salaries of the loan officers, staff and travel costs etc.) of delivering the service.

Some of the Five Talents programmes are not yet self-sustaining, such that funds from the UK or USA are still needed to cover the operational costs. This may be because the operational costs are simply very high in relation to the number of clients and the value of loans in circulation. This fits the vision of Five Talents to serve clients that are not being reached by other microfinance providers. However, there is a tension, as each microfinance is also expected to be self-sustainable in the long run. The question often revolves around how long is 'the long run'? If a programme needs an ongoing subsidy should Five Talents pull out or stay in? These are the kinds of questions that the Five Talents International Board wrestles with and which the Five Talents Programme Strategy addresses.

To date, the Christian conviction of Five Talents has led towards continuing to invest in the programmes in Burundi, Sudan, Myanmar and others where self-sustainability is a long way off. However, Five Talents has drawn back our support from the self-sustaining work in Uganda, the Philippines and Peru – preferring instead to prioritise resources towards new areas (sometimes within those countries) to reach the needy.

The interface with other providers is extremely important. For instance, in Uganda, in 2006 there were just 6 registered commercial banks. By 2011, there were 26 such banks and the landscape for financial services and financial access had changed immeasurably. In such a changing context, Five Talents is vigilant to maintain its mission to serve the poorest and maximise the impact of its donated resources.

INTEREST RATES AND FEES CHARGED

Christians often have a problem with Christian MFIs charging interest to their borrowers. The Old Testament law specifically prohibits charging interest to a fellow Jew (Ex 22:25; Lev 25:35) although it seems to permit charging interest to a Gentile (Deut 23:19). God's concern and protection for the poor is clearly spelt out in these and other scriptures. Elsewhere (Pr 28:8) it is the issue of exorbitant interest that is condemned. Other passages, of course, emphasise forgiveness (Luke 7:41) and generosity (Mt 5:42).

Five Talents Case Study

The Five Talents programmes do charge interest on the loans. As a Christian MFI, Five Talents is committed to transparency in interest rates and other charges – both to the clients and to inform the donors. The rates are not, in Five Talents' view, exorbitant or usurious. The rationale follows the path trodden by Calvin in the Reformation. It is recognised that the modern period, contrary to the biblical period, is an inflationary environment where capital has an opportunity cost associated with time.[118]

Five Talents is a member of Microfinance Transparency[119] and its Christian values drive the charity to hold high standards of integrity and openness. The Five Talents programme with the lowest rate of interest is the savings-led programme in Kenya – noted in section 5 above – which charges a flat rate of interest of 1% per month, equivalent to an APR of 20%.

The programme with the highest rate of interest and charges is the partner in Uganda, Five Talents Uganda (FTU), where they charge 3% per month (flat rate) plus 1% insurance and a small fee for membership and stationery. The equivalent APR is 63% pa. The repayment schedule for a £60 loan with Five Talents Uganda is shown below.

Principal £60	Repayment	Interest (3% flat rate)	Total repayment
Month 1	£10	£1.80	£11.80
Month 2	£10	£1.80	£11.80
Month 3	£10	£1.80	£11.80
Month 4	£10	£1.80	£11.80
Month 5	£10	£1.80	£11.80
Month 6	£10	£1.80	£11.80
Total	£60	£10.80	£70.80

Table 4 Repayment schedule at 3% per month flat rate

Someone borrowing £60 for 6 months has to repay £70.80. Compared with other microfinance providers in Uganda, FTU is mid-range in its charges and not especially unusual.[120] The Five Talents international board and office staff monitor the rates. One indicator of client satisfaction is the client retention ratio. If clients continue with the programme for several loan cycles, then that is a crude indicator that they appreciate the services. On-site visits and comparative data are also used to check rates. Five Talents makes sure the pre-loan training is conducted and there is full transparency and understanding even for illiterate clients.

Some points to note about interest rates in microfinance and Five Talents in particular are listed below:

1. Who sets the rate? The rates are set locally by the local board in the context of their local circumstances. They are not set from London or Washington D.C.

2. The rate looks high to me: Loans are unsecured (risky) and repaid over 4-6 months (short-term), so many people treat the interest charge more like a fee for borrowing the money. Interpreting the interest rate as an Annual Percentage Rate (APR) is factually correct but most borrowers do not think in those terms. To illustrate the point in Western terms, imagine that you are on a day trip and you need some cash. You might stop at a local petrol station to use the cash machine where for a £20 withdrawal it can charge a £2 fee. Depending how much you need the cash you may or may not continue with the withdrawal and pay the fee. Your judgement reflects your strength of demand and the alternatives available.

3. How easily can people pay those rates? The repayment rates on microfinance loans are remarkably and consistently high both in the Five Talents programmes and generally in the microfinance sector as a whole (barring bad practices). There are many reasons. A key one is that when loans are invested in small business activities the yield can often be very high. In South Sudan, for example, one of the Five Talents' clients buys 3 crates of Coca Cola from the big town at 50p per bottle, and transports them to his village on his bicycle where he sells each bottle for £1! Simple trade and transport can yield high returns. Other businesses like hairdressing, carpentry, and tailoring have different business models, but the principal of value added is the same. Careful business planning can ensure that returns are strong and repayments rate high. There is also a strong understanding that loans repaid in full will enable other community members to access the same loan fund when their turn comes. These factors,

combined with the group peer-pressure to repay, help ensure high repayment rates.

4. <u>What rates do commercial banks charge?</u> Domestic interest rates in many developing countries are running at between 15% – 24% pa. In the example above, the Uganda Central Bank base rate is 23% pa, the Standard Bank rate is 28% pa and inflation is running at 30% pa.[121]

5. <u>What are the alternative options?</u> For many of the poorest people, microfinance programmes such as the ones Five Talents and its partners offer, provide the first real and legitimate opportunity to save and access credit. Another option would be commercial banks, but for many of the world's poorest people, the retail banks on the high street in the nearest town are too far away to access. Additionally, they are not geared up for people without collateral, assets, and literacy, who want to save and borrow small amounts of money. The only other option that the poor have for accessing credit are loan sharks and informal money-lenders, who charge a lot more interest than microfinance institutions without the support that MFI's such as Five Talents and its partners provide. In light of these limited options, these poorest people face the serious issue of financial exclusion.

6. <u>What do I get in return?</u> Group members can access a small loan on affordable and convenient terms, based on a clear fee for service. That fee includes the provision of group and business training and mentoring by a local loan officer who visits my community

7. <u>What's to stop me getting over-indebted?</u> As part of that training, Five Talents' loan officers and the group members assess each others' business plan to determine if the person can make the repayments. Clients frequently moderate their loan application, or even withdraw their application, following advice from their fellow members or the loan officer. No-one wants a "delinquent" payer and we certainly do not want to encourage over-indebtedness or multiple borrowing.

8. <u>What is the interest used for?</u> The income from the interest is used to pay the local costs of providing the service, including the salaries of the loan officers and local MFI staff, their transport and office costs etc. Ideally, the income from the interest payments should

cover 100% of these operating costs in order that each microfinance programme becomes self-sustaining. Some programmes have finance costs too, namely their cost of capital if they have borrowed funds (debt) or invested funds (equity). So there is a measurement of financial self-sustainability where both operational and financial costs are covered. However, this is not relevant for the Five Talents programmes because our funding is grant-based (donated) capital and almost all of the Five Talents programmes rely on donated equity.

9. <u>What is special about "Flat Rate" interest?</u> All Five Talents programmes currently charge interest on a flat rate basis as opposed to a "declining balance" basis which is in fact the usual basis for charging interest in advanced economies and commercial banking. The reason that many MFIs, including Five Talents, use the flat rate basis is because it is much easier for both clients and the loan officers to calculate, explain and predict the repayment schedule – which by definition is the same each period, as in the worked examples in Tables 3 and 4. If the loans were repaid on a declining balance basis, the loan officer might have the advantage of better mathematics skills and a calculator, and could possibly deceive a client into paying too much interest. There are arguments on either side of this debate, but the Five Talents field partners have chosen the flat rate basis as the most suitable in their circumstances. As stated before, Five Talents is committed to transparency and explains these issues to the clients who understand and accept the terms.

FUNDING

Five Talents has charitable status and seeks donations from various sources. The majority of donated funds are transferred to programme activities in developing countries. The percentage of funds spent on charitable activities is monitored by the charity regulator each year and usually stays in excess of 80%. The funding sources for Five Talents UK are shown in chart 3.

IMPACT

Five Talents currently has 68,000 member clients globally, with accumulated savings of £758k and outstanding loans of £1.6m. Since its foundation in

Five Talents Case Study

1998, Five Talents has served almost half a million clients with basic business training, savings and small loans.

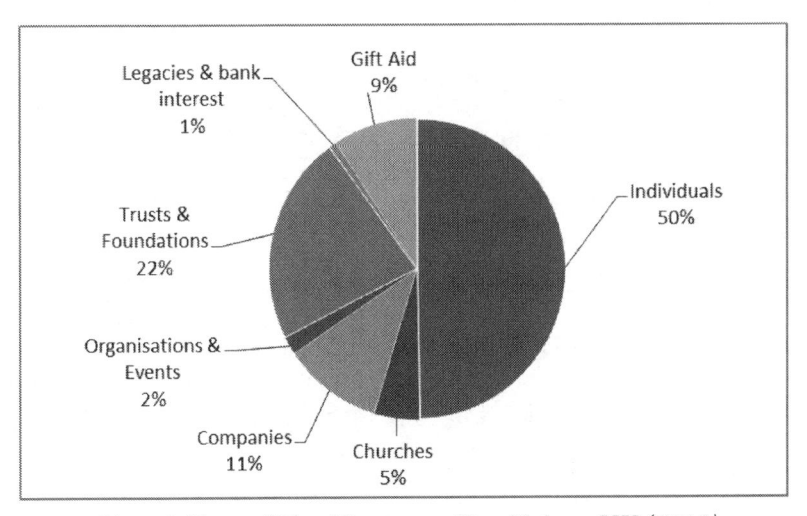

Chart 3 Share of Total Income to Five Talents UK (2012)

- Individuals 50%
- Trusts & Foundations 22%
- Companies 11%
- Gift Aid 9%
- Churches 5%
- Organisations & Events 2%
- Legacies & bank interest 1%

The numbers are obviously important to Five Talents but the principal focus is on livelihood impact, transformation and serving the most excluded. Five Talents' tag-line has become "Smaller, Poorer, Riskier" – providing smaller loans to poorer people in more risky circumstances.

In 2010, many MFIs in Andhra Pradesh in India were found to be lending aggressively to poor clients, leading to over-indebtedness and poverty aggravation – not poverty alleviation. Such MFIs were seeking profits from the poor and needing to service their investors.[122] Five Talents has worked hard to distinguish its work from such practices. The charity recognises the coercion that can take place within groups to ensure 100% repayment. Such repayment rates may look good from the outside, but masks unhappiness and bad behaviour internally. As a donor-funded NGO, Five Talents finds it hard to assign resources to expensive external evaluations and instead have relied more heavily on site visits and routine monitoring and reporting from the field partners. Five Talents has undertaken client satisfaction surveys and is developing social performance indicators and using some of the industry tools that have been

145

developed.[123] And Five Talents places a strong emphasis on its partnership approach, subsidiarity and shared Christian vision to serve the poor with integrity and effectiveness.

On Children

It may seem odd to start this section on who is impacted by referring to children, but Five Talents' experience is that children are often the priority beneficiaries for their clients. A family business is just that – a business that supports the family. Profits are most often directed to children's education – to pay fees, uniform, books, transport – but also healthcare, nutrition and clothing as prioritised by the family.

On a recent visit to Five Talents' partner in Tanzania, the Mama Bahati Foundation, the author met Zawadi pictured here with her daughter. The author could not communicate much with Zawadi a Swahili speaker, but her daughter was attending full-time school and will soon be able to speak English much better than her mother. On other visits, the author has met sons and daughters who are in university training to become doctors, lawyers or teachers. The educational attainment of the children of microfinance clients is often well above the attainment of their parents. The opportunities and aspirations of the children are also much higher. This inter-generational impact is bringing and will bring substantial improvements in living standards.

On Clients

Business owners who successfully run a small business, generate profits and employ staff literally "walk taller" than they did before their success. The self-esteem and dignity that comes from being a successful business owner is seen in the smiles, posture and confidence of many of the Five Talents clients (e.g. John the carpenter, pictured) It is a privilege to be part of this "human flourishing" although, of course, there is a relatively small percentage (less than 10%) that struggle and fail. Five Talents cares for those clients with Christian concern and a practical approach, sometimes writing off the debts and offering coaching and linkages to other programmes or Church-based initiatives where relevant help can be provided.

You are welcome to see the positive impact for yourself if you choose to come on a short visit with Five Talents. You can meet the clients and

MFI staff and hear the personal testimonies of literally thousands of clients.

On Employees
The consequence of helping the active and marginalised poor is that they often employ others in their enterprises. Stephen's car-washing business in Uganda is now employing 70 young men, as pictured, some of whom have risen up the ladder and got jobs with other employers or started their own transport or maintenance businesses.

On Families and Gender
Some of the Five Talents programmes are "women-only" (e.g. in Tanzania and India). These are designed by the local partner to address the local needs and opportunities. Five Talents is careful to understand the context and make sure that the programme is not driving a wedge between men and women. The experience is that the local MFI leaders are acutely aware of the potential tensions and misinterpretations, but the scenario and model justify a particular attention to women, not necessarily forever, but for a phase which is regularly reviewed. In fact, Five Talents' partner in Tanzania is shortly widening its criteria to accept men as group members.

Again, there are many examples from Five Talents' work where women have encouraged their husbands to join them in their enterprise, e.g. Martha and her husband Ruvis in Peru, pictured. Microfinance groups also provide solidarity and support for their members.

In the Five Talents programme in Chennai, in India, for example, one of the women was being beaten by her husband. Her solidarity group knew what was happening and they decided to confront the man jointly and tactfully with confidence. The beating has now stopped and the marriage restored. These positive stories shine an exciting light into the way that programmes such as this can restore gender and family disunity or imbalances.

On Markets
Some commentators argue that microfinance simply multiplies small enterprises that compete against each other without generating surpluses or livelihood improvements.[124] Towns and trading centres become full of uneconomic market stall holders. This might be the case where clients in

one village have chosen to operate the same business, for example, selling charcoal or selling fruit and vegetables. The margins are small and the market is small. Prices can sometimes be competed down and traders eventually wind up broke. Clients who invest in such businesses are unlikely to repay their loans and may end up needing to take another loan to repay the first loan, making the situation worse.

Microfinance, when delivered well, is better than that. Clients know better, their group members know better and the loan officers, who provide training and mentoring, know better too. Five Talents' experience is that good microfinance builds markets and stimulates economic activity. Injecting new capital helps accelerate transactions, lifting volumes and margins. Studies suggest[125] that the informal economy contributes nearly 55% of Sub-Saharan Africa's GDP and a staggering 77% of non-agricultural employment. Although governments find the informal economy hard to measure and regulate, a growing and flourishing informal economy certainly provides jobs and huge potential for broad-based development.

Although microfinance is not a panacea and the experience is not uniform, it does enhance economic growth at household level and in local markets. Some clients eventually enter the formal sector and cross the thresholds for value-added tax, income tax or corporation tax which benefits the government revenue. Five Talents estimates that up to 5% of their clients eventually enter the formal sector.

CHRISTIAN DISTINCTIVES

How Christian is Five Talents?

Five Talents was founded as a Christian Church-based initiative to alleviate poverty through microfinance. The name Five Talents is drawn from the Parable of the Talents which signals its Christian identity. The parable itself provides a worked example of microfinance and the values held. The governance and leadership of Five Talents – from patron, council, trustees and staff – profess and share the Christian faith. The motivation and energy is inspired by the Christian faith and particularly Jesus' compassion and priority for the poor.

How do our Christian foundations and values manifest themselves?

Donors might not notice Five Talents' Christian faith, focussing instead on the effective work, the ability to reach and serve the poorest, and the feedback and news from the field.

Clients in the programmes might not notice either their perspectives focussed on the services they receive, the cost (interest rate), the group formation and training and relationship with the loan officer.

Nevertheless, Five Talents is a Christian organisation, and, as such, plays its part in working towards God's "Kingdom come[ing] on earth as it is in Heaven." Five Talents is called to impact the world now, not just to sit around and wait for Jesus to come back. Five Talents is not a mission agency evangelising or a Church seeking to expand its membership. Those outcomes would, in the author's view, be good, but they are not the objective of Five Talents as an organisation. Five Talents' priority is to reach and serve the poorest with relevant and affordable microfinance services to help alleviate poverty.

The mode of operation, particularly the Church Partnership Model, is a distinctive feature of Five Talents. The microfinance programmes have helped the local Church engage with the community it serves, sharing the Love of Christ in an appropriate and practical manner. Together with its partners, Five Talents has developed tools and programmes to support the Church's abilities to reach out into the community regardless of religion or denomination. For example, in Indonesia a local Christian doctor's association has come to the community to provide healthcare alongside the Anglican Church and its microfinance partner GERHATI.

Group training sessions in any of the Five Talents programmes across the world may begin with a prayer and a hymn led by the loan officer. The parish pastor may be present at repayment meetings to accompany his "flock". Notices about the next group meetings or training sessions may be announced on Sunday at the local Church service. Group members may offer to pray for one another's needs, including the prosperity of their business. They may refer to the Parable of the Talents when discussing risk, hard work or accountability.

In many of the locations where Five Talents works – particularly Africa – the culture is predominantly Christian, so none of the above would be particularly unusual. However, Five Talents also partners with programmes in India (mainly Hindu) and Indonesia (almost 100% Muslim) where the respective Five Talents programmes focus on delivering an excellent service to the clients, both as a witness to their Christian faith but also simply because it is the right thing to do. This builds trust and friendships and can sometimes lead to evangelistic opportunities. But that is a welcome consequence and not the primary intention.

Principles for Partnership
Five Talents has adopted the following principles to clarify its Christian values and behaviour:[126]

1. We are motivated by God's love to provide financial services that empower the enterprising poor to liberate their families from poverty.
2. We are committed to serving the poorest communities, to achieve real and lasting holistic, social impact in the lives of our clients and their families.
3. We are committed to excellence in our work and relationships with our partners, to honesty and transparency, to client protection and social responsibility.
4. We do not use financial services or our influence as incentives to conversion. We believe this is unethical and dishonouring to people as well as to God.
5. We do not use our faith as a 'dividing line' in the communities where we work (e.g. providing better loan terms or larger loan sizes based on clients' faith). Five Talents, and our partners, provide financial services to the poor regardless of ethnicity, political affiliation or religion.
6. We are transparent about our Christian identity in our communication with all of our stakeholders including governments, donors, clients and partners.
7. We will work with partners who share the same Christian motivations and foundation, and who are recommended to us by and/or are in partnership with an Anglican Province or Diocese in the areas we are working in, or plan to work in according to our Programme Strategy.

8. We support partner organisations in their decision to hire indigenous staff. We treat all UK and overseas staff and volunteers, regardless of faith, race, ethnicity or culture with dignity, and grant them the equal professional development opportunities appropriate for their position.
9. We expect our senior leaders to be highly professional and competent and we desire to see spiritual maturity, reflecting Christ-like values in their life and work.
10. We recognise the sensitivities and challenges partners have in contexts of great poverty and where other world religions are in the majority. Each partner, therefore, will have their own strategy for the appropriate and effective expression of their Christian motivation in their own context.

What's so special about the Church and why Anglicans?

The strengths of the Anglican Church are as follows:
1. Reach: Its network covers almost every country in the world.
2. Scale: It has 80 million members and growing.
3. Trust: It is respected by the national government and local population as a civil society organisation.
4. Local: It is locally led and the membership is drawn from local people.
5. Stability: It has outlasted different political regimes, natural disasters and civil wars. In times of insecurity, people often run to the Church for aid and safety.
6. Infrastructure: It has buildings where community meetings can take place, usually free of charge.
7. Integrity: It promotes a message of non-corruption, transparency and accountability.

By partnering with the Anglican Church on the ground, Five Talents can take advantage of these strengths. The charity does not have to invent or establish them for itself. This gives it a head start and saves time and costs for the both initial set-up of the partnership and for future expansion of Five Talents' work to new areas.

Is there a gap between theory and practice?

Maybe there is in some areas. Neither the Church nor Five Talents are perfect. It depends on human beings who have temptations, weaknesses and compromise their behaviour for various reasons. But Five Talents aspires to be the very best and has feedback mechanisms to check on progress and is prepared to address shortcomings. The charity believes its Christian ethos is sufficiently strong and ingrained that its policies and practice are closely aligned. The board are aware of the risk of "mission drift" and regularly review their current activities and plans against their foundational documents and principles.

CHALLENGES

Debt Forgiveness

"Lord forgive us our debts as we forgive those who have debts against us."

The Lord's Prayer has sometimes caused difficulties for Five Talents' loan officers, with clients claiming debt relief. The worldwide Church is usually associated with traditional "aid" programmes and a "hand-out" approach. Indeed the word "charity" comes from the Christian virtue "*charis*" (Greek) meaning "grace" and "*caritas*" (Latin) meaning "selfless love." The Church's love of 'charity' has sometimes led to too little thought about sustainable development and discovering the root cause of social issues.

But microfinance is special, providing a "hand-up" not a hand-out. This lesson is quickly addressed at group pre-loan training, where the loan officers assert that the Five Talents programme is a professional microfinance programme, and terms of business are clearly explained.

If clients really cannot repay a loan, the first step is for the other group members to help out. Accumulated prior-savings may be used to repay. The members can apply to have the loan re-scheduled. Ultimately, if there is a risk of driving the client further into poverty, then the loan could be written-off. But this is a last resort and lessons are learnt to make sure such occurrences are rare. In particular, defaulters are best avoided by thorough prior-training, and in many ways that is what Five Talents does best.

Human Capacity

Finding qualified branch managers, loan officers, accountants and board members is sometimes difficult, especially when the Five Talents programmes are working in rural areas and pay only modest wages. This is where a shared Christian faith can help with recruitment and retention. But finding the right staff is a difficult area.

Funding

Raising donations in any NGO sector is tough. Microfinance is probably easier than most, because there is a compelling factor that one's donation keeps on delivering a benefit as loan capital rotates many times over. But the opportunities for expansion, new branches and new programmes always seem to outstrip resources. There are still approximately 1.5 billion people without access to financial services, so the resource constraints are likely to be with us for some time.

CONCLUSIONS AND FUTURE PLANS

Five Talents is a unique Church-founded microfinance initiative that is clearly focussed on reaching the most marginalised communities with relevant financial services. It has established itself as a credible organisation, with good governance, a clear mission and seeking to follow industry best practices. Its Christian distinctive affects the way they care for and train their clients, as well as leading them to operate in fragile – sometimes post-conflict or very rural communities. They have established a solid track record of effective programme partnership, delivery of relevant microfinance services and the ability to report and track progress.

The next few years will see Five Talents seeking to share their learning and expertise across the wider Anglican Communion and working alongside other carefully selected delivery partners. There are already possibilities to provide technical assistance and possibly new programme partnerships in the Democratic Republic of Congo and invitations to work in Zimbabwe and Egypt.

The USA and UK offices are excited at the prospect of future institutional grant-funding opportunities and additional donations from major trusts and individuals. There are prospects of opening more fund-raising and programme oversight offices in the coming years, possibly in

Singapore, Australia, Canada, or elsewhere, depending principally on harnessing the right people to launch those offices.

The long term vision for Five Talents is to be the microfinance partner of choice for the entire Anglican Church in low-income countries, assisting them in running effective programmes that serve the poorest communities that are yet unreached by other NGO or commercial microfinance providers. Its work involves multiplying "talents" and unlocking the talents of the poor so they can flourish sustainably and with dignity. Five Talents started with a friendship. Since its foundation, Five Talents has generated thousands and indirectly hundreds of thousands more friendships through its work and ministry. There is an exciting future ahead.

HOPE INTERNATIONAL CASE STUDY
PETER GREER AMD ANNA HAGGARD

Peter Greer is president and CEO of HOPE International, a global non-profit organization focused on Christ-centered job creation, savings mobilization, and financial training. Peter is also co-author of The Poor Will Be Glad (Zondervan, 2009), and is currently writing The Spiritual Danger of Doing Good (forthcoming 2013) and Mission Drift (forthcoming 2014) with Bethany House Publishers.

Anna Haggard is the executive writing assistant at HOPE International, where she collaborates with the president and CEO, as well as the marketing department, to share HOPE's message to donors through print and social media. Co-author of The Spiritual Danger of Doing Good, Anna is a graduate of Asbury University.

INTRODUCTION

HOPE International (HOPE) is a network of microfinance institutions and Church-based savings programmes operating in 16 countries around the world. HOPE works to empower women, men, and families to break the cycles of physical and spiritual poverty through the provision of loans, savings services, basic business training, mentoring, and discipleship. By incorporating a clear witness for Jesus Christ and by employing a variety of approaches to microfinance, HOPE is focused on maximizing its impact in addressing physical and spiritual poverty.

In its network, HOPE includes traditional microfinance programmes, microfinance plus programmes (which incorporate health care, literacy training, or other community empowerment initiatives outside the realm of traditional microfinance), savings and credit associations, and small and medium enterprise development. Programmes provide select services depending on the demonstrated economic and social need within a region.

HOPE's programmes are effectively reaching 470,000 individuals around the world with the love of Jesus Christ and the opportunity to start or expand a business.

This chapter explores HOPE's model of practising Christ-centred microenterprise development by looking at its growth as an organization, its perspective on poverty alleviation, and its impact to the underserved. Sources used include executive, operations, and board reports, as well as other internal documents. Yearly reports released to donors, such as the Annual Report, are also used.

History

Founding of HOPE

HOPE was born out of one Church's efforts to be the hands and feet of Jesus Christ. Following the collapse of the Soviet Union in 1991, the newly independent nation faced numerous challenges: Between 1991 and 1997, Ukraine lost 60% of its GDP, inflation increased to five digits, and there were protests, unrest, and riots in the streets.[127]

In the United States, many churches recognized the dire situation in Ukraine and wanted to help. One of them was Calvary Monument Bible Church, a Church in the heartland of central Pennsylvania.

Seeking to partner with a Church in Ukraine, Calvary Monument Bible Church was paired with a Church in Zaporozhe, Ukraine, a city of a million people straddling a river in the country's South East. After a successful assessment trip to Zaporozhe, Calvary Monument Bible Church supplied their sister Church with food, clothing, and medical shipments from Lancaster.[128]

One of the leaders of this partnership was Jeff Rutt. Founder, president, and CEO of an award-winning home-building company, Rutt often traveled to Ukraine on mission work. Through his travels, Rutt and other leaders built strong relationships with the indigenous Church leaders in Ukraine. One day, while he was visiting Zaporozhe, Rutt had a life-changing conversation with a Ukrainian pastor.

The pastor articulated his growing concerns about the three-year relationship: his congregation was growing increasingly dependent on the aid from the American church. They were losing the motivation to establish themselves in the new economy. Moreover, the aid shipments were beginning to harm the local economy, as businesses could not compete with the free goods flooding the community.[129]

He told Rutt, "We need a hand-up, not a hand-out."

Hope International Case Study

After working on numerous business plans to help Church members grow a sustainable business, Rutt stumbled on the idea of microfinance. Microfinance was a relatively new concept in Ukraine, and only one microfinance institution was operating in the country.[130]

Leaders from the Church in Zaporozhe endorsed the idea. In 1997, Rutt offered 12 individual loans to entrepreneurs in the church. Each one was repaid and on time. In 1998, HOPE officially registered its first microfinance institution.

From the very outset of HOPE, the staff and board were clear that HOPE existed to provide more than just loans and training; HOPE existed to intentionally and effectively build the local Church and teach the principles of Jesus.

While HOPE has used the tool of microfinance in an effort to partner with the poor in a dignified and sustainable way, ultimately, HOPE's mission is to love God, to love its neighbours, and to go into all the world to teach others to follow Jesus Christ. As formally declared by the board in November 2011:

> *The primary purpose of the Corporation is to use the tool of microfinance development to alleviate physical, spiritual, and social poverty in our world (the "Primary Purpose"). The Corporation shares the Good News of Jesus Christ unashamedly, respectfully, and sensitively in culturally appropriate manners because it is God's power to transform lives and communities. The Corporation includes Christian teaching and principles in every aspect of our work.*[131]

All of HOPE's initiatives and philosophies are an extension of this statement of purpose.

Growth

In its first 15 years as an organization, HOPE's growth has gone through three separate stages: *HOPE 1.0, HOPE 2.0, and HOPE 3.0.*

HOPE 1.0 – From 1997 to 2004, HOPE's model was characterized by growing sources of funding and start-up partnerships.

1. *Start-Ups.* By 2004, HOPE had established new programmes in three different countries, Ukraine, China (2000), and the Democratic Republic of Congo (2004).

2. *Funding.* HOPE was primarily supported through Homes for Hope, which is now a distinct 501(c) (3) non-profit organization.

HOPE 2.0 – From 2005 to 2009, the organization was characterized by rapid growth in terms of new partnerships, number of clients and staff, and increased revenue.

By the end of this period, HOPE's presence was extended to 14 countries:

Partnerships and programmes added:
- Rwanda (Urwego Community Banking), 2005
- Dominican Republic (Esperanza International), 2005
- Moldova (Invest-Credit), 2005
- Closed country (partner), 2005[132]
- Russia, 2005
- Haiti (Esperanza International), 2006
- Romania (ROMCOM), 2007
- Rwanda savings-led programme (Anglican Church of Rwanda), 2007
- Philippines (Center for Community Transformation), 2007
- India savings-led programme (partner), 2007[133]
- Burundi (Turame Community Finance), 2008
- Republic of Congo, 2008
- Haiti savings-led programme – Miragoane (Esperanza International), 2009

While metrics were more robust during this period, the emphasis was on contextualization of programmes, as well as country autonomy.

HOPE 3.0 – From 2010 to 2012, HOPE placed a higher level of emphasis on standardization and continued professionalization in staffing and technology. While HOPE still maintains the importance of contextualization, it primarily implemented practices that were used throughout its network. Similarly, it emphasized using a broad base of standards for spiritual integration across the network. Another defining characteristic of HOPE 3.0 is its emphasis on savings and credit associations. While HOPE added its first savings and credit association partnerships during HOPE 2.0, there has been much expansion with new programmes within the countries in which HOPE already operates and within the new countries in which it works.

Hope International Case Study

Partnerships and programmes added:
- India savings-led programme (partner), 2011[134]
- Peru savings-led programme (The Locker Room and Christian and Missionary Alliance Church of Comas, Peru), 2011
- Philippines savings-led programme (Center for Community Transformation), 2011
- Rwanda savings-led programme (Pentecostal Church), 2011
- Zimbabwe savings-led programme (Acta Non Verba and Coldsprings Baptist Church), 2011

Below is a graph depicting historical growth for revenue from 2003 to 2012. A second graph illustrates client growth from 2004 until 2012, as well as projections for client growth through 2015:

Growing Revenue

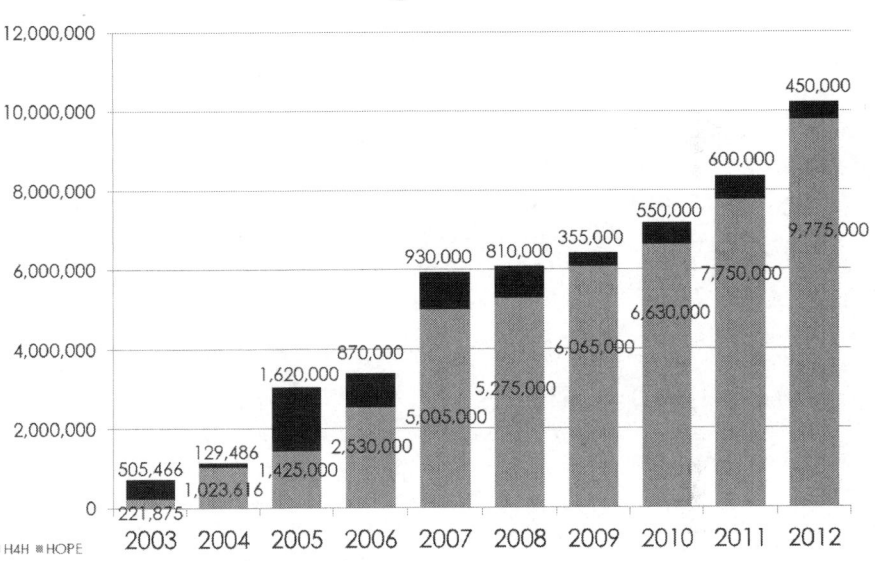

Year	H4H	HOPE
2003	221,875	
2004	505,466	1,023,616
2005	129,486	1,425,000
2006	870,000	2,530,000
2007	930,000	5,005,000
2008	810,000	5,275,000
2009	355,000	6,065,000
2010	550,000	6,630,000
2011	600,000	7,750,000
2012	450,000	9,775,000

HOPE Network Client Growth : 2013-2015 Projected

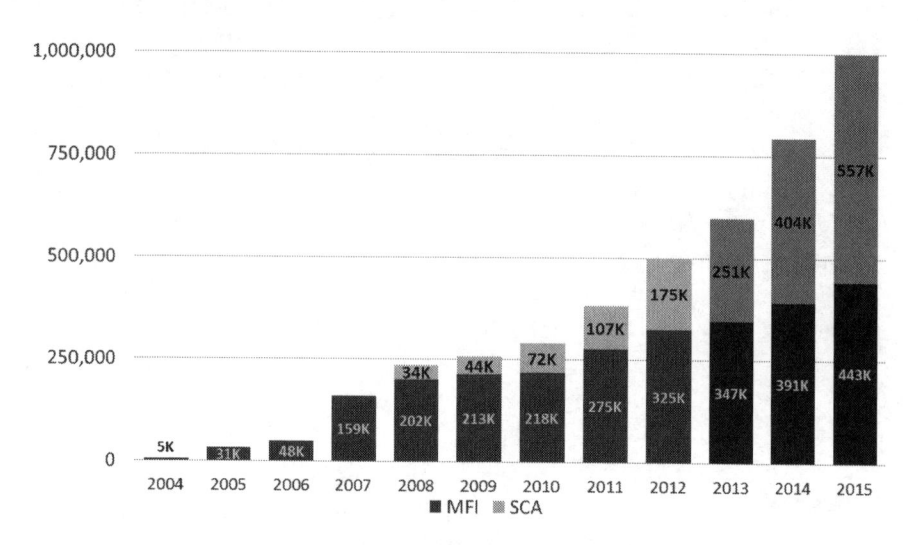

Year	MFI	SCA	Total
2004			5K
2005			31K
2006			48K
2007	159K		
2008	202K	34K	
2009	213K	44K	
2010	218K	72K	
2011	275K	107K	
2012	325K	175K	
2013	347K	251K	
2014	391K	404K	
2015	443K	557K	

HOPE's Conception of Poverty and Core Values

HOPE believes poverty alleviation without true spiritual transformation is incomplete. In 2010, the New York Times columnist, Nicholas Kristof, visited the Republic of Congo, a country in which HOPE works. Travelling around the country, he wrote about many of the positive initiatives taking place in the Congo. However, he also recognized that aid and development were not enough to change lives:

> There's an ugly secret of global poverty, one rarely acknowledged by aid groups or U.N. reports. It's a blunt truth that is politically incorrect, heartbreaking, frustrating and ubiquitous: It's that if the poorest families spent as much money educating their children as they do on wine, cigarettes and prostitutes, their children's prospects would be transformed. Much suffering is caused not only by low incomes, but also by shortsighted private spending decisions by heads of households.[135]

HOPE's mission is to invest in the dreams of the poor; therefore, HOPE believes financial tools and training equip many to work themselves out of poverty. But HOPE also recognizes that the most significant impact does not come from just financial empowerment alone.

In the 1990s, World Bank asked over 60,000 of the poor in developing countries how they described poverty. The poor did not focus on their material deficit. Rather they described social and psychological aspects of poverty: "Poor people typically talk in terms of shame, inferiority, powerlessness, humiliation, fear, hopelessness, depression, social isolation, and voicelessness," said Brian Fikkert and Steve Corbett, when analyzing the study.[136]

The study highlights that poverty is innately social and psychological. Because of this, HOPE has a holistic approach to alleviating poverty that addresses not only economic but also social and psychological needs from a spiritual foundation.

HOPE's holistic approach stems from the belief that fundamentally poverty is about broken relationships.

HOPE's philosophy on poverty is summarized well by Bryant Myers in *Walking with the Poor: Principles and Practices of Transformational Development:* "Poverty is the result of relationships that do not work, that are not just, that are not for life, that are not harmonious or enjoyable. Poverty is the absence of shalom in all its meanings."[137]

Myers' statement is rooted in the biblical meta-narrative that includes the story of creation, fall, redemption, and restoration:

1. Creation: God created a world of coherence, beauty, and order, a system best illuminated by the ancient Hebrew concept of "shalom." To the ancient Israelites, "shalom" not only meant the absence of conflict, but as Myers' writes, "just, peaceful, harmonious, and enjoyable relationships with each other, ourselves, our environment, and God."[138]
2. Fall: When man sinned, the fall occurred, and the relationship between Creator God and humanity was broken. However, brokenness extended into the natural order of the world. Human relationships and relationships with nature were broken.
3. Redemption: God's son, Jesus Christ, came to earth as a man, died on a cross, and was resurrected. Considered the ultimate mediator, the son of God took upon Himself the sins of man by dying on a cross, and reconciling mankind with God.

4. Restoration: When Christ came to earth, He ushered in a new Kingdom – a Kingdom concerned with the restoration of relationships and a return to the concept of "shalom." While He declares that ultimate restoration occurs when Jesus returns once more, in the meantime, Jesus has commissioned those who follow him to bring about reconciliation and right relationships with Him, with each other, with themselves, and with the created order.

Within the biblical meta-narrative, humans – being made in the image of God – have inherent dignity and worth. God's purpose, to restore the world to a state of "shalom," is a call to address poverty in all of its forms. That is why HOPE not only helps bring about economic prosperity, but also seeks to reconcile relationships through Jesus Christ.

Just one example of this is through HOPE's savings groups in Rwanda. Torn apart by genocide in 1994, Rwandans are seeking unity and stability as they rebuild their country. Beyond helping the poor to save, HOPE's savings groups facilitate reconciliation.

One group is called United Women. In United Women, Tutsis and Hutus save together, pray together, and rebuild their community side by side. The group decided to open its doors to both victims and perpetrators of the genocide. Though they have struggled to overcome anger, hatred, and bitterness toward one another, they are now reconciled. They attribute their love for each other to the love of Christ. Through their biblically based savings curriculum, they have learned about the power of Christ's redemption and reconciliation. Today, they are farming each other's fields, and they call each other sisters.

HOPE's core identity includes the following:

Focus on Microenterprise Development. Recognizing that focusing on one type of ministry allows us to achieve a higher level of excellence, HOPE specializes in microenterprise development. HOPE strives to implement microenterprise development's best practices to maximize impact.

Intentional Witness for Jesus Christ. HOPE is committed to effectively proclaiming and demonstrating the Gospel through every aspect of its operations. HOPE classifies its work as "Word and Deed" ministry, and HOPE staff view themselves as having the head of a banker and the heart of a missionary. They are agents of restoration in places of financial poverty. Because they have the opportunity to build sustained relationships with individuals living in poverty, loan officers are HOPE's "feet on the ground" for Christ-centred ministry. Operating out of the belief that one cannot pass on a faith that one does not have, HOPE's spiritual integration begins with hiring committed Christian staff and dedicating time for weekly devotions and periodic staff retreats. Though HOPE employs various techniques in each environment to share the Gospel, common strategies include client devotions and prayer, biblically-based business and livelihood training, service-based outreaches, and partnerships with the local Church and other Christian ministries. HOPE implements a strategic approach to spiritual integration. Each of HOPE's programmes has collaborated with HOPE's director of spiritual integration to develop a contextualized spiritual integration plan that guides its efforts in bearing witness to Christ. In agreement with the expression "you get what you measure," each programme is also developing both institutional metrics (tracking the spiritual initiatives conducted) and impact metrics (measuring spiritual outcome for clients) to replicate effective programmes and highlight areas in need of improvement.

Savings. The developing world lacks not only credit, but also more fundamentally, savings. Many of the world's poor do not even have access to a safe place to accumulate practicable sums of money. Without the ability to deposit savings, people living in poverty often resort to hiding their money, leaving it vulnerable to theft, deterioration, or forgetfulness. Keeping savings in the home increases the likelihood that family or friends will ask for it, while also creating a strong temptation to spend today rather than save for tomorrow. HOPE's savings and credit association programmes and the majority of microfinance programmes incorporate a strong savings element.

Hard Places. HOPE is dedicated to serving in under-served markets and challenging environments where poverty and suffering are at their worst. Often, this means working in areas where conflict is widespread or infrastructure and well-established banking systems are non-existent (e.g., the Democratic Republic of Congo). HOPE's countries of operation share a common lack of access to critical financial services for those living in poverty. Though the challenges in such environments are numerous, HOPE's impact can make a tremendous difference.

Organizational Structure

HOPE's Central Service Unit is based in Lancaster, Pennsylvania.

HOPE International is under the leadership of a board of directors who meet quarterly. Serving under the board of directors is the HOPE executive team. Below is an organizational chart depicting the structure of HOPE's leadership:

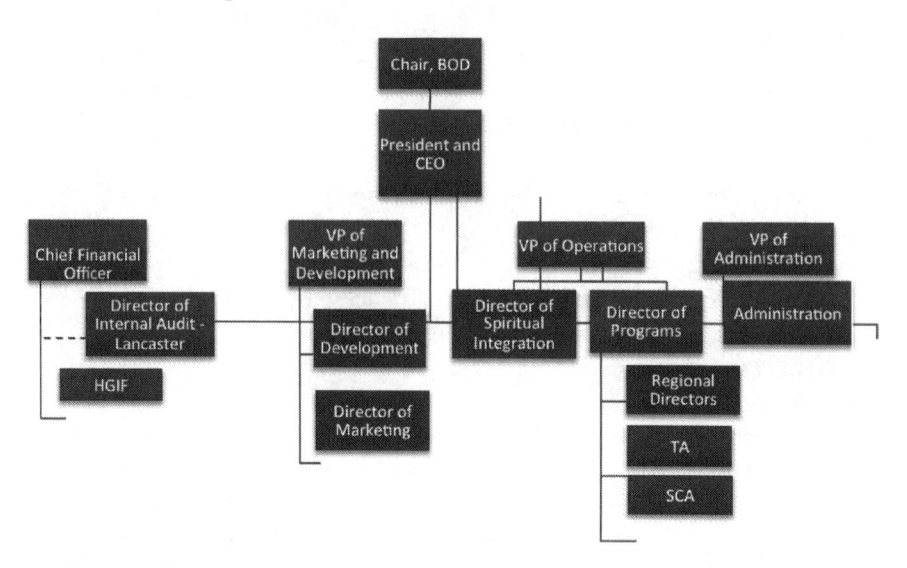

```
                          Chair, BOD
                              |
                      President and CEO
                              |
   ┌────────────┬─────────────┼──────────────┬──────────────┐
Chief          VP of         VP of          VP of
Financial      Marketing and Operations     Administration
Officer        Development
   |              |             |               |
Director of    Director of   Director of      Administration
Internal Audit Development   Spiritual
- Lancaster                  Integration
   |              |             |
  HGIF         Director of   Director of
               Marketing     Programs
                                |
                             Regional
                             Directors
                                |
                                TA
                                |
                               SCA
```

Within the HOPE International network are HOPE-led programmes owned by HOPE International, as well as HOPE partners where HOPE has varying degrees of ownership. Before HOPE partners, the organization must be determined to be a Christ-centered, operationally excellent, and financially sound organization.

Products and Clients Served

88% of HOPE clients are women.[139] HOPE offers a variety of services to the economically active poor engaged in savings and credit associations (SCAs), microenterprises (MF), and small and medium enterprises (SMEs).

The following tables and charts depict the breakdown of HOPE's active clients by region, net portfolio outstanding by region, and savings by region (MF and SCA):

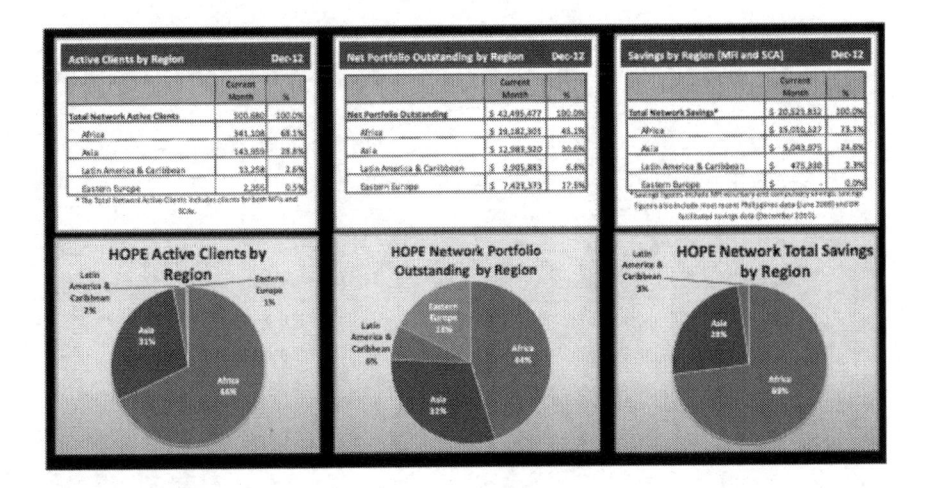

Savings and Credit Associations

HOPE defines the savings and credit association model as bringing informal financial intermediation services to rural areas and very poor individuals who lack the opportunity to save. Groups are established and meet on a regular basis and the group members decide together on an amount to save per month or week. They pool their agreed-upon savings and keep it in a locked box or bank account. Members can then apply for loans from the group's pooled savings. They agree upon an interest rate. This provides the rural poor with access to savings and credit. HOPE promotes the formation of groups by training leaders and community members in the skills they need to create and govern groups.

Methodologies used by HOPE's savings-led programmes

- *Rotating Savings and Credit Association (ROSCA):* ROSCAs are associations formed among a core of participants who make regular (equal) contributions to a fund, which is then given, in whole or in part, to each contributor in rotation. There is no accumulation of funds; rather each member gets an opportunity to access a lump sum of savings once per group cycle.
- *Accumulated Savings and Credit Association (ASCA):* ASCAs are associations formed among a core of participants who make regular (but not necessarily equal) contributions to a fund for an agreed period of time. Savings accumulate in the fund, which can then be

lent out to group members for various purposes. Many SCA groups grow their funds large enough to be transferred into bank accounts.
- *Straight Savings Group (SSG)*: SSGs are associations formed among a core of participants who make regular (but not necessarily equal) contributions to a fund for an agreed period of time. SSGs are distinct in that participants cannot withdraw more than what they have contributed at any given point. SSGs are often used to enable families to save for anticipated expenses, such as school fees, but can also be used for ongoing household or business expenses.

Financial Institutions
Microenterprises
HOPE provides small business loans between $100-2,500 to microentrepreneurs through its network of microfinance institutions. This provides a lump sum of capital to enable clients to run their businesses more efficiently or invest in productive assets, creating sustainable sources of income for one or more families.

SME
Small and medium enterprises vary in size based on different definitions, but HOPE defines its SME initiatives as benefiting clients who receive loans in the range of $2,500-$40,000. SME loans support larger businesses to further accelerate their growth and allow them to expand employment opportunities in their communities. These loans are provided to help stimulate the development of a middle class by encouraging innovation and creating jobs in contexts of pervasive unemployment or underemployment.

Methodologies used by HOPE's programmes
- *Community Banks:* A community bank is a group of approximately 15-45 individuals from within a community who come together to create a financial support group. Targeted to clients interested in small loans, the members within the group are able to borrow small amounts of money from a microfinance institution (MFI) to provide working capital for their microenterprises. Due to the members' lack of physical collateral, the group cross-guarantees one another's loans. This model is designed to reach the poor in urban and peri-urban areas.

- *Solidarity Groups:* A solidarity group is a group of approximately 5-15 individuals who are held jointly liable for one another's loans. This loans methodology can stand independently or be used to complement a community banking methodology by allowing successful clients to graduate into a solidarity group after several successful loan cycles. For graduates of a community banking methodology, these smaller groups offer more flexibility and higher loan sizes.
- *Individual loans:* This loan product provides loans to individuals who become solely responsible for the repayments with interest. These loans are often supported by guarantors or may even be collateralized. Individual loan sizes are typically larger than those of group loan products; therefore, individual loans may target clients pursuing SME initiatives, as well as clients receiving microcredit loans. Individual loans are made to clients who have an established history of repayment and can now utilize larger loans or clients who reside in countries/regions where community banking is not feasible.

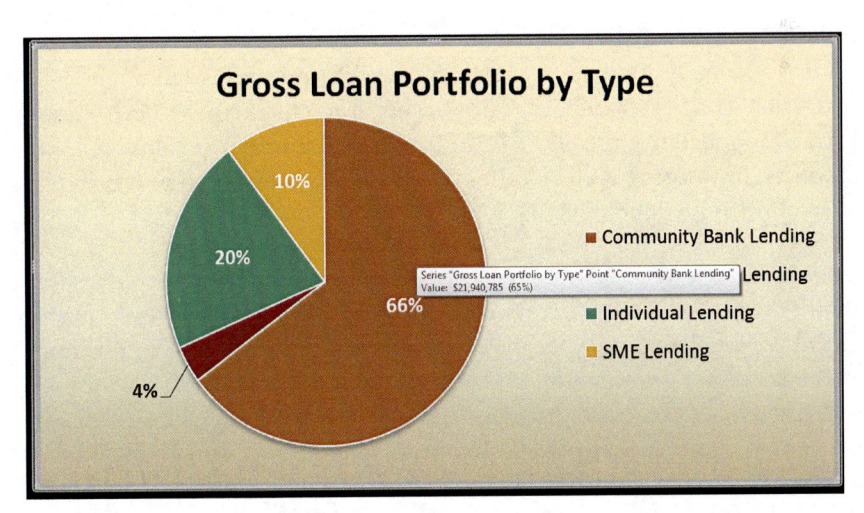

Gross Loan Portfolio by Type

- Community Bank Lending: 66%
- Solidarity Group Lending: 4%
- Individual Lending: 20%
- SME Lending: 10%

Series "Gross Loan Portfolio by Type" Point "Community Bank Lending"
Value: $21,940,785 (65%)

Traditional microenterprises make up 65% of HOPE programmes, SCAs 35%, and SMEs 5%, according to a breakdown of the number of programmes. Above is a breakdown of the gross loan portfolio by type.

Training

The majority of HOPE's clients have had limited opportunities for formal financial or business education. HOPE provides biblically-based business training to help clients understand the value of saving and record-keeping, giving to the Church and community, and running an ethical business. Topics of training include personal finances, preventive health, and business management. Loan clients also receive a clear explanation of interest rates and other terms they need to understand to make informed borrowing decisions.

One curriculum used throughout HOPE's network in both credit-led and savings-led programmes is the Chalmers Center for Economic Development's *Business, Home, and Health* (BHH) materials. The curriculum provides basic business and home and healthcare principles from a Christian worldview that affirms clients are made in the image of God, and so they have dignity and capacity.[140]

Funding

Below is the breakdown of HOPE's primary sources of funding:

Family Foundations

HOPE's primary funding resource comes from private, family foundations that value HOPE's model of Christ-centred microenterprise development. Private foundations provide HOPE with the freedom to invest in the products, in the geographic locations, and the spiritual direction it believes is most effective to uphold its mission.

Homes for Hope

Homes for Hope (H4H) invites builders and their trade partners to alleviate global poverty by doing what they do best: building a home. The mission of H4H is to work within the building industry, forming partnerships with builders and their trade partners to create Homes for Hope: income-generating projects that provide financial resources to benefit HOPE and like-minded organizations working to alleviate physical and spiritual poverty in developing countries throughout the world. As a home-builder and entrepreneur, HOPE's founder and chairman, Jeff Rutt, started Homes for Hope in 1998 as a way to galvanize the building industry to use their skills to fight against poverty.

Interest Income

Despite generous support from HOPE donors, the largest contributors to the model are the entrepreneurs served by HOPE. Each client pays interest income on loans, which enables the local institutions to cover their local operating costs and fund expansion.

HOPE's funding by sources

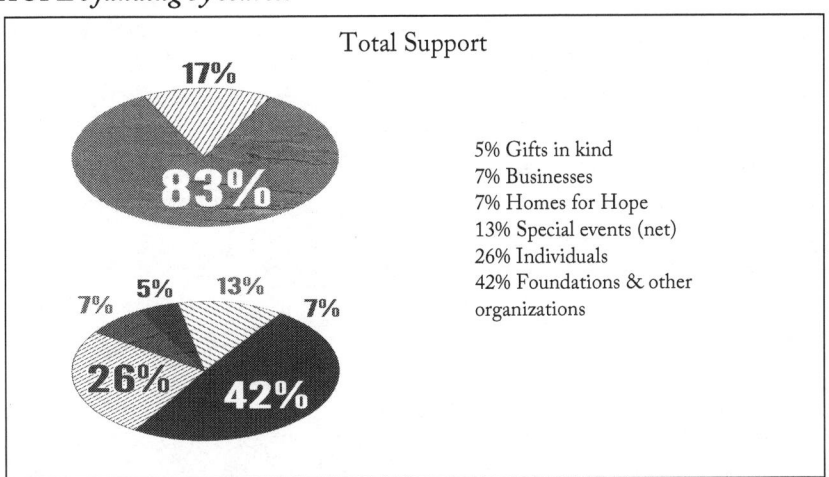

Total Support

- 17%
- 83%
- 7%
- 5%
- 13%
- 7%
- 26%
- 42%

5% Gifts in kind
7% Businesses
7% Homes for Hope
13% Special events (net)
26% Individuals
42% Foundations & other organizations

Christian Distinctives

Proclaiming and obeying Jesus Christ is at the heart of HOPE's mission. This decision is reflected in HOPE's 2010-2012 strategic plan:[141]

- Proclaim and obey Jesus Christ in all aspects of our work
- Excellent microenterprise development & financial services
- Scalable microenterprise development & financial services

As an organization whose primary purpose is to share the Good News of Jesus Christ to the poor, HOPE is committed to the following aspects of corporate culture:

(1) Believing in a prayerful dependence upon the Holy Spirit for eternal impact

HOPE embraces the Holy Spirit's powerful role. The Holy Spirit is the one who guides hearts to respond to God's love. HOPE believes lasting change requires supernatural intervention.

(2) Believing in including spiritual integration and effective outreach in specific country-level planning

As mentioned previously, HOPE sees its commitment to alleviating spiritual poverty as the core of its identity. Therefore, HOPE does not view its spiritual component as compartmentalized from its work, rather, HOPE incorporates its spiritual component into the structure of its services.

Building on the positive relationships and credibility gained through microfinance, HOPE is able to lovingly and effectively share the Good News of Jesus Christ. HOPE does so without coercion but with the full conviction that people need to know and live out spiritual truth. HOPE issues loans to individuals of any faith background (or no faith background) and does not discriminate on the basis of faith. HOPE offers no incentives for clients to follow Jesus.

The spiritual integration model differs depending on whether it is for group-based, individual lending, or savings and credit associations (SCAs).

Group-based lending model:
5W's community bank structure. First championed by HOPE's partner in the Philippines, the Center for Community Transformation (CCT), the bank structure provides an intentional platform for spiritual formation within the structure of the repayment meetings:

- *Welcome (5 mins.):* Loan officers take time to greet and build rapport with clients.
- *Worship (5 mins.):* Opening in prayer, the entire group then worships together in song.
- *Word (20 mins.):* Biblically-based business training, Crown Financial films, and teachings from spiritual impact co-ordinators and loan officers enable clients to hear the Word of God and acquire life skills.
- *Work (30 mins.):* Loan officers share best practices on repayment policies and collect or disburse loans and savings.
- *Wrap-up (5 mins.):* Loan officers emphasize final takeaways from the biblically-based training and any outstanding collection issues, and then close in prayer.

Training materials
HOPE capitalizes on prudent financial management principles based on the Bible. Emphasizing savings, proper planning, good stewardship, and a strong work ethic leads to a more productive use of loans and greater income generation. By teaching biblically-based ethical principles, HOPE contributes to combating corruption and teaching a higher standard for business.

HOPE uses the Chalmers Center for Economic Development's *Business, Home, and Health*, or BHH materials in both savings-led and credit-led programmes.[142] Using a Christian worldview, BHH teaches clients basic business and home and healthcare principles.

In the Dominican Republic, *Doing Business God's Way (DBGW)*, is a curriculum developed in-house by Esperanza International, HOPE's microfinance partner in the Dominican Republic and Haiti (Esperanza). Esperanza is now implementing DBGW across its 9 branch offices in the Dominican Republic. Like the BHH curriculum, DBGW affirms that individuals are made in the image of God and also teaches foundational business principles.

Individual lending model
Relationally based, the individual lending spiritual integration component is a three-step model.
1. Loan officers and cashiers from every office pray for the welfare of each of their clients.
2. If clients are interested, HOPE offers curriculum and training on business management, personal finance, and marriage and family to meet daily needs of clients and their families.
3. Finally, if clients are interested, loan officers and cashiers will share their faith with clients and/or they will invite them to their local Churches and Church communities.

Savings and credit associations (SCAs) model
By partnering with the local Church to implement its savings programmes, HOPE's spiritual component is thoroughly integrated in its SCAs. (More about HOPE's Church partnerships is listed in V. "Believing in partnering with the local Church.") Through the programme, clients also use the 5W

methodology and BHH materials being used in HOPE's traditional microfinance services.

Measurement

According to Matthew Rohrs, HOPE's director of spiritual integration, there is a tension in measuring spiritual integration, but one that HOPE readily navigates:

> *While admittedly difficult, at HOPE we desire to regularly assess our effectiveness in spiritual transformation. We are motivated to be as fruitful as possible and recognize that in general "what gets measured gets done." Thinking biblically about measurement, we affirm that there are aspects of our spiritual integration efforts for which we are accountable, even as we recognize that fruitfulness, life change, and eternal impact come only from the Lord. We see this as an unsolvable tension that requires prayerful dependence upon the Holy Spirit, humility, and great effort to do all we can to be faithful to our mission.*[143]

Each of HOPE's 16 countries of operation collaborates with HOPE's director of spiritual integration to develop a contextualized spiritual integration plan to guide its efforts in bearing witness to Christ.[144]

Every year, each HOPE network programme submits a spiritual integration plan, detailing how they aim to carry out their holistic mission. Some objectives include, but are not limited to, having devotions with clients and with staff, employing a full-time SI staff member, encouraging prayer between loan officers and clients, and carrying out client service projects, as well as committing to partnerships with local Churches.

Specific spiritual integration plans have been developed with prayer and reflection by full-time staff working in each local context. Those who develop the plan are those who best know the situation and the culture and also those who will be responsible for carrying it out.

Goals also vary depending on the nature of the restrictions on religious freedom in some countries (see 7.2 "Christ-centered identity"). Every year, HOPE includes spiritual integration expenses in its yearly budget. HOPE also receives reports on the execution of these yearly plans from managing directors.

Leadership
HOPE's director of spiritual integration is on the executive team, and HOPE also hires spiritual integration co-ordinators in the countries in which it operates. These co-ordinators help to train staff to carry out the 5W's group structure and implement biblical business training. They also meet regularly with clients to hear clients' needs and they establish relationships with local pastors and ministries.

(3) Believing in recruiting Christian staff

HOPE's success in holistic ministry hinges on its employees being fully on board with its mission.[145] Since the spiritual component of HOPE's programmes is woven into the structure of its model, HOPE hires staff members who not only accept the mission, but also identify themselves as fully devoted followers of Jesus Christ.

"The Board Strategy for Spiritual Integration" presented by HOPE's sub-committee for spirituality and culture, declares the following:

1. We will recruit people, whenever possible who both profess faith in Christ and have the requisite technical skills.
2. We will train and develop staff to contribute to the whole mission of HOPE, including the effective communication of the Gospel.
3. We will require all CSU staff and in-field directors to sign HOPE's Statement of Belief.[146]

Each department plays a vital role in fulfilling HOPE's mission, and, therefore, the requirement for Christ-following staff extends to the entire organization. Again, in order to effectively carry out its mission, it is absolutely crucial that all HOPE staff members, at all levels and in all functions of the organization, are followers of Jesus Christ.[147]

HOPE recruits employees regarding faith fit, technical fit, and mission fit. Some of the characteristics embodied by HOPE employees are listed below:

- *The **heart** of a missionary – a passion for helping people to come to know and follow Christ.* HOPE is looking for individuals who believe Jesus Christ is the Son of God who came to earth to restore relationships.
- *The **soul** of a development worker – the mentality of enabling people to help themselves.* HOPE is looking for people interested in not only giving a hand-out, but also looking at a long-term approach to

addressing poverty, one that gives people dignity. Because the poor are made in the image of God, they have dignity and worth, abilities and talents, purpose and calling. HOPE is looking for individuals who recognize that hand-outs can foster dependency among the poor, which takes away from the poor's ability to use their God-given gifts and skills.
- *The mind of a business person – the skills in management, finance, accounting, systems, etc.* HOPE is looking for individuals with backgrounds in business, accounting, and management to lead its programmes overseas.

(4) Commitment to spiritual formation for its staff and clients

In a Church in Brazzaville, HOPE facilitated the showing of a film based on the life of Joseph, as depicted in the Old Testament, to clients, their families, and friends.

Upon seeing the film, one man stood up and said, "It is difficult for me to forgive, but when I saw this video, I was touched and wanted to forgive those who had offended [me]."[148]

During that same session, another client shared that "the life of Joseph is a reflection of Jesus Christ's life of forgiveness and humility."

This is just one example of how HOPE intentionally seeks to bring about spiritual transformation in the lives of its staff and clients. Spiritual formation is at the heart of HOPE's mission to alleviate poverty holistically.

Staff

To carry out its mission, HOPE understands that staff members need to have an active, personal faith. If staff members are sharing the Good News, it can only be authentic if they have a personal relationship with Christ in their own lives, an acknowledgement that God is real though unseen, and the Holy Spirit is guiding and working through them.[149] HOPE intentionally seeks to encourage spiritual growth in the lives of its staff members:
- *Annual departmental spiritual integration goals.* These goals are created to ensure that the way HOPE accomplishes its tasks and the way it treats fellow employees, donors, and the community is thoroughly biblical. Progress is analyzed yearly.

- *Alpha Course.* HOPE staff members in Lancaster, Pennsylvania, and around the world, have been given the opportunity to participate in the world-renowned course exploring fundamental elements of the Christian faith to enable them to better articulate their faith to clients. This has also been piloted with clients in the Democratic Republic of Congo and the Republic of Congo.
- *Weekly devotions and prayer times.* This time of fellowship helps to bring HOPE staff closer to God as a community of faith.
- *Relationship.* Directors will regularly address spiritual formation issues with their staff members.

Clients

- *Partnership with Crown Financial Ministries.* Crown Financial Ministries and HOPE International have partnered to bring HOPE staff and clients access to the Gospel in a new way with the *God Provides Film Learning Experience.* Depicting such familiar biblical narratives of faith, hope, and trust, as the widow's oil, Jeremiah's call, Abram's reward, Abraham and Isaac, the rich man and Lazarus, and Nicodemus' talk with Jesus, the six-part film series is used in HOPE's staff devotions and community bank meetings. With its rich, visual storytelling, the videos are a particularly effective means of sharing the Gospel with HOPE's clients in places where literacy rates are low.
- *Relationship building.* Staff members build relationships with clients, seeking to know their life circumstances, offering encouragement and counsel, and "making the most of every opportunity" to communicate Christ.

Below is one story of how the relationships between staff and client helped to facilitate transformation in the lives of one of Esperanza's clients.

Client Story – Jose Luis Rincon

"When there isn't capital, there isn't work," says José Luís Rincón, a successful Dominican wheel-barrow manufacturer.[150] José knows from experience. Over a decade ago, Jose dreamed of turning his craft of wheel-barrow making into a successful enterprise, but he never had enough capital to put his skill to work. To finance his dream and provide for his family, José had mortgaged nearly everything he owned, but it was not enough.

José discovered HOPE and partner microfinance institution, Esperanza, and applied for a small loan. He also started hearing about Christ and seeing the love of God in action through the relationship with his loan officer.

By seeing God's love through his loan officer, Jose said he came to know Jesus as his personal saviour.

"I found Jesus," he said.

Little by little he received and repaid six loans. Putting this simple "hand up" to good use, José expanded his business by over 500%. He purchased a truck, paid for all his own tools, and hired five employees who were formerly out of work. Today, José has built a modest but sturdy concrete block home for his family. He can provide for his wife and two daughters without wondering where their next meal will come from. Though his family and business are now entirely self-sufficient, this talented entrepreneur isn't done yet. He built a full-fledged factory where he can continue to produce wheelbarrows and even manufacture tires, cutting his production costs dramatically.

Each day José and his team manufacture ten wheel-barrows. Because he believes God calls him to do excellent work through this business, José has become the first wheel-barrow manufacturer in the Dominican Republic to offer a one-year warranty on his product. José considers himself a changed man. He has dignity in being able to provide for his family. He takes pride in working hard and producing a quality product. He also has been able to support his Church, provide food for hungry individuals in his community, and in turn show the love of God to others.

(5) Believing in partnering with the local Church

In 2007, the Anglican Church of Rwanda began a partnership with HOPE to meet the needs of people living on less than $2 a day. They asked HOPE to help them start SCAs within the region. Through the churches' involvement, start-up costs have been low, which has allowed for rapid growth: in 2008, there were just over 32,000 clients; in 2012, there was over 100,000 group members.

The Anglican Church provides an optimal distribution system to offer financial services: they have decreed that every diocese must have at least three SCAs per Church. The Church provides the human capital (volunteer trainers) and the meeting place (group members can meet in the Churches). HOPE trains the volunteers and provides the biblically-based curriculum group members use, the BHH curriculum created by the Chalmers Center for Economic Development.

Another benefit of the programme is that there is zero capital injection into the SCAs. HOPE donors provide capital for the training of the trainers and the curriculum but the group members receive no outside aid to start saving.

There is an ongoing concern about integrating the Church with microfinance. However, savings groups are an ideal partnership between the two: Church members do not handle money; they only help to facilitate meetings.

By partnering with Churches, HOPE's savings programmes are combating spiritual, physical, and social poverty.[151] HOPE provides technical expertise to partnering Churches and ministries to create and manage savings and credit associations in locations where partners already have relationships with local indigenous Churches.

Partnering with Churches not only reinforces HOPE's mission of spiritual transformation but also provides an effective distribution system for microfinance services. Pastor and author Rick Warren pointed out in a map of the Western Province of Rwanda that there are 26 hospitals, but over 700 Churches in the same region. In places like sub-Saharan Africa, where the church hierarchy plays a greater role in daily life than in Western culture, the Church is a great platform to reach the community with their large networks and scale.[152]

- *Spiritual Transformation*: By facilitating Christ-centered savings and credit associations, Churches help build the Kingdom of God by addressing physical need, social brokenness, and spiritual poverty. Savings and credit associations provide a valuable financial service that attracts people from diverse social and religious backgrounds and places them in direct contact with local Churches in a non-threatening way, opening doors for Christians to build relationships and proclaim the hope of Christ.

  The community-focused nature of the group structure creates an instant community. Relationships replace isolation, and neighbours become family. Savings and credit associations also promote the practice of giving. Generosity replaces dependency and self-interest, and Christians are given tools to tithe and to care for their own communities. Finally, savings and credit associations pave the way for reconciliation between family members and neighbours. Trust and interdependence replace fear and suspicion, and the community begins to be restored.

- *Physical Transformation:* Members receive access to a lump sum of capital that they can use to cover everyday expenses and save for major purchases. This leads to greater access for the entire family to improved nutrition, healthcare, and education. Members who use savings and credit association savings to start small businesses will have increased household income, and in turn, more productive, stable, and self-sufficient household enterprises. Finally, savings and credit associations provide members with a basic safety net, giving them the ability to guard their families and assets against emergencies like illness, death, and natural disasters, enabling members' families to enjoy a more sustainable livelihood during difficult times.
- *Social Transformation*: Through savings and credit association elements like biblical teaching, livelihood training, community interaction, and the actual act of saving regularly, savings members come to have a better understanding of their own self-worth and value as children of God. When they see themselves as capable of meeting their own needs and the needs of their families, they are empowered. Savings programmes also provide a venue for community leadership, creating a local forum for addressing common problems. By creating a close network of people who share interests and work together to ensure each member has a safety net, savings members experience a sense of social support and "belonging," perhaps for the first time.
- Programmes of traditional microfinance (microenterprise) and SME development work are also committed to finding a local Church partner. There are mutual benefits to such partnerships: HOPE connects its clients to the local Churches, and in countries like Haiti, the Church has used the microfinance programme as a vehicle to offer healthcare and literacy training to those in the

community, while the Church often provides a venue for spiritual integration plans initiatives to take place, such as HOPE's showcasing of the *God Provides Film Learning Experience.*

(6) Upholding the dignity of its clients in all of its dealings
When many clients of high-profile micro-lenders in the region of Andhra Pradesh, India, committed suicide due to over-indebtedness and ill-treatment from some institutions,[153] donors called HOPE, questioning the extent of this sort of abuse.

In response to provocative headlines like "India's Major Crisis in Micro-lending: Loans Involving Tiny Amounts of Money Were a Good Idea, but the Explosion of Interest Backfires"[154] in *The Wall Street Journal* and others in leading publications, people wanted to know if the tool was broken and if HOPE had a different model.

Although the scandal was limited to certain provinces in India, the wide-ranging effects went outside the region, undermining microfinance's credibility globally.

Ironically, amid the scandal, HOPE's savings clients in the neighboring state of Maharashtra were still gathering to save as before and experiencing a positive impact. In geographic proximity to the scandal, HOPE's savings programme – being Christ-centered and client-focused – was philosophically and programmatically far removed from the crisis.

Different in approach from many microfinance institutions in the region, when HOPE India first arrived in Maharashtra, some clients were sceptical of its approach: "Why are you wasting your time with us?" they asked HOPE staff. "We're poor. We're stuck here, and there is no way out for us."[155]

HOPE India's message to the poor is that they are made in the image of God – that they have dignity, talents, and potential. By partnering with local churches, offering Bible studies, providing outreach to youth and children, and offering first-rate financial services, HOPE India is seeing lives transformed.

A HOPE client stepped forward in a recent meeting and said, "Before, we were called slum dwellers, but this is no longer how we view ourselves in our hearts. We have hopes, we have dreams, and we want to continue moving forward in God's vision."[156]

HOPE actively supports the creation of profitable microfinance institutions – but never at the expense of these institutions' social mission. Recognizing the growing gulf between a client-focused approach to microfinance and one that focuses primarily on shareholders' returns, HOPE declares that it exists for the purpose of the client and has made the following commitments:[157]

- *HOPE has forsworn profits from its programmes.* Although the concept of a development programme generating profit is not antithetical to HOPE's philosophy, and profits are indeed a positive and desirable outcome from HOPE's microfinance activity, HOPE's board members each sign a "Declaration of Non-Personal Use of or Gain from HOPE International's Microenterprise Development Activities," which states that "no individual investor, staff member, or board member [will] experience any direct personal financial gain from the profit of the microfinance institutions in HOPE's network."[158]
- *Partnership with MicroFinance Transparency.* In 2008, Chuck Waterfield – an industry leader with over 25 years of experience in microfinance as a practitioner, teacher, and developer of Microfin (the most widely accepted financial planning tool in the sector) – invited HOPE to help launch MicroFinance Transparency.[159]

Now endorsed by over 800 industry leaders, MicroFinance Transparency is "the venue for the microfinance industry to publicly demonstrate its commitment to pricing transparency, integrity and poverty alleviation."[160]

Not only was HOPE influential to the start-up of the organization but HOPE was also the first microfinance network to endorse MicroFinance Transparency publicly.

CEO of MicroFinance Transparency, Chuck Waterfield, took HOPE's executive team aside after personally assessing the interest rates of HOPE's programmes and described how HOPE was a lower-cost provider of quality services. He summarized, "Your interest rates could be higher."[161]

(7) Believing in corporate and social responsibility at the organizational level
Within the first year of its founding, HOPE had itself started a children's ministry in Ukraine. Cindy Marty, the wife of HOPE's first president, Paul

Marty, founded Tomorrow Clubs, which are similar to Awana, a well-known Bible club for children in the United States.[162]

Started in Zaporozhe, Ukraine, the burgeoning programme now operates in every region of the country. It has extended into Russia as well. By transforming lives, Tomorrow Clubs teach a biblical curriculum to children; offer hobby classes, such as cooking, sewing, and woodworking; and provide sports and activities in which children can engage. Now a separate entity from HOPE International, Tomorrow Clubs receive their primary funding from the profits of HOPE's microfinance institutions in Ukraine and Russia.

Giving is not a secondary part of HOPE's mission. As HOPE's microfinance institutions become sustainable, they are encouraged to support a local Christ-centred children's ministry through funding and volunteering.[163] HOPE's desire for a lasting impact and the transformation of communities underlies its commitment to giving. 10% of HOPE's surplus income goes to children and youth programmes, according to Brian Lewis (2011), a HOPE board member, in a memorandum to the 2011 board of directors.[164] Herein, he shares about the element of giving that permeates every part of HOPE's organizational culture:

> But institutionalizing giving – making giving to children and youth programs part of the DNA of local HOPE offices – does not imply a second strategic focus for our ministry. Our focus is not divided between micro-enterprise development and child and youth programs. Giving is rather part of our core teaching and modeling effort with micro-entrepreneurs. As Jesus modeled Kingdom Living for the 12, and as Paul said, "Follow me as I follow Christ," so being a model and example to new micro-entrepreneurs is an essential part of our mission.[165]

As Lewis wrote, HOPE's culture of giving extends to HOPE clients:

> What then do we intend to model? For the nearly 400,000 emerging entrepreneurs in the HOPE network, we intend to model that business people are givers. Businesses grow, and they give. They grow some more, and they give some more. The best way to have a generational impact on the communities where we work is to raise up a new generation of local givers – to replace Western dollars with local dollars, to multiply giving as fast as we multiply loans.[166]

HOPE has seen in countless cases that once their families' basic needs are met, clients have the freedom and confidence to participate in community transformation through projects like feeding the hungry, supporting their Church leaders, adopting orphans, opening Christian schools, and employing ex-convicts.

(8) Commitment to funding its mission in ways that enhance the proclamation of the Gospel

HOPE has historically relied on a constituency that supports the full mission of impacting lives physically, socially and spiritually. In 2007, HOPE's board of directors issued the following statement regarding financing:

- HOPE is committed to funding its entire mission in ways that do not restrict but rather enhance its proclamation of the Gospel. Therefore:
- We will communicate our mission to all potential donors, anticipating that the vast majority of our support will come from those who share our spiritual convictions.
- We will welcome financial partners who do not personally share our spiritual commitment provided they understand it and choose to contribute regardless.
- We will decline funding which would shift our spiritual priorities or stifle our Gospel proclamation. The mission to proclaim Christ is at the core of our identity.[167]

Not only is HOPE's prerogative to fund its mission in a way that enhances the proclamation of the Gospel, but it also sees fund-raising as ministry. Interactions with donors are not just transactions but part of the process of transformation on the part of the staff and the individual donor. As HOPE recognizes that humanity suffers from a common poverty – and that poverty is innately spiritual – it believes that all people are on a journey to better understand Jesus Christ's redemptive grace.

CHALLENGES

The primary challenges HOPE faces are because of its commitment to hard places and its dedication to its Christ-centred mission.

Hard places

HOPE seeks to work in areas that are under-served, not saturated by microfinance services – regions considered difficult to do business. For example, two countries ranked as having the lowest human development by the 2011 UNDP's Human Development Index, Burundi and the Democratic Republic of Congo, are countries in which HOPE carries out its mission.[168]

Because of its commitment to working in hard places, HOPE faces the following challenges:

Foreign exchange risk

Fluctuating currency values in countries often plagued by economic instability pose an obstacle to growth. During the global financial recession in 2008-2009, HOPE Ukraine experienced extreme difficulty: the Ukraine *hryvnia* depreciated from 4.7 to 8 per 1 USD.[169] Because HOPE Ukraine had not been able to hedge external hard currency debt, the programme had to nearly double the amount of *hryvnias* it repaid investors.

There are few hedging mechanisms for currencies like the *hryvnia* or the Congolese *franc* due to the political and economic instability of countries HOPE serves with only a small number of investors willing to make local currency loans.

Besides highlighting the challenge of foreign exchange risk within Ukraine, the global recession also targeted HOPE's primary sector of clients: market and retail vendors. Until 2009, clients were primarily involved in retail sales and small market and neighbourhood stalls.

In order to continue to serve the poor within Ukraine, HOPE Ukraine sought to diversify its portfolio to include greenhouse and agricultural loans. Agricultural loans also enabled HOPE to better serve rural communities.[170]

By 2010, HOPE Ukraine's portfolio grew once more, fueled by the addition of agricultural loans and the increasing number of housing loans offered by HOPE through a partnership with Habitat for Humanity, reported by HOPE Ukraine.[171]

By 2011, greenhouse loans made up about 20% of HOPE Ukraine's loan portfolio at the peak of growing season. HOPE's portfolio diversification, in 2011, is illustrated by the chart below:[172]

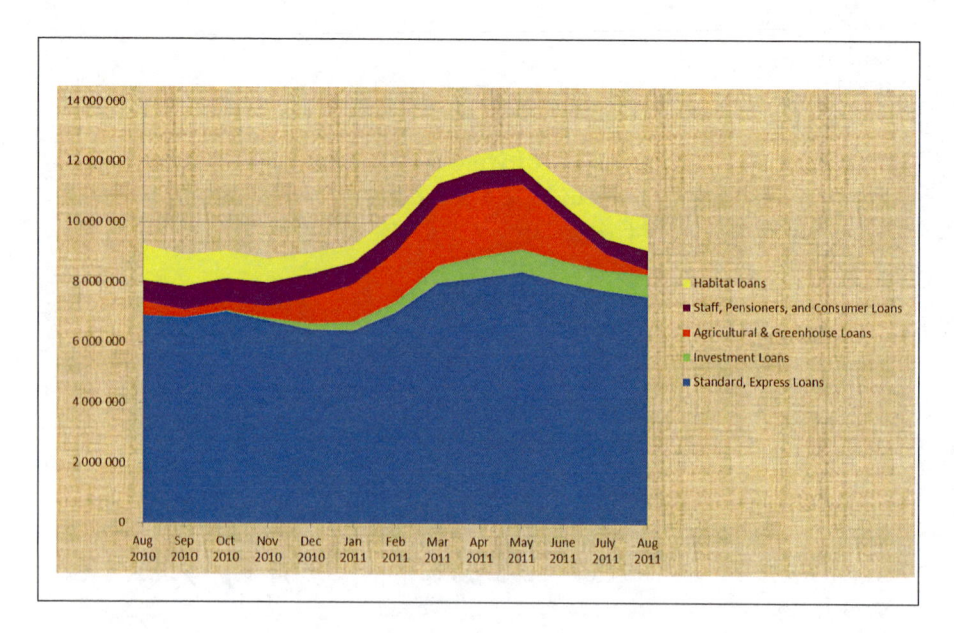

[Chart: Stacked area chart showing loan portfolio from Aug 2010 to Aug 2011, with categories: Habitat loans; Staff, Pensioners, and Consumer Loans; Agricultural & Greenhouse Loans; Investment Loans; Standard, Express Loans. Y-axis scale 0 to 14,000,000.]

Registration

Even before formally operating, the challenges of working in under-served areas begin. Because of the need to receive approval from local, state, and federal government, registering microfinance institutions in regions often beset with political instability and civil war can be fraught with challenges.

For example, HOPE's most recently launched microfinance institution in the Republic of Congo took over a year (from 2008-2009) to be formally registered. In the case of HOPE Congo, beyond registering locally, microfinance institutions require state and federal approval from the Central Bank and approval from the Commission Bancaire de l'Afrique Centrale (COBAC), which regulates banks in six African countries of the Central African Zone.

Other

Cultural and religious norms place restrictions on HOPE employees in some of the countries in which HOPE works. For example, in one closed country, it is culturally appropriate for female loan officers to administer loans to women whereas male loan officers lend to male entrepreneurs. This increases costs and decreases efficiency.

Working in countries often hostile to the Christian faith poses other challenges.

A managing director of a closed country said in a staff meeting, "When HOPE staff join, they recognize that the risk that comes in their spiritual life naturally extends into their work life."[173] While this is true, HOPE takes precautions to ensure that its staff members are safe, complying with all of a country's legal restrictions.

Christ-centred identity

HOPE intentionally seeks to alleviate not only physical poverty, but also spiritual poverty. All functions of the organization's operations – from funding to loan payments – integrate its spiritual mission. Because of its emphasis, HOPE faces unique challenges regarding funding and recruitment.

Funding

Because of HOPE's overt Christian mission, it has received little support from corporations and secular foundations. For example, in 2011, HOPE was denied the ability to participate in a major proposal because the implementing partner was uncomfortable with HOPE's clear emphasis on addressing spiritual poverty.

In the same way, a foundation of a significant corporation in Europe called a meeting in Houston, Texas, in 2008, and pledged to give significant support to HOPE. Their intended gift during the early stages of HOPE's history would have provided a catalyst for enormous growth.

HOPE's desire to reach the most financially under-served and its commitment to do business in the world's most challenging business environments were directly allied to the foundation's mission. Ultimately, the foundation decided not to partner with HOPE, citing HOPE's uncompromising position to implement its holistic mission.

While HOPE has been passed over by large foundations due to its public allegiance to Jesus Christ, HOPE has had a great opportunity to engage a still largely untapped Christian community. According to Scott Todd, chairman of North America's largest network for Christian relief and development organizations and the senior ministry advisor at Compassion International, the number of American Church-goers is 138 million, and in sum, they make over $2.5 trillion every year.[174]

American Church-goers are an ideal demographic for HOPE as they statistically give more: Mark Hrywna of The NonProfit Times writes that "people who give to a religious group are almost three times more likely to give to another charity than those who do not give to religion. They will also give to more charities, according to a recent national survey by *The NonProfit Times* and Infogroup."[175]

Recruitment
HOPE aspires to hire corporate industry leaders who are strongly invested in their faith. For example, its upper-level management includes leaders with executive roles from organizations like Capital One, JP Morgan Chase, Arthur Anderson LLP, and Price Waterhouse Coopers. Because of HOPE's unique niche – and its particular dedication to working in challenging environments – recruiting those with technical expertise and mission fit is often difficult. As mentioned previously, to achieve success, HOPE sees it as imperative to hire employees who are both a technical and mission fit.

MICROFINANCE-PLUS SERVICES AND IMPACT
Networking with local Churches affords HOPE access to free venues for client training, repayment meetings, etc., and a larger base of volunteers who can cost-effectively deliver supplementary business and livelihood training. Partnerships with other Christian ministries allow HOPE to provide clients with complementary services like healthcare, education, and HIV/AIDS prevention.

More than providing loans, HOPE's objective is to facilitate social, physical, and spiritual transformation in the lives of its clients. In 2012, HOPE hired an outside consultant, the Metrix Research Group, to do network-wide impact assessment and monitoring and evaluation of HOPE operations, in order to streamline operations and to provide a better customer experience – helping HOPE to most effectively achieve its mission to enact change in the lives of its clients.

Below are summaries of two impact assessments carried out through HOPE's network:

Rwanda SCA – Impact assessments conducted in Kigali (2010) and Byumba (2011), two districts in Rwanda, found the following:[176]

- An increase in ownership of productive assets in Kigali, especially goats (increase of 101%), chickens (140% increase) and cows (114% increase).
- Increased school attendance in Byumba: 27% more children were attending primary school, and 104% more children were attending secondary school after parents joined savings programmes.
- The number of families who reported having three meals a day in Byumba increased from 7% to 42%.
- Before joining savings groups, 65% of families attended church regularly while 96% attended regularly after joining the savings programmes.

Moldova SME – In 2011, Invest-Credit, HOPE's partner in Moldova, conducted a client survey to assess the social and spiritual impact of its program on clients' lives. Staff surveyed 23% of its 566 active clients on the social impact of Invest-Credit loans on business and family life, and 8% of clients on the spiritual impact of Invest-Credit's services.[177]

- Spiritual impact: What the survey found was that 80 new Christians were led to Christ by Invest-Credit clients. 85% of clients were investing 6 or more hours per month in a local Church ministry. 94% of clients attended Church at least once a week.
- Social impact: The average growth in business income due to a loan from Invest-Credit was 21.6%. Lastly, 128 new employees were hired by clients after taking a loan from Invest-Credit.

CONCLUSION

In 1997, HOPE offered financial services to 12 people living in Ukraine. While its scope has increased to include over 450,000 clients in 16 countries, HOPE, in its intent, has changed little. As it did in 1997, HOPE invests in the dreams of the poor.

Offering a variety of financial services, HOPE is committed to serving the poor in areas that are under-served financially. As a faith-based organization, HOPE incorporates a clear witness for Jesus Christ. Client-focused and Christ-centred, HOPE's microenterprise development services offer basic business training, mentoring, and discipleship to equip the poor to break the cycles of physical and spiritual poverty.

FAULU KENYA DEPOSIT TAKING MICROFINANCE INSTITUTION CASE STUDY

JOHN MWARA AND JACQUELINE NYAGA

John Mwara is the Managing Director of Faulu Kenya. He holds a Master of Business Administration, and is a Certified Public Accountant (CPA-K) and a Certified Public Secretary (CPS-K). He has over 20 years' experience in strategic planning, financial and business management, and microfinance.

Jacqueline Nyaga is currently Human Resource Manager, Faulu Kenya Deposit-Taking Microfinance. She has 17 years' work experience as a microfinance and human resource practitioner. She holds a Master of Business Administration degree, in addition to a Bachelor of Commerce degree and Higher Diploma in Human Resource Management. She is also a Certified Financial Literacy and Microfinance Trainer of Trainers.

HISTORY

Kenya is the 47th largest country in the world in terms of land area, and is the regional hub for trade in East Africa. The country has a market-based economy with agriculture, industry and the service sector, especially tourism, being the key economic contributors to the country's Gross Domestic Product [GDP],[178] which was at $33.6 billion in 2011.[179] The Kenyan economy has had its share of ups and downs, since independence, with GDP increasing annually at an annual average of 6.6% from 1963 to 1973 followed by a period of declining economic performance between 1974 and 1990, with the worst years ranging from 1990-1993 when growth in GDP stagnated, and inflation rose due to among others the negative effects from the political environment and unstable agricultural performance.

However, Kenyans are a hardworking people, and are rated the most optimistic people in the world[180] and this is evident in the return to higher economic growth. To further propel the country to middle-income status by 2030, there is in place a robust national long term strategy named Vision 2030 founded on three key pillars: economic, social and political governance. The economic pillar of vision 2030 seeks to achieve a 10% Gross Domestic Product (GDP) growth rate per annum, and the financial services sector is one of the 6 priority areas that will facilitate this. Successive government policy has, therefore, prioritized sector reforms in the financial services sector,[181] geared towards expanded financial inclusion of Kenyans, in an effort to reduce the 32.7% Kenyans that are excluded from access to any form of formal or non-formal financial services (Central Bank of Kenya in partnership with Central Bank of Kenya, FSD Kenya and FAP, 2009) as at 2009.[182] This has led to among others the passing of legislation to promote and regulate microfinance, providing great opportunities to increase outreach within the sector which focuses on the transformation of those at the bottom of the pyramid (Prahalad, August 5 2004).

The financial services sector is vibrant, with 43 licensed commercial banks, a SACCO movement with 2,959 active institutions,[183] and 9 licensed Deposit Taking Microfinance Institutions, not to mention the semi-formal and informal providers of financial services. Deposit taking Microfinances had a total loan portfolio $218 million and deposits base of $150 million,[184] as at mid-2012, with Faulu Kenya Deposit Taking Microfinance ("Faulu") among the market leaders, who include Kenya Women Finance Trust, and Jamii Bora.

Faulu began in 1991 as a programme for Food for the Hungry ("FH"), an international non-governmental organization [NGO] to offer financial services on a sustainable development approach. This led to the conceptualization of a microfinance programme that was aimed at financing small businesses, with the driving force behind the formation of the then "Faulu loan program", being *"they die one at a time, we can help them one at a time"*.[185] The pilot project began with a seed loan capital of $ 8,000 with micro-loans to the traders in the Mathare slums, East of Nairobi. As methodologies and systems were defined, and the programme grew, the initial focus from 1991 to 1994 was learning the ropes of micro-financing and building capacity. Initial funding from DFID [UK Department for International development] of $2 million in 1995 led to Faulu's growth and by 1997 the institution sought to move towards profitability and away from dependence on donor funding for sustenance.

To facilitate this focus, Faulu changed its legal status from Non-Governmental Organization [NGO] into a limited liability company in 1999, and formally became Faulu Kenya Limited ("FKL"). By 2004, momentum to expand business gained with focused strategic plans by the

Faulu board, who sought to "Dream into the Future", and sourced partnerships and financing that saw the issuance of a 5 years' bond in 2005 of $ 6.25 million from the capital markets as capital injection. This was the first bond issued by an MFI in Africa, and there was excitement at both staff and client level:

"30 customers were invited to witness as Faulu rang the bell to start trading on the trading floor of the Nairobi Stock Exchange in April 2005.....There was excitement and awe as they visited the *'money market'*, and the loan officers explained to them that money was traded here similar to trading their wares in the physical market place, and that Faulu was coming to this market to 'buy' money to open more branches and enable other clients' access financing like them. Commented one... *'I never thought that one day I would walk into the Nairobi Stock Exchange! Faulu has brought me far!"* [186]

A further $18 million was raised through various partnerships with Deustche Bank, Overseas Private Investment Corporation [OPIC], International Finance Corporation [IFC] and Financial Sector Deepening-Kenya [FSD-K], leading to an unprecedented growth from 14,000 clients at the end of 2004 to 90,339 at the end of 2007, with an outstanding loan balance of $21 million, enabling Faulu to commence its next transformation phase.

In 2009, Faulu became the first Deposit Taking Microfinance [DTM] registered in Kenya under the Micro-Finance Act, regulated by the Central Bank of Kenya [CBK], allowing it to take deposits from the public. The institution had taken an active role in lobbying for this regulation, as a means of furthering the transformation agenda of poor people in Kenya. With regulation in place, Faulu evolved from a programme that targeted an under-served market with unique needs and is currently one of the top 3 Deposit Taking MFIs in Kenya having successfully developed a platform aimed at banking the previously unbanked through a variety of savings, credit, micro-insurance and mobile banking solutions, with advisory services and education deeply embedded.

From its humble roots as a loan scheme in 1991 to its conversion to the first DTM in Kenya in 2009, Faulu has demonstrated a consistent track record of enviable growth in its assets and loan book, currently standing at $ 54 million in outstanding loan balance and $ 51 million in deposits as at November 2012. (Faulu Kenya Annual Report and Financial Statements, 2008-2011, & Management Report 2012).

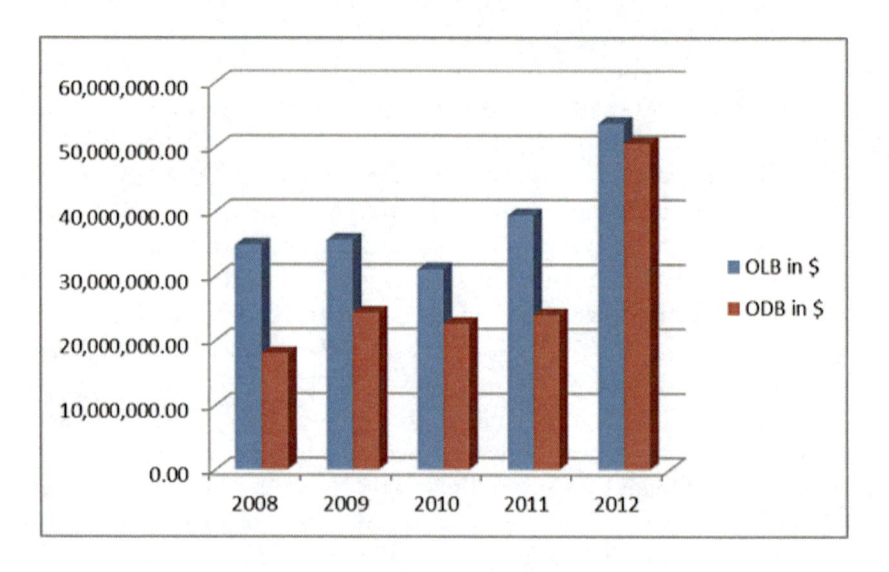

Figure 1 Faulu Kenya Performance of Loan and Deposit books

Following transformation (conversion to regulated deposit-taking), Faulu has been able to work with more development partners, to position itself as a financial institution offering holistic transformation. Its unique business model provides a highly attractive platform for sustained growth and improved profitability. The institution currently serves over 350,000 customers, almost equally split between urban and rural residents, with growth increasingly coming from the rural customer base. To effectively serve its customer base, Faulu has established over 100 service outlets comprising 27 banking branches with strategic service provision partnerships that make its services available countrywide. The company currently has more than 700 members of staff, representing a rapid growth from only 10 employees and one business unit in 1991.

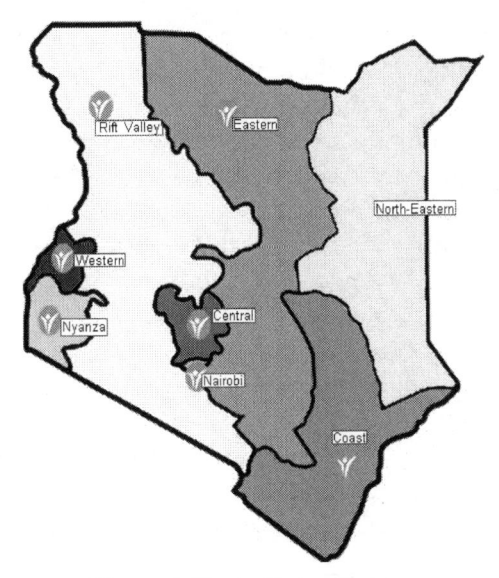

Figure 2 Faulu Kenya Presence

Among other notable *"Faulu Firsts"* have been:
- 2006: Faulu participated in the successful pilot of the now world renowned M-Pesa money transfer service. The pilot ran for over 6 months in Kenya with Faulu as the local microfinance institution testing the micro-payment platform.
- 2009: Faulu was the first microfinance institution to structure and roll out a financial literacy programme, named 'Elewa Pesa' [Understand your money], under the Financial education Fund Challenge [FEF] for its customers and communities. 52,000 end-users were trained in the programme, which innovatively combined classroom training, video and visual aids and group coaching to promote a lifestyle of saving, budgeting, prudent debt management and investment. This added to the portfolio of customer education programmes that Faulu has offered for its customers since inception.
- 2010: Faulu launched the "Faulu Popote" [Faulu Everywhere] mobile platform, the first of its kind in Kenya, where customers

enjoy fully-fledged banking services through their mobile phones regardless of their mobile service provider.
- 2010: Faulu launched a low-cost in-patient and out-patient medical cover for its customers, where premiums are financed from cash, savings or credit facilities.

These initiatives are in line with the institution's goals and objectives that seek to become the financial services provider of choice for the MSME [micro, small, and medium] sector. Faulu seeks to:
- Transform the economically active and their communities through provision of relevant financial services
- Provide profitably quality service to clients through technology and presence
- Reach 10% of the un-banked population in Kenya by increasing outreach to the unbanked
- Become a recognized and compelling financial brand in the region

KAMAU... A LIFE TRANSFORMED

Kamau lived in Mathare, a large slum area in Nairobi, Kenya, where his business was not making enough for him to feed his family...

One day he walked into the Faulu office and talked to a loan officer, who took him through the process of getting a loan to improve his business....Today, Kamau is an employer and a landlord who has several business outlets including a supermarket and a thriving grocery, egg and dairy business.

...Says Kamau, "Faulu trusted me when my business was small. My life has changed"![187]

VISION, MISSION AND CORE VALUES

Since inception, Faulu's has endeavoured to adhere to its calling as an institution founded on a Christian ethos seeking the transformation of society holistically through the provision of financial services. The original institutional vision of Faulu at inception was of "*a nation where all people are able to work toward fulfiling their dreams and potential for the future, and have the dignity of being able to provide for their own needs and the needs of others.*"[188] The board and management realised early in Faulu's history that for transformation to occur, Faulu would need to become "a leading provider of financial services; to further holistic nation building and maximize shareholder value."[189] This was its original mission statement.

Following Faulu's transformation journey, and with the evolvement of the microfinance sector and strategic focus, the institution further refined its vision and mission to communicate clearly its focus. Faulu's current vision, mission and core values reflect a determination to transform Kenyans.

VISION: "GIVING KENYANS HOPE AND A FUTURE"[190]

Derived from Scripture, the Faulu Vision has been elaborated to guide Faulu staff in living out the vision:
- GIVING: Proactively seeking to enrich others through service
- KENYANS: Belief in our people's potential, home-grown indigenous solutions for Kenyans by Kenyans
- HOPE: Motivation for optimism
- A FUTURE: Facilitate the fulfilment of Kenyans' aspirations and dreams

MISSION: "TO LISTEN AND EMPOWER KENYANS BY PROVIDING RELEVANT FINANCIAL SOLUTIONS"

- TO LISTEN: Actively engaging others with a view to know them better, hence meet their needs
- TO EMPOWER: Going beyond financial services by equipping with knowledge, skills and reaching out through the vision of community
- KENYANS: Belief in our people's potential, citizens and residents, home-grown indigenous solutions for Kenyans, by Kenyans
- RELEVANT FINANCIAL SOLUTIONS: Financial products and services that respond to customer needs

The Faulu workforce is guided by its core values, which every staff member is expected to understand and embrace to ensure that high standards are upheld.

Core Values: The Lordship of Jesus Christ, Listening, Learning, Excellence and Integrity.

As with the vision and mission, Faulu values are well elaborated to ensure that there is a focus and standardization in how they are lived out.

THE LORDSHIP OF JESUS

The institution has maintained its commitment to a Christian ethos, with the first value being the "Lordship of Jesus Christ."

This value is exemplified by hard work, love, compassion and commitment in the transformation of lives by being plugged in to God Himself.

Jesus said to them, "My Father is always at his work to this very day, and I too, am working."[191]

Entrenchment of a performance-based work culture has honed staff consciousness that results will be demanded especially from those whose standard is commitment to Christian values, as articulated in the Bible. Every year, performance targets are set out at every level of staff, and aligned to the corporate goals, with quarterly measurement systems in place to ensure that staff *'walk the talk'* and transform lives through the provision of financial services.

This value is also lived out in corporate sponsorship of Christian activities like the annual prayer day and structured devotions for staff, where emphasis is provided for all Faulu staff to submit to the Lordship of Jesus Christ through their personal devotion, their relationship with each other and in the provision of a professional service to all stakeholders.

Faulu's growth and success since inception from an informal to a formally regulated corporate business while maintaining this value has in many ways endorsed and validated that Christian approaches to providing financial services do work, and leads to the provision of microfinance with a difference.

LISTENING

There are 3 ways that Faulu will listen, or "pay attention to" in line with the direction in the Bible, *"Therefore consider carefully how you listen."*[192]

- To God – "Now, my son, listen carefully and do what I tell you"[193]
- To each other – "Listen to advice and accept instruction, and in the end you will be wise"[194]
- To our clientele – We will be sensitive to our clients and communities' needs, and respond with appropriate financial solutions

LEARNING

Learning means 'To gain knowledge or skill, to gradually change your attitude through acquiring of information and knowledge. `
- The fear of the Lord is the beginning of knowledge[195]
- Apply your heart to instruction and your ears to words of knowledge[196]

Faulu realizes that to remain competitive we will need to remain a <u>learning institution</u>, open to ideas and implementing creative and innovative plans.

EXCELLENCE

Faulu embraces this value that may be described as the *"quality of being extremely good, pleasing and outstanding.* Transformational initiatives embrace a 360 degrees approach to ensure a positive and outstanding impact that result in efficiencies and improved quality of life for all. By embracing the use of technology amongst other innovative initiatives, the organization has been able to provide banking services with ease, and the introduction of the mobile banking platform, 'Faulu popote' [Faulu everywhere] has been a foundation for reaching out to more customers with ease, through the mobile phone.

Excellence is an attitude that is manifested through behaviour, and Faulu is committed to strive for quality and endeavour to get better with time, in line with the spirit of excellence. It has resulted in various awards, from various partners, such as:

1. Best Insured Microfinance Institution in successive years, from 2003 to 2010[197]
2. Distinguished Tax Payer award from Kenya Revenue Authority – first runner-up 2008
3. Outstanding support in financing education through diligent remitting of statutory loan payments for loans taken by staff to the Higher Education Loans Board [HELB]

This is in addition to supporting various causes through its corporate social responsibility initiative, Vision of Community [VOC].

Excellence in service has seen Faulu take its place as one of the respected providers of financial services in Kenya: "Do you see a man skilled in his work? He will serve before kings, and not obscure men":[198]

INTEGRITY
"Complete honesty!" Walking the talk as guided by the Bible:

> *"Whatever is.... true, noble, right, pure, lovely, admirable, if anything is excellent and praiseworthy, think about such things."*[199]

Faulu's vision, mission and core values are articulated in a series of values documentation,[200] designed to introduce staff to the institution's core beliefs as part of a well-designed leadership development strategy that prepares staff to impact society through a professionally delivered service.

ORGANIZATIONAL STRUCTURE
An organization is only as excellent as its leadership. Faulu has over the years sought to ensure a seamless achievement of its mandate by harnessing staff abilities and focusing the organization through the practice of good governance and effective organization. Throughout, the board of directors has been composed of a balanced mix of proficient God-fearing individuals, who are guided in their work by a board charter. The board has 7 professionals who provide capability from their experience, drawn mainly from the business, finance, human resource, and development professions.[201]

Led by the chairman, the board gives broad direction and leadership to the company and plays a key role in funding, corporate governance and compliance. It meets 4 times a year and whenever necessary to ensure that Faulu Kenya management receives adequate guidance and direction. Board decisions are guided by the values of the organization, with percentages provided in the board charter on voting and attendance at meetings.

Various board sub-committees ensure that every board member is able to utilize his competence in guiding decision making in critical areas. In keeping with regulator guidelines, Faulu has embedded the executive risk management, credit, and human resource committees within the board structure, to ensure effective practice of corporate governance.

The management team is made up of key managers, who have broad experience in the financial, microfinance and other sectors, and have steered the institution into its current market position by passionately believing in Faulu's transformation mandate and value system:

1. **Managing Director:** A member of the board whose main responsibility is to implement the strategic plans and policies as established by the board and link the board and the management to provide leadership and direction to the business. The managing director also provides liaison with external stakeholders.
2. **Head of Internal Audit and Risk:** oversees compliance to governance structures, both external relating to the regulator, and internal with regard to operational policies and procedure. Functionally, the role reports to the board and administratively to the managing director, and has a key role in policy development, review and adherence.
3. **Head of Legal and Human Resource:** This main role is to resource, develop, reward, motivate and manage the employment relationship in addition to offering legal and statutory advice to the management and the board. The role also designs sound staff management and development systems and procedures that ensure that Faulu Kenya attracts and retains skilled and highly motivated personnel capable of delivering the organization's strategic objectives. The position is responsible for staff development initiatives, and is the custodian of Faulu's core values of transformation and implementation of best human resource practice.
4. **Head of Risk:** This role ensures compliance with prudent lending standards while working constructively with other departments to grow the business and managing portfolio quality and portfolio performance against defined limits. It contributes to the overall risk management strategy of maintaining/ reducing the level of risk as business expands.
5. **Head of Business Development:** The role is expected to drive business growth by increasing the customer base, loan book, and portfolio quality and products usage.
6. **Head of Retail Banking:** The role is in charge of branch network, encompassing the administration and management of branches to ensure efficient service delivery and customer satisfaction.
7. **Head of Finance:** ensures the accountable use of resources and works closely with management, the board, and other external stakeholders, to monitor the day-to-day cash flow management

and sourcing of financial resources, as it supports the business growth and management decision-making process by providing timely and accurate financial information.

8. **Head of Commercial Services:** Reporting to the Managing Director, the role manages the ICT resources and processes and ensures continuous support to the business. It is also charged with the responsibility of supplying the business with the requisite equipment, materials and premises both timely and cost effectively.
9. **Head of Operations:** provides leadership in banking operations by ensuring development and establishment of systems and procedures that comply with internal policy, CBK regulations and International Financial Services Regulations.
10. **Head of Marketing and Research:** This role oversees the implementation of the marketing strategy in line with the overall corporate strategic direction to ensure value delivery to Faulu clients and to develop a positive corporate image that results in business growth through implementation of the agreed action plans. It also comprises a research unit that utilizes both quantitative and qualitative research to ensure that decision-making is fully informed.

These key managers lead teams comprising of section heads, branch managers, and officers who work in various roles, i.e. field officers, tellers, customer service and operations. The role of front line supervisors and staff is to interact with customers and the external public and spread the word about Faulu and its product offering, to ensure excellence in customer care and provide financial services, whilst remembering that Faulu is called to give hope and provide for a future.

The management structure has a minimal hierarchy, with the business council and leadership team taking a responsive role in policy-making and implementation, with the employment of a culture of teamwork ensuring the participation of all levels of staff. There are deliberate initiatives to optimize the contact time between management and staff, through annual prayer and team building events, quarterly management field visits and staff participation in building Faulu's business plans every year.

All members of staff are expected to take responsibility for their assigned work, and ensure that the company meets its promise to Kenyans. This balanced scorecard is the performance tool that is utilised to align all departments and staff with the corporate business plans, resulting in synchronized delivery of service to the customer. This alignment and expectation of performance is appreciated by staff members, who have found individual fulfilment in working for an organization that demands accountability. *"I want to work with this organization that fears God, and brings economical social and spiritual transformation...I believe I have the skills and competence and will use my God given talent to make a difference"* [202] (Staff, 2010).

Methodology

Types of clients served and products offered

Faulu has adapted a holistic approach to the development of financial products and accompanying services by adhering to its slogan *'your bridge to success.'* The institution seeks in its product portfolio and methodology to promote success in life through life's seasons, and has credit and saving products that enable customers meet their basic, social, security, health and other needs, in line with the hierarchy of human needs.

Over the years, Faulu has experienced growth in their clients and portfolio because of offering relevant, client-driven loan and savings products that seek to transform the lives of clients and their communities.

Loan services

Loans are accessed through:
1. The group methodology, where self-selecting groups commit to co-guarantee each other's loans.
- The average size of groups ranges from 15 to 50 members, who are trained to govern their group operations in a transparent manner. A Faulu group, named 'Kikundi', Swahili for 'group' has a team of officials, chairman, secretary and treasurer, who are elected annually.
- Groups meet regularly depending on their maturity and need and are charged with screening each member's loan applications to ensure that the amount provided complies with the credit policies.
- Loan access and repayment has been eased through the use of technology, which ensures receipt of loan monies within 12 hours of approval, through individual customer accounts. In addition,

repayment is eased by the options available for repayment including cash collection at group level, use of banking branches or use of mobile phone technology for money payments.
2. Individual borrowing to cater for individuals who are able to offer formal collateral and for group members who have good credit rating who 'graduate' to individual status.

Loan facilities in Faulu have been tailored to include:

- **Business loans:** This is Faulu's flagship product and the envy of the microfinance sector. That has been tailored to meet the needs of the Kenyan business person (i.e. micro, small and medium) at all points of their growth continuum. Having been refined over time, it exudes relevance and suits particularly the Kenyan micro and small enterprise market.
- **Salaried employees' loans:** This is an unsecured facility extended to salaried employees allowing them the choice to achieve desired goals by financing the purchase of assets, business capital or even meeting emergency needs.
- **Consumer loans:** This is a multi-purpose loan designed in response to client needs that were particularly expressed through a diversion of business funds. It allows clients the benefit of home and lifestyle enhancement e.g. through purchase of domestic assets, such as solar energy solutions, generators, and farm machinery. Consumer loans are also acquired for the purpose of funding education through the payment of school fees.
- **E-cash advance facility-'Pesa Chap Chap':** This is available to all our group clients enabling them to meet unexpected cash demands. Application, disbursement and repayment are eased through the use of the mobile phone application.
- **Market traders loan – 'Soko Cash':** the Swahili word for *'market money,'* this is a short-term loan facility extended to small and micro traders in various market centres country-wide who need a reliable source that is easily accessible to provide daily working capital in order to take advantage of opportunities that arise in their operations.

Savings Services

In addition to the loan facilities on offer, Faulu recognizes the need to embed a culture of saving amongst the Kenyan population. The institution has a variety of savings products that appeal to customers from all walks of life, ranging from the transactional savings account to **Hazina [Swahili word for 'savings'] Account**, which offers one a great opportunity to save in small amounts for a rainy day and enables an individual to meet his/her day to day financial obligations such as food expenses, rent, medical bills, emergencies and any other bills in a stress free manner. It is affordable and convenient to operate. This account has a variant, named **Lengo**, meaning 'goal' that was guided by research that allowed guided withdrawal structuring, offering the Faulu clients a pure savings solution, with restricted withdrawals, enabling them to cultivate a savings discipline and accumulate their savings in order to achieve their life's aspirations.

Faulu savings products are also structured to provide a contractual savings product, designed to blend into ones desired short term, medium term and long term goals. This offers flexible self-determined options at all levels of income with particular sensitivity to the low-income client. For those wishing to invest in competitive returns, the **Faulu Faida Fixed Deposit Account** is a highly ranked savings solution with an opportunity to give back high interest earnings, per annum.

Experienced and amiable staff members are on hand to assist in customers in accessing the right service that will be their bridge to success, translating their dreams (big or small) into reality.

The interest rates charged for loans are market led and competitive, ranging from between 16% per annum to 22% per annum, to ensure organizational sustainability and alignment to the market. Interest provided for customer savings have an attractive range from 2% to 13%, depending on the type of savings accessed, to ensure that customers receive a justifiable return on their savings. Faulu's robust research initiatives ensure that interest rates are responsive to specific customer niches and dependant on specific credit and saving products.

Insurance services

Faulu has a double bottom-line approach to its service provision, desiring that the communities among which it works are transformed holistically, as directed: *"Dear friend, I pray that you may enjoy good health and that all may go well with you, even as your soul is getting along well."* [203]

Faulu's health insurance solution, 'Faulu Afya' – was developed as an innovative micro-insurance solution to unlock health care for the masses. "The program...offers elaborate medical cover for Faulu clients and their families at the lowest premiums in the Kenyan market, $82 per year."[204] The health cover offers in-patient, life and an unprecedented unlimited out-patient benefit to Faulu clients, and is predictably causing waves in the Kenyan financial sector and of course in the country's insurance industry because it is designed to cushion poor households against financial emergencies during illness, surgery and accidents. In 2010 alone, 19,000 lives were covered under the scheme.

Value adding non-financial services

Faulu's value proposition and promise to Kenya is threefold: Loans, Savings and Advice. Education of clients, therefore, forms a major component of Faulu's service, in recognition that to transform a society, there is need to entrench knowledge and learning, to ensure that communities are able to make informed financial decisions.

Research has shown that in Kenya, the extent of financial inclusion approximates 67.3%, meaning that 32.7% of Kenyans are financially excluded and unreached by financial services,[205] (Central Bank of Kenya in partnership with FAP, 2009) largely due to ignorance and inaccessibility to well-articulated information to enable decision-making.

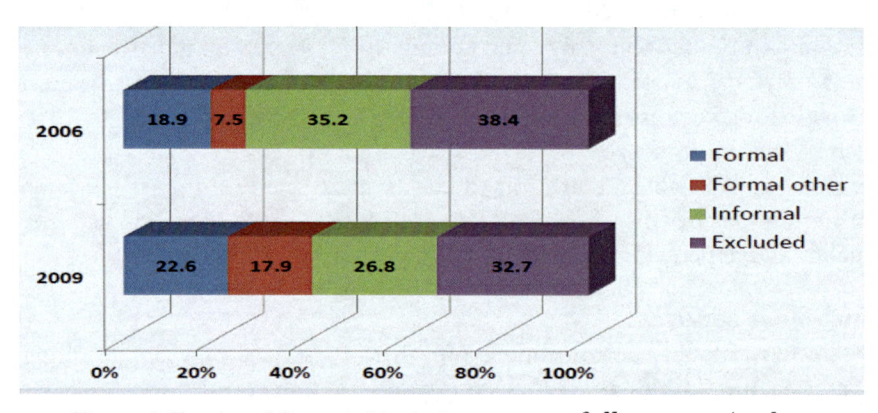

Year	Formal	Formal other	Informal	Excluded
2006	18.9	7.5	35.2	38.4
2009	22.6	17.9	26.8	32.7

Figure 3 Extent of financial inclusion – www.fsdkenya.org/updates

It is also acknowledged that the use of financial services increases with education and it is with this in mind that Faulu has embraced a provision of education in business and entrepreneurship, financial services and personal financial management and life skills for its clientele and communities.

Faulu Kenya has historically provided educational services for its clientele, aimed at improving their quality of life and ensuring that they make prudent financial decisions. The core client education programme revolves around providing entrepreneurship and business education and financial literacy, under the brand name, *'Masomo'*, Swahili for *'education'*.

Every Faulu customer who wishes to access a loan is entitled to a loan orientation seminar, where sessions are provided on business planning, marketing, record and book-keeping and on loan policies and procedures, to guide the customer on prudent debt management and business enterprise.

Faulu customers also have access to financial management sessions of saving, budgeting and investment and to date, 40,000 customers and 12,000 members of the public have benefited under an intensive financial literacy programme named 'Elewa pesa', meaning 'understand money', which was co-funded by Financial Sector Deepening [FSD] Kenya and the financial education fund to further financial education.

Training sessions are facilitated by well-prepared trainers versed in adult training methodology, and the use of various adult friendly training aids, i.e. visual aids [comic strips and videos], and group discussions and coaching sessions that promote the change of attitudes and behaviour towards money management.

A recent evaluation of the financial literacy programme to measure its impact was concluded in 2011 (Faulu Kenya, financial literacy project evaluation report 2011), where the use of a longitudinal study approach with comparison and treatment branches for clients and a cross-sectional approach for the general public component, including a qualitative survey that included focus group discussions, showed that the education programme that was rolled out from 2009-2011 increased awareness of customers of financial issues through the provision of skills and knowledge.

For example, the proportion of those who were surveyed at baseline and end-line showed an increase of those who use a household budget from a composite index of 15% to 31%, meaning that training contributed to the change of behaviour regarding the use of a budget plan.

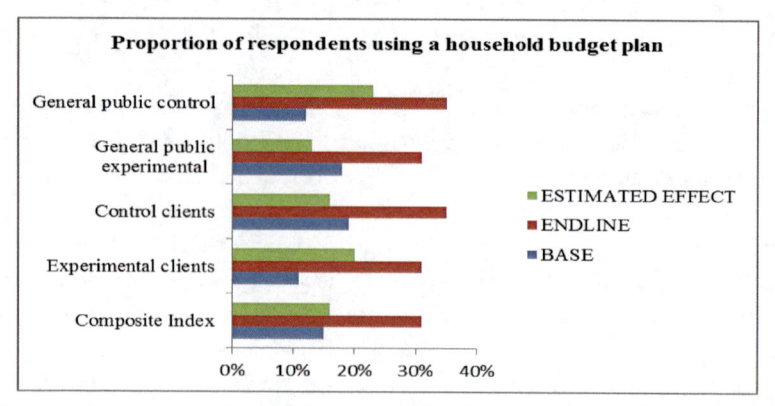

Figure 4 Proportion of respondents using budget during evaluation of Faulu Kenya's financial literacy programme – 2011

A customer who attended the training commented, "I was invited to attend training. Afterwards, I sat my family down and we did a budget. They were so happy and said that we must continue to follow it." – Charles K.[206]

In addition, training customers on savings showed that even 12 months after the end of training, customers surveyed could still mention the four main things that must be in a savings plan, which was impressive as it indicated a growth in the knowledge level with regard to savings.

Another comment from a customer going through the sessions on saving as a lifestyle: "I discovered that my 'drinking' was wastage and confessed that I needed my family's help to reduce the money I waste through beer, and begin saving." (Kenya, Case Studies, financial education program, 2011)

Faulu Kenya intends to utilize the lessons learnt from customer education programmes to embed and scale up the provision of training and advisory programmes as part and parcel of its agenda to improve the quality of lives for its customers and other members of the public. This decision is informed by the evaluation report on Faulu's financial literacy report, conducted by Microsave Consulting, a leading research firm, which showed that a consistent and sustained approach at providing customer education will bear results and ensure that Faulu has played its part in providing responsible finance for Kenyans.

Types of clients served

The business model and diverse approach by Faulu ensures that it serves the micro, small, and medium sectors [MSME] and has positioned itself to also serve institutions, both corporate, Church and para-Church, and the government institutions, from its diverse product portfolio.

Faulu serves Kenyans from all walks of life, and has over the years grown its definition of a customer from those having businesses to include all sectors, i.e. those in formal employment, civil servants [government workers], and farmers. The constitution of customers by gender and sector is as reflected below, with a composition that shows a slightly high male to female ratio, mainly because Faulu targets Kenyans without specific gender skewing and, therefore, attracts the main decision-makers in society and families, i.e. men. Once these join Faulu, it then becomes relatively easy to access the female and youth population as well.

Customer ratio by gender

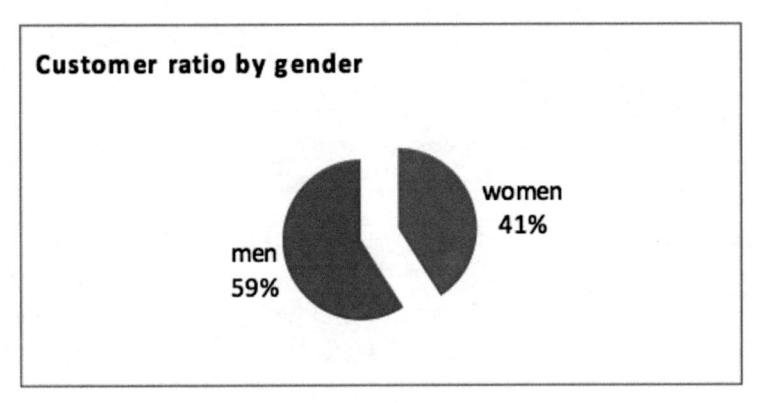

men 59%

women 41%

Figure 5 Customer ratio by gender in 2012

The institution has well defined products for the manufacturing, retail, service and agricultural sectors, and its mandate is to serve those in the micro, small, and medium sectors with tailor-made services. On entry into an area, Faulu develops partnerships with market associations that serve the manufacturing and retail [commercial] sectors and, therefore, attracts a large number of clientele in this area, that have manufacturing enterprises such as metal works, food and clothes works, light industries, amongst others. By targeting these sectors, Faulu supports growth and employment in the micro-sector where a large percentage of Kenyans find their livelihood.

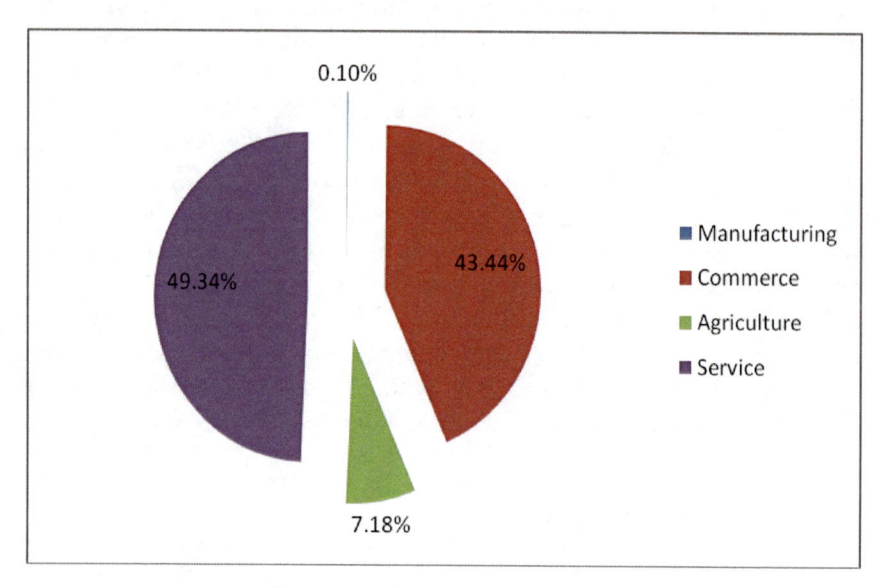

Figure 6 Sectors served by Faulu

- Manufacturing: 0.10%
- Commerce: 43.44%
- Agriculture: 7.18%
- Service: 49.34%

Technology
To achieve the exponential outreach that will result in transformation through Faulu's presence in a community, investment in innovative technology has been core for Faulu, with the following notable achievements:
- 2009: Faulu introduced the first instant e-loan product in the market. This loan is applied through mobile phones and is available to all of Faulu's group-based credit customers. The loan is mainly meant to meet unexpected cash demands and is payable within 10 days.
- 2010: Faulu became the first MFI to offer fully-fledged banking services on mobile phones through its borderless mobile banking

platform (Faulu Popote) that provides easy access and convenience to its customers in a cost efficient manner through a mobile platform.
- 2010: Faulu recently introduced a savings product (Pesa Chap Chap) that was developed to allow for small value deposits at the convenience of micro clients.

Faulu is intent on providing financial services innovatively following its commitment to increase financial access to those who would otherwise find it difficult to access formal banking services. Even with over 100 physical outlets, the institution recognizes those that may be unable to access these, and investment into the robust T 24 banking system ensured that the institution was able to customize and innovate platforms that ensured access to financial services. To date, Faulu continued to do this with the recent introduction of technology that enables customers to commence the process of opening an account through their mobile phones using major local languages. Faulu will continue to utilize technology to drive financial inclusion and key channels are already in place to drive access to financial services through group meetings, formal banking halls, partnerships with other financial providers, and through the use of mobile technology e.g. the famous M-pesa money transfer system that was first piloted by Faulu.

Impact

Faulu as an organization and the staff who serve portray a strong sense of mission in a corporate environment where Faulu is a valued contributor and business leader in microfinance. Some of the Christian distinctives that position Faulu as Christian include a commitment to social, economic, and spiritual transformation of society through participation in the financial sector as Christian microfinance and in community development and the embedding of value-adding social services such as customer education [discussed extensively above], and involvement in community development.

Community Development

Faulu has an active Vision of Community initiative that is geared towards partnering communities to improve their social and spiritual welfare, even as financial services are provided. These tailored corporate social responsibility initiatives are funded from 10% of Faulu's profits, which are invested in sustainable community projects ranging from funding the building of water points, and schools to prison outreach. Notable evidence of Faulu's involvement include national rebuilding and reconciliation efforts: Following the post-election violence that rocked Kenya following 2007, Faulu contributed resources towards the internally displaced persons welfare, and consequently visited camps to motivate and to identify Faulu clients and facilitate their resettlement.

The institution urges all staff to utilize their skills and gifts in reaching out to the communities around them, and has participated in building schools and shelters for children, and in various community training initiatives.

Faulu Kenya was among the key institutions that lobbied aggressively with the government and other stakeholders to ensure that the Microfinance Bill was passed into law in 2006, leading the way for microfinance institutions to continue their efforts of financial inclusion for all by being the first licensed deposit-taking institution.

The institution has, as a result of its services, directly impacted the lives of over 1 million Kenyans through the provision of financial and non-financial services as described in detail in previous sections.

Education

While this has been elaborated in earlier sections, it is important to note as a distinctive that most customers and community members surveyed in areas where Faulu is a key player cite that Faulu is a distinct institution in that it provides training and information on financial services. The recently concluded evaluation of Faulu's financial literacy programme showed that most respondents received their training from Faulu, showing that the institution's programme continues to make an impact in society, especially with the recent training of 52,000 trainees on financial literacy.

This training at end-line was from Faulu (84%) and relatives, friends and family members (4%). Apart from receiving information from Faulu that maintained its high rating, the transfer of information through other MFIs dropped by 16% to a negligible figure. (Kenya, End Of Project Financial Education Evaluation Report, 2011)

Faulu Kenya Deposit Taking Microfinance Institution Case Study

Where did you receive your most recent training/discussion/information?			
Baseline (N=507)		**End line (N=655)**	
Faulu	71%	Faulu	84%
Other MFIs	17%	Relatives or Friends and family members	4%
At school	4%	Newspapers	1%
Radio	3%	Television	1%
Newspapers and magazines	2%	Radio	1%
Friend, family and relatives	2%	Other MFIs	1%
Television	1%	Community opinion Leaders	1%
Community opinion Leaders (Headmen, Chiefs, sub-Chiefs)	1%	Church organised training	1%
		Banks	1%
		Co-operative societies	1%

Figure 7 Training providers:
Where did you receive your most recent training?

CHALLENGES

Faulu has grown progressively and consistently as a financial institution that is passionately driven by the need to see communities that are able to make prudent financial decisions and utilize financial services to improve the quality of their lives. The institution has faced several challenges in ensuring that it continues to serve Kenyans:

1. Stagnated business performance due to the country's economic, social and political challenges The post-election violence following the 2007 general elections and recurring drought have affected provision of financial services, with the institution remaining at the same levels between 2009-2011, with a slight drop in 2010 as it sought to maintain stability even with the effect of the macro factors.

In response to this, the institution supported its customers and communities that were affected by the post-election violence through its vision of a community initiative, and as part of prudent financial management, wrote off its loan portfolio that had been provisioned for in line with its policy. Product innovation enabled a response to the environmental effect, where the agricultural product was re-launched to take into account crop failure and animal deaths through insurance to cushion both the customer and institution.

The lack of a level playing-field governing deposit-taking and banking institutions, caused Faulu as a key player to continuously lobby the regulator on policy issues, resulting in a realignment of regulations to facilitate a friendlier environment with the enactment of the Microfinance Act, and the passage of agency banking regulation which allows the use of partners in the community to provide banking services cost effectively.

2. Poor infrastructure in the areas with the highest target customers, which creates barriers in tapping the unbanked customers. Faulu responded to this challenge through the implementation of a robust Management Information System [MIS] and the setting up of banking facilities to enable the provision of banking services, as part of its transformation agenda. It enabled the innovation of mobile banking solutions to enable access as has been described previously.

3. Internally, Faulu has faced its share of situations that have challenged the institution. The decision to transform into deposit-taking status resulted in staff capacity gaps to handle business in a realigned model, as most staff had a credit only microfinance background and required up scaling of skills to fit in a credit and deposit-taking environment. External and internal capacity building efforts were rolled out to develop a learning curriculum and also engage staff with banking experience to resolve the challenge and trigger internal job learning.

In addition, a vibrant cultural realignment programme was put in place in 2010 to ensure that Faulu maintained its commitment to transformation through the Christian approach, and stayed true to its vision and mission. The programme led to the retraining of all staff on institutional values, to maintain the staff's focus on organizational philosophy even with institutional growth and expansion at all levels of the organization.

CONCLUSION

Faulu Kenya Deposit Taking Microfinance ("Faulu") has been in existence for the last 20 years, with the consistent focus on transformation of the total person through provision of relevant financial solutions. The institution, which began as a pilot project by Food for the Hungry [FH], has evolved over time, and is now one of the leading regulated microfinance institutions in Kenya, with a loan book of $ 54 million and $ 51 million in deposits as at 2012, and a clientele of over 350,000 served by more than 700 staff situated in over 100 outlets, representing a rapid growth from only 10 employees and one branch at its inception in 1991.

The institution is driven by a culture for innovation, and the embracing of new ways of delivering superior service to its clientele, resulting in a history of *"Faulu Firsts,"* such as being the first regulated microfinance institution in Kenya, piloting the world renowned M-pesa money transfer service and launching the first structured financial literacy programme in Kenya.

All the strides Faulu has made are because of a firm foundation in a Christian ethos, with a vision and values that show the place of faith in propelling business success:

"For I know the plans I have for you," declares the Lord, "plans to prosper you and not to harm you, plans to give you hope and a future."[207] The Lordship of Jesus is among its core values, with all staff exemplifying passion, hard work and compassion that the Lord would have shown in transforming communities.

The corporate governance structure is designed to ensure that accountability and prudent management are advocated, with minimal hierarchy and responsiveness ensuring the participation of all levels of staff. A performance management system has been instituted in the last few years, with all staff taking responsibility for their work, ensuring that the company meets its promise to Kenyans. The results have shown that Faulu staff work with dedication and focus, as a result of this work culture, leading to impressive business results and a reputation as an attractor of talented and passionate staff.

A look at Faulu Kenya's products shows a philosophy of developing solutions that are aimed at meeting the basic, social needs of Kenyans, resulting in the provision of core financial products like loans and savings, and value-adding and life-transforming services like health insurance and education, in line with its double bottom-line approach to service provision, desiring that the communities among which it works are transformed holistically, as directed in the Bible: *"Dear friend, I pray that you may enjoy good health and that all may go well with you, even as your soul is getting along well."*[208]

The business model and diverse approach by Faulu ensures that it serves the micro, small, and medium sectors [MSME] and has positioned itself to also serve institutions, both corporate, Church and para-Church, and the government institutions, from its diverse product portfolio. This resolve has resulted in service to Kenyans from all walks of life without discrimination, earning itself the reputation of being the *'bridge to success.'*

Even as Faulu strives to accomplish its mandate, it endeavours to overcome challenges such as a fluctuating business performance due to the country's economic, social and political situation. The institution has always responded appropriately to this challenge by implementing a strategy that is supportive to both its business and the communities it serves, to ensure sustained business stability. It has at several times lobbied the regulator on policy issues that have affected the microfinance industry, resulting in a realignment of regulations to facilitate a friendlier environment with the enactment of the Microfinance Act, and the passage of agency banking regulations which allow the use of partners in the community to provide banking services cost effectively.

The board, management and staff of Faulu foresee a robust future where the institution will continue to spread its influence and entrench itself deeper in the financial services sector.

The focus for Faulu into the future is in line with the parable of the mustard seed, which is the smallest of all seeds, yet when it grows, it is the largest of garden plants and becomes a tree, so that the birds [i.e. communities] come and perch in its branches."[209]

MICROFINANCE CRITICISM AND CHRISTIAN RESPONSE

MAKONEN GETU

Makonen Getu (Ph.D.) is Vice President of International Business Development at Opportunity International. Makonen has also taught at both under- and postgraduate levels in development studies at Stockholm University and the Oxford Centre for Mission Studies, where he currently examines and supervises Ph.D. scholars. Makonen has published several books, pamphlets and articles on topics related to development, foreign aid, microfinance, HIV/AIDS, human trafficking, faith and development.

This chapter is devoted to presenting some of the core criticisms of microfinance and related responses with reference to the programmes and experiences of the five CMFIs covered in this book. In most cases, the responses are made in a more synthesized and generalized form and readers are encouraged to read the five cases as thoroughly as possible for specific evidence.

GENERAL

Until recently, scarcely a voice was raised against microfinance. It was regarded by governments, by academics and, increasingly, by the wider public as an unalloyed public good.[210]

For over three decades of its life in the 20th century, the microfinance industry enjoyed an era of celebration. Donors, governments, NGOs, and the media recognized microfinance as a powerful tool in the fight against poverty and financial exclusion of the poor in the developing world. For most of that time, the industry consisted predominantly of one single product: microcredit. There were little or no substantive criticisms made that would cast doubt about the role of microcredit in alleviating poverty, increasing income, improving the well-being of and empowering the poor. The industry received high accolades in 2006, when the Nobel Peace Prize was awarded to Professor Yunus and Grameen Bank both of whom were at the forefront of the innovations and practices that made the microfinance industry what it is today.

During the last decade, microfinance has been subjected to an increasingly growing series of criticisms.[211] There were three major reasons that lay behind the rising criticism:

(1) The Mexican MFI, Banco Compartomos, went public in 2007 (i.e. listed on the stock exchange), about six months after Yunus' Nobel Prize award, selling 30% of their existing stock, resulting in a total earning of $450 million, making its shareholders as well as board and staff members "microfinance millionaires." The total cost of stakes was $6 million and the entire institution was valued at $1.4 billion. This sent a shock wave throughout the microfinance world and attracted widespread negative reactions.

(2) The collapse of microcredit in Bosnia, Morocco, Nicaragua and Pakistan in 2008-2009 due to fast growth, global recession, debtor revolts and political backlash caused doubts about the effectiveness of microfinance as a poverty alleviation tool. A study conducted by CGAP established three vulnerabilities in the microfinance industry lay behind the crises:

1. Concentrated market competition and multiple borrowing, (ii) overstretched MFI system and controls, (iii) erosion of MFI lending discipline. This was followed by another microfinance crisis in India in 2010 when (i) SKS went public creating a situation in which private investors and staff sharing profits in tens of millions of dollars, including the founder who earned over $80 million; and

2. Many borrowers were reported to have committed suicide as a result of over-indebtedness and an aggressive repayment collection methods applied by MFIs. Consequently, the government of Andhra Pradesh, accused the MFIs there of exploiting clients "through usurious interest rates and coercive means of recovery resulting in their impoverishment and in some cases leading to suicides."[212]

(3) The emergence of several randomized impact studies with findings that showed the absence of evidence to support the foundational claim made about microfinance as a poverty reduction tool. These academic

studies dismissed the long-standing claim by arguing that, on average, microcredit has not reduced poverty.

Special reference is made to the voices of three critics: Bateman (2010), Roodman (2012) and Sinclair (2012). The reason being that these studies: (i) are relatively more comprehensive in coverage than many other critical perspectives, (ii) have drawn more media attention and popularity, (iii) generated more debate, and (iv) caused more stir.

Although they unite in their criticism against the microfinance industry, it is important to mention at least two major differences:

Firstly, Bateman applies a neo-Marxist approach and sees microfinance as a "local-neo-liberalism" and finds faults in the industry accordingly. Roodman and Sinclair apply a liberal approach and find faults in the industry within the bounds of a market economy. Roodman conducts his critical analysis of the role/impact of microfinance using a combination of three approaches: development as escape from poverty, development as freedom a la Amartya Sen and development as industry building a la Joseph Schumpeter. Sinclair does not refer to any specific approach as he bases his criticism on a "detective-like" insider account of motives, standards, practices and operations.

Secondly, Bateman takes an extreme view seeing microfinance as "local neo-liberalism", "harmful" and "a powerful 'poverty trap'" designed by the West to "de-industrialize" developing countries and claims that it "does not work and is also *known* not to be working," is "preordained to do no good for the poor" and is no more than 'lipstick on the pig.'"[213] He claims that microfinance is a "delusion" and throws the baby out with the bathwater. Roodman and Sinclair, on the other hand, try to bring out both the "bad" and "good" sides of the industry in a relatively balanced way by admitting the positive role it has played, is playing and can be playing in the lives of the poor and holds that microfinance works. For Sinclair, "The problem is neither that the entire microfinance sector is evil, nor the basic mode is fatally flawed ... The model does work."[214] Although he does not see microfinance providing an escape from poverty, Roodman argues that microfinance has strength that "lies in *building self-sufficient institutions that can give billions of poor people an increment of control over their lives*, control they will use to put food on the table more regularly, invest in education, and yes, start tiny businesses." And "poor people are diverse, and so are the impacts of microcredit upon them.

Thus, microcredit undoubtedly helps many people."[215] Roodman's study is relatively more comprehensive and his criticism is more objective and constructive. On many occasions he has debated against Bateman and expressed his disagreement to Bateman's approach and conclusions.

The overall message of the criticism is as follows: MFIs have lied to the public so that supporters (individual citizens, donors and investors) can continue pumping in money into the industry and to clients so that they can keep on borrowing. They have told the stories that the public wants to hear, portraying "the half-good" they claim to have achieved in poverty reduction through colourful client success stories. The success story that has been painted by the MFIs is all an "illusion" and an overhyped "myth".[216]

Specifically, the three critics make the following claims:

> Bateman: "... Unfortunately, after thirty or so years of unparalleled easy access to microfinance, its [Jobra, the village where Yunus started lending] hapless inhabitants still remain trapped in extreme poverty and deprivation."[217]
>
> Roodman: "... The evidence of the direct impact [of microfinance] on poverty is spotty and muted."[218]
>
> Sinclair: "Maybe, just maybe, the reason for the scarcity of any evidence supporting the claims of poverty alleviation made by the MFI industry was simply that there was none."[219]

The critics do not only argue that there is no proof that microfinance has not had any impact on poverty reduction, in terms of *average benefits*. They go further and state that microfinance cannot play the role it has been given by donors and MFIs as a poverty reduction tool:

> In truth, microfinance represents an anti-development policy – a development policy that largely works against the establishment of sustainable economic and social development trajectories and so also against sustainable poverty reduction.[220]
>
> Microenterprise helps people survive poverty more than escape it. Next to the poverty-reducing power of industrialization, microfinance is a palliative.[221]
>
> It [microfinance] is not the miracle cure that its publicists would have you believe.[222]

Overall, unlike the last three decades of the 20th century, the first decade of the 21st century marked a phase in which microfinance was confronted by these and other critics. However, the industry has not been weakened nor deterred, and in fact has probably benefited from such strong challenges. For example, new campaigns related to client protection, financial inclusion, microfinance transparency and social performance management have been undertaken by MFIs to jointly strengthen and maintain the reputation and impact of the industry.[223] Although this is not the place for going into polemics and providing a detailed response to the critical message voiced by the writers, it might be worthwhile to point out some of the main defensive arguments:

First, the criticism is based on the claim that MFIs and their leaders hold microfinance as "a miracle cure" or as "a panacea" to poverty. The critics make references to what some MFIs write on their websites and marketing literature and Yunus' talk about the poverty museum. Yes, MFIs have promoted and do promote microfinance as a poverty solution tool and Yunus dreams of a time when people will be freed from the grinding grip of poverty. All MFIs are designing and implementing microfinance interventions to alleviate poverty, not to keep it. None, however, claims that microfinance alone will solve poverty. MFIs treat microfinance as one of many intertwined social, economic, political, and cultural interventions and never as the only one. Nor do they claim every individual that participates in microfinance programmes will become a successful entrepreneur. And less so among CMFIs which attach a significant role to spiritual and related behavioural transformation in poverty reduction. Who in this day and age, let alone veteran development and anti-poverty activists like Yunus, would think that poverty would be solved or banished to the museum only through one intervention: microfinance? Talking about the role of microfinance in reducing poverty is not the same as claiming that it is "a miracle cure". In 2009, just before the scandal broke in Andhra Pradesh, a book entitled, *The Poor Will Be Glad* co-authored by two Christian microfinance practitioners, Peter Greer and Phil Smith, was published. In the chapter, *"It Can't Be That Good, Can It?"* Peter Greer (the co-author of the chapter on Hope in this book) discussed the limitations of microfinance, pointing out that microfinance was "an *opportunity*, not a total *solution*" and argued that lasting change and development would require structural changes.[224]

Yet, one of the claims the critics apply is that MFIs falsely spread the view that microfinance ends poverty: they tell the public that, "microfinance is not a miracle cure as MFIs would have you believe."[225] This is simply an unfounded claim. Moreover, the ultimate performance and overall impact of microfinance is determined by the international and local socio-economic contexts in which it is implemented.

Second, the criticism rejects the impact of microfinance on the grounds that there are no rigorous impact studies showing *average benefits (gains)* and the few independent Randomized Control Trials (RCTs) to measure the poverty impact reveal no positive impact. Unlike Roodman, who takes a cautious position, Bateman and Sinclair consider RCTs as the litmus test judging the impact of microfinance. Sinclair, for example, asserts, "rigorous research by independent, qualified academics and practitioners on the actual impact of microfinance on the poor is the only way we will gather the data to understand what is actually happening and how we can improve."[226] Bateman, for example, dismisses all hitherto impact studies, including academic ones, as "flawed", "incomplete" and "fads" deliberately designed by donors and high profile MFIs "to secure a broadly favorable impact assessment."[227] One cannot be more arrogant and pretentious than this. And I ask with Stuart, "Are all the people, who generate evidence about what works and what does not work without using RCTs, not doing rigorous work? Are RCTs the only way to get to the truth of the matter?" And I answer no, they are not. The irony of this claim is that Bateman and Sinclair do not provide any solid evidence of *average losses (harms)* which microfinance is claimed to have caused among the poor. And "absent strong evidence of harm, it would be the height of arrogance to dispute their [150 million microcredit clients] judgment."[228] Moreover, an average increase in gain or loss does not necessarily mean it works or does not work for everybody, just as an average increase/decrease in per capita income does not.

Third, the criticism undermines the role of successful client stories presented on the websites and literature of MFIs and dismisses them as marketing tools, colourfully created to gain support among the public, donors and funders. In other words, the criticism looks down at the voices and thoughts of clients and qualitative indicators in favour of "academic or expert" voices and quantitative indicators. They brush aside that "what is real is what the people say." Yet, the critics make use of a great deal of anecdotes related to stories of clients, individual MFIs, investment funds and countries in advancing their respective criticisms.

Fourth, the criticism is mainly focused on the credit component and not the full suite of services offered, including savings, money transfers, insurance and non-financial services. Most of the "harm" claimed by the critics is related to the credit (loans) services. It is very difficult to attach any claim of "harm" to the other components.

Fifth, the criticism claims that the microfinance industry has promoted itself by telling and over-hyping the "half good" or the "half success" story. Yet, the criticism does exactly the same thing albeit taking the opposite side. It tells the "half bad" or the "half failure" story in an over-hyped manner.

SPECIFICS

The section below makes reference to some of the specific criticisms made by Roodman, Bateman and Sinclair and the responses derived from the work of the five CMFIs presented in this book.

Interest rate and fees

Lending money costs money. When MFIs deliver financial services to their clients, they incur operational costs in addition to the investment they make in innovations. The interest rates and fees are meant to contribute towards covering these expenses. The rate of interest charged by the microfinance industry has generally been recognized as higher than commercial rates but lower than the rates charged by local moneylenders or loan sharks. While it has been easy to understand the latter, the former scenario has been relatively less understood and less accepted.

The comparison of rates charged by commercial banks and MFIs is "artificial" and unjustified as the two serve clients of different socio-economic scales and use a different operating model. The former serve high-income clients, large loan sizes, less risky loans involving little or no training and monitoring activities and incurring lower operational costs. On the other hand, MFIs serve poor clients through small, risky loans that involve intensive training and monitoring activities. They not only provide loans to groups, but also to individuals in rural and scattered areas, resulting in higher operational costs. In view of this, the comparison should be made between those (MFIs and local moneylenders) that lend to poor clients and not between MFIs and commercial banks that serve different constituencies – poor and rich clients respectively.

Although the high, and some would say exploitative, interest rates charged by some MFIs, like Compartamos and SKS, have hit the media and given rise to the belief that the entire industry does the same. But that is not the case. Roodman, one of the main critics of the industry, finds that most rates do not seem to be exploitative. "Worldwide, 63% of MFIs, accounting for 83% of the loans, charge less than 30 percent over inflation."[229] In the case of the five CMFIs covered in this book, the average rate for group loans stands around 29%.

Generally, interest rates and fees charged by MFIs are determined by contexts and relative costs of capital and service delivery (staff salaries and benefits, equipment, systems, training, travel, etc.) as well as inflation, loan sizes and products. For example, the cost of delivery for MFIs that apply a minimalist approach is likely to be lower than those that apply a holistic approach. Loans with larger sizes and longer terms are charged lower interest rates than those with smaller amounts and shorter terms. The reason is that the former cost less to deliver than the latter. For CMFIs that invest in non-financial services focused on facilitating whole-person development, delivery costs are bound to be higher than those that follow "minimalist" approaches. Newer, smaller and technologically less equipped MFIs dealing with smaller scale outreach are also more likely to incur higher delivery costs than more mature, larger and technologically better equipped ones due to the economy of scale. Moreover, deposit-taking CMFIs, including banks like Opportunity International and Faulu Kenya, incur heavy costs, in terms of developing infrastructure, human resources capacity, back office systems and security, in order to meet regulatory standards and provide quality services. In this regard, interest rates might be higher than those charged by commercial banks, but much lower than the exorbitant rates charged by the local moneylenders who do not offer any other service and incur little or no operational expenses.

CMFIs exist to fight exploitative moneylenders and do not wish to become loan sharks themselves. Their purpose is not to greedily make as much profit as they can at the cost of the poor, but to help the poor make a profit and prosper. They charge interest and fees to cover their costs and stay financially solvent, so that they can keep on serving the poor on a sustainable basis and not to accumulate profits and enrich themselves. In addition to being guided by contexts and market trends, CMFIs determine the interest rates and fees they charge in accordance with Christian principles. Opportunity and World Relief individually studied the Biblical perspective of interest, in order to establish whether or not charging interest was Christian and to seek guidance.[230] The principle they learnt was: charge interest on loans, but do not practice usury by charging an interest rate that is excessive and oppressive and is likely to harm the borrower.[231]

CMFIs recognize that interest expenses are a cost to clients and reduce the income that accrues to them. Therefore, they neither have the intention nor the ethical mandate to ruthlessly charge as high an interest rate as possible in the pursuit of profits. On the contrary, their intention and ethical mandate is to keep interest rates as low as possible and continually seek to lower them. Opportunity International strives to use a range of tools, including appropriate MIS technology, hub and spoke model (mobile banking, cell-phone banking, branches, satellites, point of sale devices) and partnerships with other players. This approach enables Opportunity to improve its accounting, data collection, decision-making process and delivery (implementation) and thereby increase its performance and efficiency.[232] Although investing in technology and infrastructure is expensive and costly in the short term, this mode of operation enables Opportunity to reduce its delivery costs, resulting in the reduction of the interest rates and fees paid by clients in the long run. Technology investment is, therefore, an investment in cost reduction.

Roodman points to another aspect: transparency. While acknowledging that the quotation of "flat" rates which allow people to calculate their weekly installment payments as fixed percentages of their opening loan amount, he holds that "complex fee structures still hide the full cost, and APRs are not typically quoted" and that this is "low-hanging fruit if a goal of microcredit is empowerment."[233]

In an attempt to reduce the interest rates and fees they charge, CMFIs are (i) continuously increasing their efficiency through improved technology as delineated above with reference to Opportunity, (ii) shifting from "flat" rates to declining rates, especially for longer term loans and (iii) actively participating in implementing the principles advanced by the Smart Campaign and Microfinance Transparency to protect clients. These are two complementary efforts aimed at ensuring that clients' overall well-being is preserved with the latter focusing on responsibly and transparently priced products by MFIs.[234]

According to Roodman, some of the practices that need to be avoided include: (i) requiring borrowers to deposit a percentage of their loan amount in a savings account that pays an interest rate lower than on the loan; (ii) over-charging for life insurance bundled with the loan; (iii) imposing fees or other requirements that effectively raise interest rates without seeming to; (iv) explaining contracts in ways that are incomplete, confusing and misleading; (v) unwritten loan rules; (vi) loan rules written in languages foreign to clients.

All the CMFIs, in the case studies, accept and are addressing these points. Opportunity has made significant strides by investing in technology, conducting financial training and producing training materials including videos in local languages, explaining contracts during training and loan appraisals and writing contracts in languages that people understand.[235] The five CMFIs in this book have all endorsed the Smart Campaign and MF Transparency, and make a great effort to build financial literacy and explain obligations to clients in order to avoid inappropriate or unscrupulous lending which would be counter-productive to their clients and business model.

Moreover, CMFIs are increasingly moving into focusing on savings, money transfers and insurance products in addition to credit. Opportunity International has helped over one million rural and urban poor in several Sub-Sahara African countries to open savings accounts with as little as $5, whilst most commercial banks require $100 as a minimum opening balance. This is far beyond the reach of poor clients. In Malawi and Ghana, for example, the ratio of Opportunity savers to borrowers is 3:1.[236] The clients do not only keep their monies safe but also earn interest and can use their savings during times of crisis and to smooth out their irregular income flow. Insurance services help clients to protect their businesses and families during calamities, while money transfer services help facilitate safe and convenient transfers and transactions.

Flexibility

The standards and practices of microfinance have been established by MFIs and clients have been receiving services following their willingness to abide by those rules. For a long time, MFIs have "religiously" followed their set terms and systems for making loans to and collecting repayments from clients. The practice worked well for both parties. In his study, Roodman found that "Microfinance offers more reliability to clients and usually demands more of it from them. By nature, it is reliable and inflexible."[237] In fact, Roodman finds that although MFIs charge lower interest rates than local moneylenders, the latter show more flexibility and empathy in times of calamities and difficulties that are appreciated by clients. Banerjee and Duflo too hold that moneylenders "allow their borrowers to choose how they borrow and the way they repay – some repay one a week, but others repay whenever they have money in hand." In other words, while MFIs "rigidly" expect clients to repay their loans as per the agreed contract regardless of their circumstances, local moneylenders allow their borrowers to skip paying when they find themselves in financial distresses caused by funeral and wedding expenses or other forms of emergencies. These are some of the reasons why moneylenders still operate side by side with MFIs to this day, contrary to the belief that they would be out of business due to microfinance services that offer cheaper loans.[238]

The "rigidity" or "inflexibility" criticism made by the microfinance critics is a thing of the past. CMFIs have been and are increasingly becoming more client-friendly and are performing better by striving to practice a system that is client-driven and sensitive to client voices. Opportunity conducts regular client surveys to assess client satisfaction and establish their perspectives on products and terms. Hope audited its community bank meetings and restructured its meetings, clarifying processes, retraining staff, and creating a system that would better benefit clients by providing value-added services.

Although weekly meetings and loan repayments are still practised among group clients, CMFIs have begun to allow bi-weekly and monthly meetings and repayments. In certain instances, even loan terms are decided in consultation with clients. In other cases, clients who find working in groups inhibitive to the growth of their business because of the small loan sizes are allowed to access individual loans. CMFIs also cancel debts in some critically stressful cases and pray with and for clients who are in distress. The Christian priority to put the clients' needs first and foremost translates into practices that are client-centric. CMFIs seek to protect and enhance the living standards of the client, often ahead of the financial imperative to repay and meet targets.

Client empowerment

The critics find several cases in which clients have been mistreated and experienced a sense of disempowerment, contrary to the claim made by the industry. In his examination of the impact of microfinance on clients' agency, Roodman finds that it both increases and reduces freedom, and that "credit is both a source of possibilities and a bond."[239] He also asserts that the "peer pressure implicit in group credit appears more oppressive than liberating"[240] and "individual credit is more apt to enhance agency than group credit."[241] Bateman goes on to say that (i) it is "quite wrong to suggest that microfinance is associated with either genuine *intention* to empower the poor or any meaningful *outcome* having been achieved in this direction"[242] and (ii) "... self-employment and microenterprises have most often been promoted as part of the programmed disempowerment of the poor."[243] Sinclair, in his turn, says "... in the sector's quest for relentless growth we have lost sight of the human element at stake: the poor are people. They may deserve access to credit, but they certainly deserve respect and fair treatment."[244]

The argument is based on two major references: the basic nature of microfinance, particularly the credit component, and the treatment of clients, particularly women, by MFIs. It is hard to believe that microfinance is by nature a disempowering intervention. Theoretically speaking, microfinance, including its credit component, is inherently empowering and gives people choices and opportunities.

Firstly, microfinance fulfils what some say are basic human rights, related to access to financial services, just as the right to having water, education and health services. The lack of such services disenfranchises the poor while their availability empowers them. Microfinance recognizes and embraces those marginalized and excluded by the mainstream financial sector as deserving and capable citizens. That, in itself, is empowerment.

Secondly, microfinance brings with it the "hand-up" culture breaking away from the "hand-out" culture of many development aid interventions that has stigmatized and continues to stigmatize people living in poverty as "pitiful" and "hopeless" by society. As a means of development, charity is "toxic" as it patronizes, disempowers and breeds dependency, while a loan aimed at unleashing potential has a more dignifying element to it.[245]

Thirdly, microfinance is based on trust and recognition of the ability and creditworthiness of the people living in poverty. The mainstream financial system kept people living in poverty at the periphery and treated them as unable, untrustworthy and "unbankable". Microfinance has demolished that derogatory and disempowering perception and practice and embraced people living in poverty as capable and trustworthy. This is empowerment, not disempowerment.

Fourthly, when the poor develop a business plan and a loan application and sign a contract with MFIs, the lenders, there is a sense of being treated as a business partner and not a charity recipient. This is another form of empowerment that gets stronger when the loans are paid back with interest. Credit neither disempowers the people living in poverty, nor is it programmed to do so.

The practical side could result in different scenarios. Depending on how it is translated in practice, microfinance could, as Roodman points out, expand or contract people's freedom. In this regard, the problem seems to revolve around the nature of group lending and the power exercised by some loan officers, some leaders of joint liability groups and some husbands, in the case of women.[246]

In some cases, loan officers tend to resort to their power as representatives of money and can manipulate and or even bully clients struggling with repayment problems. They can apply negative methods including threats and/or blackmail and come with their own rules, often contrary to the MFIs', in order to get people to repay their loans on time. They might hound and harass those who fail to repay. Very often, they tend to resort to such methods, in order to achieve their targets that would secure maximum bonuses.

This type of behaviour among loan officers is more prevalent in circumstances where MFIs set goals for each loan officer and correlate bonuses and performance reviews according to the rate of achievement. Underperformance makes the loan officers concerned vulnerable to missing their targets and consequently being sacked or losing bonuses.

In the same vein, dominant group leaders can mishandle members with repayment problems. They may also resort to coercing others, often those who are relatively "better off", to cover for peer repayments or take their cows or chickens, in order to pay off their debts.[247] Such practices cause unintended conflicts and disharmony within communities. In situations where women experience business failures or increased debts, they tend to face domestic violence and humiliation by their husbands.

CMFIs attempt to mitigate these problems by ensuring that:
- Groups are always formed through a self-selection process in which clients select members, often neighbours they know, and are given training to make them aware of such occurrences and how to address them;
- Groups (large and small alike) work and take whatever is required to revitalize and make them strong centres of learning and empowerment, and not only transaction meetings. CMFIs recognize that the more boring and less beneficial the group meetings are seen by clients, the less attended and effective they become as tired clients begin to absent themselves and send their repayments through dependents or colleagues. Efforts are made, therefore, to use some of the weekly, bi-weekly or monthly meetings for conducting innovative non-financial training events, including spiritual nurturing, often as identified by the groups themselves.
- The movements and interests of loan officers and clients alike are well managed and met. Both loan officers and clients come and go. Loan officers have personal (bonuses) and organizational (increased number of clients and 100% repayment rate) interests to juggle. Clients too have group and personal interests to balance. How best these various interests are met determines how conducive the groups become for client empowerment. Moreover, these movements among loan officers and clients also create cultural and knowledge gaps that weaken the group dynamics. Despite the difficulties in effectively managing this, CMFIs have put in place mechanisms that help them retain both staff and clients. All the five CMFIs follow a policy of keeping lower client-to-loan officer ratios to ensure that loan officers get more time to build relationships with their clients, and invest in the professional, spiritual (discipleship) and financial well-being of their staff. They also show care towards their clients in times of loss, marital problems and financial distresses. For instance, Five Talents does not expect 100% repayment rates, since that would indicate lending

to low-risk groups, whereas the mission of Five Talents is to serve marginal groups and, as such, the organization accepts a reasonable level of default.

- The capacity of loan officers is developed. These are the most important personnel of CMFIs as they interface with the most important people in the business, the clients. The loan officers are often young and fresh graduates with limited experience of working with people. In addition to microfinance skills, CMFIs invest in the development of facilitation and people skills among their loan officers, so as to enable them to treat clients with respect and work in empowering ways. Group leaders are also trained in leadership skills, so as to exercise democratic practices and harmony within groups. CMFIs also attempt to ensure that loan officers have reasonable case-loads to enable them to fulfil their role as agents of transformation by spending more quality time with clients.
- A mixture of both material and non-material or quantitative and qualitative bonuses is applied. CMFIs recognize that when bonuses are only in monetary and quantitative forms, loan officers are likely to value money more than other aspects of the business and focus on recruitment, in order to increase the number of new clients at the cost of former/existing clients. Therefore, they combine material incentives with non-material ones, such as recognition and educational opportunities. Some are also introducing social impact monitoring of clients, measuring non-financial goals alongside financial ones.
- Gender training is conducted to establish better awareness and understanding of gender matters among loan officers, group leaders, women and men. Married women are asked to invite their husbands to orientation events, so they are aware of the wife's involvement and their internal family dynamics. In some cases, both wives and husbands, or the whole family, including children, are made aware of the loan taken, so as to enhance joint responsibility in the households concerned. Cultural and traditional practices that impede women's participation are also addressed during gender training events. In this way, CMFIs ensure that the role of women in decision-making is properly recognized and

respected both within and outside the home. The general guiding principle followed by CMFIs is: "There is neither Jew nor Greek, slave nor free, male nor female, for you are all one in Christ Jesus."[248]

- Managers and loan officers gain a better understanding of the portfolios of the poor. The study by Collins et al. has, for example, revealed so many complex aspects of how the poor manage their meagre financial resources, loans, savings and assets that practitioners need to know, in order to do their job well. It is not only clients that need to receive financial education, but also the employees of MFIs.[249] CMFIs attach value to this and seek to enable frontline staff to know their clients' conditions better. Opportunity's "Living the Opportunity Brand" and "Hire Right, Train Right and Treat Right" and Hope's "Doing Business God's Way" and "Business, Home, and Health" training materials are some examples of the efforts made by CMFIs to equip their staff with Christian business principles and practices.

- Clients are being trained in financial literacy, transformational development, and family life, as well as their rights and responsibilities, so as to increase their overall awareness and participation in decision-making processes and socio-economic affairs that affect their destiny.

- Through training in value formation, the clients' faith is strengthened and in contexts where idolatry, witchcraft and superstitious practices often tend to create fear among people and become inhibitive to development, faith-based values release people from such practices and related fears, enabling them to embrace innovative undertakings. This is the other critical component of empowerment facilitated by CMFIs that is not considered by any of the critics as something positive.

Multiple borrowing

Roodman finds, "Borrowing from several MFIs may have gotten people into debt trouble, or trouble may have led them to borrow from several MFIs, like people juggling credit card balances.... Behind statistics showing full repayment may lie a haphazard pattern of paying off old loans near the end of each one-year cycle, possibly via bridge loans from moneylenders, in order to quickly obtain new ones."[250]

Very often, clients borrow from other sources for several reasons:
- Inadequate loans from the service providers where they get their first loans, repayment pressure and lack of flexibility
- Ignorance of implications
- Availability of several loan opportunities
- Competition and related eagerness among service providers to lend no matter what, calamities/personal misfortunes
- Immediate needs (funerals, wedding, school fees, medical fees, etc.)

Easy credit leads to multiple borrowing which, if badly managed, leads to increased indebtedness with the likelihood of making credit a "poverty trap," particularly when the loan is taken for non-wealth creating purposes. This becomes worse when MFIs operate in competitive environments where the market is saturated and they provide loans without taking full consideration of the total loans outstanding and multiple sources clients are dealing with. In other words, MFIs are partially responsible for increased client indebtedness and this crudely undermines client freedom and becomes a source of enslavement and destruction.

CMFIs recognize the destructive consequences of multiple borrowing and undertake the following measures to protect clients from being lured and snared by a cycle of unmanageable debt traps:
- Share information about clients/borrowers with other service providers via credit bureaux, where they exist, and network to establish them where they do not, in partnership with national microfinance networks
- Train clients on the risks and dangers involved in multiple borrowing, so as to help them make the right choice. This is important because clients often borrow from various service providers without understanding the financial implications. The problem gets worse when clients borrow more in order to repay other loans and to meet immediate consumption needs, such as funeral and wedding expenses. Five Talents has found that the best trainers in this respect are the clients themselves who share their stories with their groups and explain the pitfalls of multiple

borrowing to each other. Opportunity and Faulu Kenya have developed training modules and DVDs covering the meaning and risks of multi-borrowing
- Help client businesses to be profitable, so they meet their repayment requirements by using part of the profits they make and not by using other loans be it from MFIs, friends, relatives or local money-lenders. This is often communicated during financial education events in groups
- Provide adequate loans, so clients do not need to go to other lenders to meet their need for working capital
- Establish where clients divert their business loans and create loan products to meet those needs, so as to mitigate the problem of diversion. Very often clients divert their business loans to pay school fees for their children, home improvements, and emergencies
- Inform clients about credit bureaux and how they work, including the accessibility of their business data to any lender they approach for loans
- Monitor loan utilization regularly and consistently to ensure that loans are utilized for the intended purposes, or determine the reason why they are not
- Demand and train clients on how to keep proper financial records, including invoices
- Avoid making credit easy. CMFIs undertake serious loan appraisals to ensure that the loans for which clients apply are based on sound business plans and due diligence
- Emphasis on the client screening process could be noted here. Through client screenings, CMFIs evaluate whether clients have access to the right amount of capital to generate business growth
- Emphasis on savings as a way to encourage clients to manage their money wisely

Mission drift

Bateman claims that commercialization is increasingly forcing MFIs "to pressure and hoodwink their clients in order to obtain new business", which is "a very serious case of 'mission drift'" and concludes that, "the 'new wave' commercialization model has added enormous impetus to the ongoing abandonment of the social mission [poverty reduction] aspect to microfinance."[251] Commercialized microfinance diverts "a nation's valuable savings flows into simple 'no-development' uses, and concomitantly out of all *other* uses that we know are likely to be of much higher development value to society – principally SME lending."[252] Commercialization has also led to the "rise of a group of 'microfinance millionaires,'" consisting of Western social investors as well as key MFI employees/owners which in itself has become "a major 'feedback' driver behind the increasing commercialization of microfinance."[253] He concludes, "The light at the end of the 'commercialized microfinance-as-poverty-reduction' tunnel is actually an oncoming train."[254]

Sinclair claims that microfinance has been "hijacked by profiteers" and "morphed into a means of exploitation." As evidence, he gives a detailed insider account of LAPO, a Nigerian MFI and Investment Fund, particularly Triple Jump, that supply it with capital loans. He holds that "mission drift is the risk of an MFI forgetting its own mission and pursuing purely commercial ends to the detriment of the poor. It is serious and rampant."[255]

Much of the discussion on mission drift was heightened, following the initial public offering (IPO) of Compartamos, a Mexican MFI, on the stock market in 2007 bringing about $450 million to its investors and making its Founding Co-CEOs the first "microfinance millionaires". This was followed by another IPO in India, when the flotation of SKS earned its founder and another venture capitalist $80 million each.[256] The 2011 annual survey report, *Microfinance Banana Skins*, published by the Centre for the Study of Financial Innovation (CSFI), brought out the worries surrounding the industry about the drift away of microfinance from its original mission and being co-opted by the pursuit of size and profitability.[257] Together, the critics have done a good job in exposing profit-driven commercialized MFIs, founders, directors and investment funds, which have permeated the industry with profit-making agendas, who are out to make money for themselves by taking advantage of the vulnerability of the poor for their own gain. I agree that, "profiting so egregiously from the suffering of poor individuals is morally and ethically wrong."[258]

However, these are only the bad apples or "wolves in sheep's clothing", to use Sinclair's expression. They are not all the apples in the market and should not be used as a basis for undermining the entire industry.

233

Compartamos and SKS were strongly criticized by the wider microfinance community as soon as their actions were made public. Yunus, for example, identified Compartamos with "loan sharks" or "moneylenders" and described its priorities as "screwed up." He also described SKS leader as being in the business of "exciting people to make money off the poor."

The good apples, the shepherds of the poor, are greater in number and the industry should be seen and judged through their eyes. CMFIs are not out there to make profit at any cost but to serve people living in poverty with additional services including non-financial ones.[259] CMFIs are not motivated by profiteering, accumulation and individual gains, but by the call of Jesus Christ to serve people in poverty. CMFIs are driven by three bottom lines (economic, social and value). The proceeds are re-invested for more and better service. There are no "microfinance millionaires" among CMFIs.

As Roodman says, "microfinance is a boon and a bond". It has two edges: good (benefit) and bad (harm). Commercialization has all the elements and potential to cause MFIs, including CMFIs, to drift from their poverty reduction (social) mission. Keeping the balance becomes a challenge. When NGO CMFIs commercialize their operations, they undergo a whole range of changes: boards, senior professionals, business plans, operations and standards have to be approved by central banks; daily reports have to be submitted to central banks; dividends have to be shared among shareholders, etc. All these bring about changes in pace, culture, language and social composition and have the potential to gradually diminish the original social mission

In an effort to prevent commercialization from becoming a bane to the preservation and realization of the original social mission of microfinance, CMFIs continue to ensure that:
- Shareholders are social investors not driven by profit-maximization for personal gain alone, but ready to fund non-dividend and non-loss making social businesses, allowing profits to be reinvested for more growth and more and better services.
- Lenders (investment funds and commercial banks) are ethically minded and non-interventionists – they are not in a position to influence policies, values and practices.

Microfinance Criticism and Christian Response

- Social mission is clearly defined and a deliberate strategy for its realization is developed, fully understood/owned, and implemented.
- Christian principles and standards are developed and adhered to.
- Seasoned professionals are recruited and regularly trained and equipped to facilitate value-driven transforming microfinance.
- Clients are consulted and their voices are heard on how business is conducted, including recommendations for improvement.
- Regular reviews, evaluations and reflections are made to assess progress in the realization of social and value goals and overall direction. It must, however, be pointed out that the evaluations referred to here are often internal and qualitative, and not academically rigorous in nature.

To ensure that they stay true to their original mission, CMFIs have clearly defined their core business to be facilitating the transformation of their clients. This policy focus is what drives the board, management and staff to facilitate the development of tools and indicators for transformational development and to train both loan officers and clients to ensure that mission drift does not creep in. Staff and divisions engaged in financial, operational and non-financial work closely to ensure that they operate within the established mission and value frameworks.

Utilization of Loans

One of the main grounds of microfinance criticism is the contention that only a very little portion of the loan capital disbursed by MFIs goes to business development. The contentions made include:

- The overwhelming portion of the loan portfolio provided by MFIs is given for financing consumption. Bateman holds that consumption, not business lending, represents the vast bulk of microfinance lending. He estimates that "... between 50% and 90% of microloans are actually accessed for simple consumption purposes, rather than to support income-generating activities."[260] The most commonly quoted evidence given to support this claim is what John Hatch, the founder of FINCA, is reported to have publicly said: "90% of the microloans are used to finance current consumption rather than to fuel enterprise."[261]

- Clients divert part (commonly 30%-40%), and sometimes even 100%), of their business loans to meet other needs like food, funeral expenses, school fees, hospitalization, household goods, wedding expenses, gifts, etc. The other form of implied diversion happens when clients use the loan to import goods, resulting in the utilization of the loan for transactions in other countries and not in the intended ones.
- The overwhelming microfinance loans are given to "buy cheap, sell dear" type of microenterprises: traders. Even worse is when these traders are in the business of buying and selling imported goods. Microfinance is not only turning nations into economies of traders and hawkers, but also increasing their import dependency that is harmful to both development and independence. With reference to Africa, Bateman cites, "the continent is fast becoming instead a vast reservoir of self-employed traders, and not so much else"[262] and "microfinance support for such 'quick and easy to enter' shuttle trading and importing activities thus leads to import dependence. Local production possibilities get wiped out too. Microfinance thus underpins an import-dependency dynamic that is pretty much irreversible."[263]
- The critics claim that the poor who take microloans make little or no re-investment in their businesses. The common practice is that the little money they make is used for non-business expenses. This contention is based on some of the results of the rigorous studies conducted by Abhijit Banerjee and Esther Duflo, founders of the Poverty Action Lab at MIT, on the economic lives of the poor across 13 countries that was summarized by Beck and Ogden as follows: "Regardless of country or continent, very little of each additional dollar of disposable income is spent on any form of investment, or even on food and shelter."[264]

CMFIs recognize that these are important findings and seek to direct their financial services, so as to enhance sustainable economic transformation by:
- Re-focusing on business loans. Originally MFIs came into being with the mission of providing working capital among people living in poverty for strengthening and expanding businesses to create

employment and generate income and not for financing consumption. Authentic microfinance is about making available working capital that generates income and contributes to wealth creation and not just for wealth depletion. Two of the five CMFIs studied do not give consumption loans at all, while the average consumption loan among the other three is about 15%-20%, much lower than the 50%-90% the critics refer to.

Moreover, the consumption loans are not for buying TV sets or food and other immediate consumption goods. In most cases, these relate to loans given for school fees to enable parents to pay for their children's education, housing loans to improve access and quality and utility loans (water, electricity and sanitation) for improving living conditions. Such improvements are also indirectly linked to business, as they are likely to increase performance. This is under the control of CMFIs and they can deliberately ensure that their primary focus continues to be on wealth-generating activities, while limiting their consumption lending to selective and business-enhancing activities.

It must, however, be noted that people living in poverty have as much right as the rich to have access to consumption loans and to make their own choices as long as such loans are not all they are given. The problem is not the consumption loan in itself; rather, the problem is in the type of consumption the loan is used for and the means used to finance it. Clients with business loans benefit more from such types of loans than those without.

- Strengthening monitoring, training activities and record keeping. Money is fungible and loans can be used by clients for different purposes than initially intended. This is practiced across all socio-economic levels – rich or poor. CMFIs endeavour to strengthen monitoring and training activities already being done and also help clients to keep proper records of business activities, including in- and out-goings to make it easier for loan officers to monitor and provide meaningful technical assistance. Observing activities on the site by itself does not inform the loan officers much about the utilization of loans. The story told by Roodman says it all: "We take a loan to buy a cow. The first half goes for paying another loan. And the other half goes for buying land. When the loan officer visits to check, we show him our neighbor's cow." (Roodman) Onsite observations become more effective if accompanied by recorded accounts and invoices. Only the combined application of these three elements is likely to mitigate the risk of diverting business loans to unintended purposes and that is what CMFIs are attempting to do.

- Creating loan products to meet the needs for which diverted loans are used. In many instances, clients tend to use part of their loans for meeting the educational needs (school fees) of their children, housing finance (home improvement and incremental) loans. CMFIs have already responded by creating such products, so that clients do not need to use part of the business loans for paying school fees and improving their homes. These include school fee loans, home improvement loans, and transport loans.

- Applying a deliberate policy of re-directing business loans from trading to production-focused enterprises. These are the activities that generate new and more wealth, employment opportunities and innovations. They also have more positive forward and backward linkages than trading enterprises which are more for distributing goods and services, already created by buying where they are available and cheap and selling them dear, where there is demand. In an attempt to promote a production-oriented microfinance operation, CMFIs do not only provide financial education to raise general economic awareness among clients, but also deliberately aim to direct their loans towards productive activities such as agriculture, agro-processing, carpentry, metal work, shoe-making, textiles, crafts, basketry, and less towards trading and services.

- Helping clients to develop investment plans. Many clients do not keep general business records of in-and-outgoings, let alone investment and savings plans. These are difficult things to do for people with no literacy and business skills. Hence, the tendency of spending money as it is generated. In most instances spending and not saving/reinvesting comes first. Even with the financial education most CMFIs offer, this does not occur that easily. CMFIs do, therefore, attempt to create a situation in which clients would be able to access technical support in developing and implementing investment plans, so as to enable them to re-invest into their businesses on a regular basis. The focus is on developing a savings culture and enabling clients to save. Siphoning or repatriating profits from the communities, as claimed by Sinclair, is something not done by CMFIs as any profits made are reinvested in the business they conduct.

Conclusion

According to Roodman, effective MFIs are those which: (i) offer a comprehensive package of financial products and services including credit, savings, money transfers and insurance, (ii) focus on savings and insurance rather than credit, (iii) combine financial services with non-financial services (iv) apply telephone banking, and (v) create sustainable local financial institutions. Such MFIs are likely to produce better impact results.

The five CMFIs together satisfy, or are on the way to satisfy, all the characteristics listed here. Although they are at different stages and a lot more is still to be done, all the five CMFIs are savings-led, offer insurance and other non-financial services, apply mobile technology and endeavour to create sustainable financial institutions. Opportunity and Faulu Kenya have deposit-taking licenses and can mobilize savings under the regulation of central banks. Hope, VisionFund and Five Talents, also run savings-led programmes which are done through grassroots-based informal organizations (see the various chapters).[265] They all provide financial and non-financial services including value formation. The same thing applies to their application of telephone banking and the creation of sustainable local institutions.

Moreover, although at varying degrees, the five CMFIs provide multi-sectoral (agriculture, value chain, trading and service industry, cottage industry, housing, health, education, water and sanitation, and energy), services aimed to promote long-term development. CMFIs do not offer only microfinance; rather, they facilitate transformational development through microfinance and have elevated the industry to a higher purpose. Microfinance is the means and not the end of their business.

In view of this, it can be said that many of the microfinance criticisms do not fully apply to CMFIs as they seem to move beyond the conventional and narrow microfinance in a way that is economic- and material-centric.

Four issues about the future of CMF/CMFIs

Lessons from microfinance criticism: interest rate and impact assessment

Despite the negative portrayal the critics have painted of the microfinance industry, their studies have exposed several weak links to which CMFIs need to pay attention. The criticism is not something to fully deny, ignore, brush aside or be discouraged by. Many of the findings I have referred to here, emanated from these studies. Many of the measures I have listed as part of the response to the criticism with reference to the five CMF programmes described in this book are on-going and in progress. There is so much useful material produced by the various studies and they should be constructively channeled in the improvement of the industry. CMFIs should be wise enough to take stock of what have been identified as weak points, draw lessons to do better while they also celebrate what they do right and correct false allegations made against the industry they represent. A learning organization values criticisms and uses them for strengthening its work and reputation. As any learning organization, CMFIs should not only satisfy themselves with the way they see themselves, but also consider how others see them.

The microfinance industry as a whole has responded positively to the overall criticism by taking corrective actions: The Smart Campaign, Client Protection, Microfinance Transparency, Social Performance Management Indicators constitute some of the post-criticism initiatives taken by the industry and CMFIs have and are actively participating in implementing these.

The two major criticisms of microfinance relate to the high interest rates charged and the absence of rigorous impact studies. The efforts that CMFIs have made and are making in keeping interest rates as low as possible, within market and Biblical standards, have been described above. This is not something CMFIs take lightly. It is a thorn in their flesh and they are doing the best they can in the various contexts and stages in which they operate. CMFIs are implored to keep on doing what they are doing in more aggressive ways, so as to reduce clients' costs without undermining their efforts to be sustainable.

Knowing the difference microfinance programmes make in a more scientific and rigorous way is not only the concern of academics or donors, but also the concern of CMFIs. However, CMFIs have not done much in this regard in the past mainly because conducting rigorous impact studies is time-consuming and expensive. CMFIs recognize that assessing the positive and negative impact of their programmes on the clients and communities supported will not only produce knowledge about current performance, but also help to reflect on progress and draw lessons for reshaping future programmes and practices for attaining better performance and increased impact on clients' lives. As noted in the case studies covered in this book, some of the CMFIs have developed and continue to refine indicators for measuring the impact of their programmes.

In this regard, many of the critics of microfinance have tended to advance RCTs as the right way of evaluating the impact of social interventions including microfinance. However, these are not without weaknesses: their contribution to knowledge is limited as they only "tell a bit about what happened to particular groups of people at particular places and times,"[266] and do not often inform us enough about the long-term impact of, for example, behavioural changes (quitting alcohol consumption, smoking, gambling, stealing), love, harmony, respect, dignity, faith, freedom, etc., and also they do not successfully capture the effects of cultural and contextual factors. According to a recent paper, "RCTs are often ill-suited to evaluating social innovations"[267] and propose what the authors call "developmental evaluation." This emerging approach is defined as:

> *Developmental evaluation informs and supports innovative and adaptive development in complex dynamic environments. DE brings to innovation and adaptation the processes of asking evaluative questions, applying evaluation logic, and gathering and reporting evaluative data to support project, program, product, and/or organizational development with timely feedback.*[268]

Development evaluation is said to focus on seven questions listed as follows:
- What is developing or emerging as the innovation (e.g. microfinance) takes shape?
- What variations in effects are we seeing?
- What do the initial results reveal about expected progress?

- What seems to be working and not working?
- How is the larger system or environment responding to the innovation?
- How should the innovation be adapted in response to changing circumstances?
- How can the project adapt to the context in ways that are within the project's control?

Both RCTs and Developmental Evaluation approaches involve longitudinal studies. As described above, CMFIs are in the microfinance world, but not of it. There are objectives, standards and indicators that they have in common with the rest of the industry but also that set them apart. So, the choice of approaches, tools, indicators and questions will have to reflect these scenarios. In other words, CMFIs will have to develop their own approach that is rooted in and reflective of their Christian values

Longitudinal, rigorous impact studies are expensive and require complex administration and skills/tools. CMFIs should not allow this to deter them from conducting such studies. One solution could be for CMFIs to form a joint Christian think tank that will develop common indicators and undertake joint impact studies by taking an equal number of samples from each of the interested CMFIs. This will generate scientific knowledge about the impact made by CMF interventions on the transformation of clients' lives and provide the basis for directing future programmes.

The history of nations and the experience of CMFIs have shown that there is a positive correlation of impact between Christian faith and wholistic development, with the former having a positive impact on human flourishing. Max Weber showed the positive role Protestant ethics played in the development of Europe. In her examination of Biblical Christianity and its socio-economic consequences in Guatemala, Amy Sherman finds that the conversion to Protestant Christianity creates a fertile environment conducive to freedom, development and enhanced well-being. CMFIs should be committed to conducting rigorous studies and providing evidence to substantiate the positive impact of Christian faith on the socio-economic development of the clients they serve.

"Salt and light"

As part of the microfinance world, CMFIs deal with money and are obliged to go by the laws and principles that govern money management. CMFIs mobilize (grants, donations, deposits, equity) or borrow money. They lend (disburse) money and they collect (repayments) the money they have lent. In other words, they talk, teach, disburse and manage money. Conventionally, microfinance is all about mobilizing money, accounting for money and making (profit) money. As the saying goes, actions speak louder than words and while CMFIs rightly do all this, it is likely that their actions could unintentionally make money appear as the single most important thing in life, and thereby lead to two unintended consequences: clients easily develop love for money and idolize money (mammon) as their master. This is not what CMFIs believe and stand for as it goes against two Biblical principles: "the love of money is a root of all kinds of evil"[269] and "you cannot serve God and mammon."[270]

Money is important and has to be managed and generated with full integrity, accountability, stewardship and excellence, and CMFIs must do this in ways that are even better and exemplary, so as to play the role of being "salt and light" in the microfinance industry. Mobilizing and managing money with a high level of accountability and excellence requires investment in technology, systems and human resources: professionalization. This should be accompanied by investment in enhancing knowledge and practice of Christian values and standards among staff and directors who should be transformed by the renewing of their minds. They should not just follow the standards set by the microfinance industry, but set standards to lead the industry.

Advocacy

Christians believe in a God who is just and righteous, loves justice and righteousness, executes righteousness and justice for all who are oppressed and treats justice as the measuring line and righteousness the plummet.[271] He commands us to "love justice" and do justice to the afflicted.[272] Setting the captives and oppressed free was part of the mission of Jesus Christ.

CMFIs operate in a world where injustice and corruption are rampant. The poor are subject to economic injustice, social injustice, political injustice, and spiritual injustice that are constantly constraining them from unleashing their potential to the full and living an abundant life.

The impact of CMF programmes does not depend only on what CMFIs do through microfinance, how they deliver their services and how they relate to their clients. It does not depend on what and how their clients use the services offered either. While it is important that both the CMFIs and their clients do the right thing, in the right ways and at the right time, the success and ultimately the impact of CMF interventions, just like any other, will also depend on the economic, social, political, environmental, religious, and cultural policies and practices applied by the governments of the countries in which they operate. For example, governments may (i) decide to move or close down market places where clients run their resulting in coerced evictions and demolitions without compensations, (ii) increase prices on commodities (imported and local alike) and taxes on income, (iii) make getting business licences cumbersome (e.g., requirements and bureaucracy) and costly (e.g. bribery) and (iv) artificially devalue or revaluate currencies thereby creating instabilities in commodity and capital flows.

Fighting against such injustices is part of the fight against poverty and oppression. God is not indifferent to injustices and this suggests that CMFIs have no option but to actively engage in campaigning for their abolition. Injustice and poverty go together and their solution is justice and development that also go together. CMFIs cannot take on the fight against material and spiritual poverty and be indifferent to injustice. They have to fight both and advocacy is a vital tool for so doing.

While the most sustainable way of empowerment is enabling people to advocate for themselves and that is what CMFIs are partially doing through financial, leadership and spiritual training, it is also important that they advocate and lobby on their behalf and alongside them at all levels. This does not mean that CMFIs turn into full-time campaigners of justice on their own. They can do this in different ways: They can hold discussions with the relevant national authorities (e.g. Central Banks, Ministries of Finance and Planning, Trade, Social and Gender Affairs, etc.) and international agencies on issues, including globalization, that affect the lives and businesses of clients individually or collectively. They can also advocate and lobby as part of national, regional and international networks. Moreover, CMFIs could also indirectly influence local and national leaders using their strong links with Church leaders as the latter are often revered and listened to by the former.

Because their business is in the financial sector, CMFIs might fear that engaging in advocacy is likely to compromise and restrain their relationships with governments. Although the fear might be justified, CMFIs ought to recognize that not doing so will also compromise their relationships with God who is just, loves them and will bring justice. Some even identify advocacy with politics and think that Christians should keep out of such an engagement. Advocacy is not always equated with politics, nor should Christians see politics as peripheral and alien to their work. Advocacy leverages freedom and development. The intention of advocacy is not to antagonize and create problems that will be counter-productive. The purpose is to reconcile and bring harmony through bold love, without being inimical, and through constructive dialogue, so as to influence policies and practices of governments and donors for the benefit of the poor. Silence and indifference only do harm to the cause of justice and restoration that CMFIs aim to bring about through microfinance. "Open rebuke is better than love carefully concealed."[273]

CMF Coalition

Since 1997, the microfinance industry has built a movement of its own: global, regional and national networks of MFIs have been established during the last 15 years for mutual learning and advocacy purposes. Most CMFIs have been and are active players in these networks. However, these forums have been used for discussing and strategizing issues related to conventional microfinance. CMFIs have benefited from and contributed to these discussions and to the general evolution of the industry. However, CMFIs have not been and are not able to use these forums for discussing all the issues related to their entire programmes as faith-based concerns are often avoided as "sensitive" and "inappropriate".

As much as it is appropriate for CMFIs to be part of the general microfinance movement for mutual learning and advocacy through conventional coalitions, it is equally important to form a coalition of CMFIs for openly pursuing the Christian agenda with like-minded organizations. In other words, without necessarily leaving the wider microfinance movement, CMFIs should create a CMF network at global, regional and national levels to enhance mutual learning, and develop common standards and impact indicators applicable to Christ-centric microfinance. It is important that CMFIs recognize that, in many ways, they offer a better and stronger microfinance alternative as they are pursuing a higher purpose and that they will be able to strengthen their global influence and contribution by seeking to interact and work together.

Such collaboration is already in the making: Opportunity and Hope co-own the Opportunity Bank of Rwanda. Opportunity and VisionFund are collaborating in DR Congo, whereby Opportunity provides financial services to World Vision's clients. Opportunity co-owns Opportunity Bank of Uganda and Opportunity Tanzania Limited with Faulu Uganda and Faulu Tanzania respectively, while the chairperson of Faulu Kenya serves on the two boards. Five Talents partners with Opportunity's former partner in Tanzania: Talanta Trust that is now known as Mamma Bahti.

A Christian Coalition is likely to serve as an indispensable advocacy tool since it is likely to help CMFIs speak the same language, come closer in unity and raise one voice that is relatively more powerful than many scattered voices.[274] Moreover, the coalition is likely to serve as a vehicle for the production and dissemination of knowledge and learning among CMFIs.

The Carpenter's Fund: Brief Profile

The Carpenter's Fund is a senior, collateralized lender investing in projects designed to increase wealth through investment in sustainable development projects. TCF specializes in small business and Church infrastructure projects in emerging markets. TCF endeavors to promote sustainable transformational development that allows people to seek fulfilment spiritually, physically, intellectually and materially.

To realize its mission, TCF provides loans and capacity building services to Christian organizations which are unable to access affordable loan capital from existing financial sources.

The programme of TCF focuses on four key areas:

Health – construction or expansion of clinics, hospital and water facilities

Education – primary schools, secondary schools, vocational training institutes, colleges and universities

Church – buildings and other facilities

Small & medium businesses – entrepreneurs operating in manufacturing, agro-processing, eco– tourism, and trade and service industries

Since 2001, TCF and its predecessor have made $11 million in loans to organizations on five continents. Each investment made by TCF must stand on its own merit and meet minimum financial standards. Qualifying organizations have a successful operating history, management and board capability, clear strategy, and have demonstrated commitment to environmental care as well as a sustainable transformational development impact.

More information can be found on www.thecarperntersfund.org.

SELECTED BIBLIOGRAPHY

African Economic Outlook *Youth Unemployment* http://www.africaneconomicoutlook.org/en/in-depth/developing-technical-vocational-skills-in-africa/tvsd-in-specific-contexts/youth-unemployment/

Allen, H. *Care International's Village Savings & Loan Programmes in Africa: Micro Finance for the Rural Poor that Works.*

Armendáriz, B. and J. Morduch *The Economics of Microfinance.* Cambridge, Mass.: MIT Press, 2005.

Aziz, N. *African cellphone so get free Wikipedia access* http://www.bet.com/news/global/2012/02/15/african-cell-phones-to-get-free-wikipedia-access.html

Banerjee, A., and E. Duflo *Poor Economics: A Radical Rethinking of the Way to Fight Global Poverty.* New York: Public Affairs, 2011.

Bankable Frontier Associates *Land Title for Ghana's Poor Project.* Boston, Mass.: Bankable Frontier Associates, 2011.

Bankable Frontier Associates *Mid-Term Evaluation of the Housing Finance.* Boston, Mass.: Bankable Frontier Associates, 2011.

Bateman, M. *Why Doesn't Microfinance work? The Destructive Rise of Local Neoliberalism.* New York: Zed Books, 2010.

Bateman, M. "The Microfinance Delusion." *Global Labour Column.* http://column.global-labour-university.org/2012/01/microfinance-delusion.html

Bellman, E. and A. Chang. "India's Major Crisis in Microlending: Loans Involving Tiny Amounts of Money Were a Good Idea, but the Explosion of Interest Backfires." http://www.sksindia.com/downloads/The_Wall_Street_Journal_Article_No-2.pdf

Belshaw, D. et al. *Faith in Development: Partnership between the World Bank and the Churches of Africa.* Oxford: Regnum Books International, 2001.

Bolton, B. *The Entrepreneur and the Church.* Cambridge: Grove Books, 2006.

Briney, A. "History and development of the Green Revolution." geography.about.com/od/.../a/greenrevolution.htm

Bussau, D. and R. Mask *Christian Microenterprise Development: An Introduction.* Carlisle: Regnum Books International, 2003.

Bussau, D. and M. Getu *Sustainable Transformational Development: A Diagnostic Tool.* Manila: CTRC, 2003.

_____ *Wealth Generation & Kingdom Building through CMED: A Biblical Reflection.* Manila: CTRC, 2003.

Calum, S. 'A Roadmap towards Social Performance Management'. Blue Print: Shaping Opportunity's Future. Paper presented at Global Leadership Conference. Oxford: Opportunity International, 2012.

Campion, A. and White, V. *Institutional Metamorphosis: Transformation of Microfinance NGOs into Regulated Financial Institutions.* The Microfinance Network Occasional Paper No.4, 1999.

Centre for the Study of Financial Innovation (CSFI) "Microfinance Banana Skins: The CSFI

survey of microfinance risk 2012."
http://www.creativemetier.com/news/microfinance-banana-skins-survey-2012-published/
CGAP "The New Moneylenders: Are the Poor Being Exploited by High Microcredit Interest Rates?" CGAP Occasional Paper, no. 15, 2009.
CGAP "Microfinance Overview." http://www.cgap.org/about/microfinance.html
CGAP "Strategic Directions 2008-2013: Building Local Financial Systems That Work for the Poor's Equity and Efficiency", p. 6.
sitersssources.worldbank.org/.../Resources/CGAP_strategy.pdf
Chen, G. et al. "Growth and vulnerabilities." *Focus Note*, no.61. Washington D.C.: CGAP, 2010.
Cheston, S. and Reed, L. "Measuring Transformation: Assessing and Improving the Impact of Microcredit." *Journal of Microfinance*, v.1, no.1, 2001, pp. 20-43.
Christen, R. *Commercial and Mission Drift: The Transformation of Microfinance in Latin America*. Washington D.C.: CGAP, 2000.
Collins, Daryl *Portfolios of the Poor: How the World's Poor Live on $2 a Day*. Princeton, N.J.: Princeton University Press, 2009.
Daley-Harris, S. and A. Awimbo *New Paths Out of Poverty*. Sterling, Va.: Kumarian Press, 2011.
Daley-Harris, S. and A. Awimbo *More Pathways Out of Poverty*. Bloomfield, Conn.: Kumarian Press, 2006.
Demirguc-Kunt, Asli and Kapper Leora *Measuring Financial Inclusion: The Global Findex Database*. Policy Research Working Paper Series. Washington, D.C.: World Bank, 2012.
Dearborn, T. *Reflections on Business and Micro-enterprise Development*. Monrovia, Calif.: World Vision International, 2009.
Dichter, T. and M. Harper. eds. *What is Wrong with Microfinance?* Rugby: Practical Action Publishing, 2007.
Drake, D.and E. Rhyne, eds. *The Commercialization of Microfinance: Balancing Business and Development*. San Francisco, Calif.: Kumarian Press, 2002.
Dunford, C. "Building better lives: sustainable integration of microfinance with education in child survival, reproductive health, and HIV/AIDS prevention for the poorest entrepreneurs." In Daley-Harris, S. ed. (2002) *Pathways Out of Poverty: Innovations in Microfinance for the Poorest Families*. Bloomfield, Conn.: Kumarian Press, 2002.
Dupas, P. and J. Robinson. "Savings Constraints and Microenterprise Development: Evidence from a Field Experiment in Kenya." *American Economic Journal: Applied Economics*, March 2012: 1.
Dupas, P. and J. Robinson. "Savings Constraints and Microenterprise Development: Evidence from a Field Experiment in Kenya." *Grameen Foundation*, 2009: 1.
Facts on Women at Work http://www.ilo.org/wcmsp5/groups/public/---dgreports/---dcomm/documents/publication/wcms_067595.pdf
Faulu Kenya. Annual Reports and Financial Statement,& Management Report (2008-2011 & 2012). Nairobi: Faulu Kenya, 2012.
Faulu Kenya *Board and Management Reports*. (2010, 2011). Nairobi: Faulu Kenya, 2011
Faulu Kenya *Case Studies,financial education program*. Nairobi: Faulu Kenya, 2012.

Selected Bibliography

Faulu Kenya *End-of-Project Financial Education Evaluation Report*. Nairobi: Faulu Kenya, 2011.
Five Talents *Impact Report* 2012. www.fivetalents.org.uk
Fikkert, B. and S. Corbett *When Helping Hurts: Alleviating Poverty without Hurting the Poor...and Yourself*, 2009.
Good News Translation Bible. New York: American Bible Society, 1965.
Greer, P. "A Hand Up, Not a Handout." *Mission Frontiers*, July/August, 2011.
Greer, P. *Putting Client above Profits*. Lancaster, Penn.: HOPE International, 2010.
Greer, P. and P. Smith *The Poor Will Be Glad: Joining The Revolution To Lift The World Out Of Poverty*. Grand Rapids, Mich.: Zondervan, 2009.
Griffiths, B. and K. Tan *Fighting Poetry through Enterprise: The case for social venture capital*. London: Transformational Business Network, 2007.
Harper, M. et al. *Development, Divinity and Dharma: The Role of Religion in Development and Microfinance Institutions*. Rugby: Practical Action, 2008.
Heslam, P. *Transforming Capitalism: Entrepreneurship and the Renewal of Thrift*. Cambridge: Grove Books, 2010.
Higginson, R. *Faith, Hope & the Global Economy*. Nottingham: Inter-Varsity Press, 2012.
Hobson, E. "The importance of the informal economy for local economic development (LED) in Africa." LED Network Africa, no. 2. www.ledna.org
Hokans, J. et al. 'Mid-term Evaluation of the Housing Finance and Land title of Ghana's Poor Project.' Bankable Frontier Associates, August 2011.
Homes for Hope *Homes for Hope Brochure*. Lancaster, Penn.: HOPE International, 2008.
HOPE International *About HOPE: History* http://www.hopeinternational.org/site/PageServer?pagename=about_history, 2010.
HOPE International *Board Strategy for Spiritual Integration*. Lancaster, Penn.: HOPE International, 2007.
HOPE International. *Board Strategy for Spiritual Integration (March 2007)*. Sub-committee for spirituality and culture. Lancaster, Penn.: HOPE International, 2007.
HOPE International *Declaration of Non-Personal Use of or Gain from HOPE International*. Lancaster, Penn.: HOPE International, 2008.
HOPE International *Microenterprise Development Activities*. Lancaster, Penn.: HOPE International.
HOPE International *Hiring Christian Staff*. Lancaster, Penn.: HOPE International, 2011.
HOPE International *HOPE and Ambassador Enterprises – the 2020 Project*. Lancaster, Penn.: HOPE International, 2011.
HOPE International *HOPE International 2010 Annual Report*. Lancaster, Penn.: HOPE International, 2010.
HOPE International *HOPE International Intern Orientation: HOPE 101*. Lancaster, Penn.: HOPE International, 2009.
HOPE International. *HOPE International Strategic Plan 2010-2012*. Lancaster, Penn.: HOPE International, 2009.
HOPE International *Minutes from the Board Meeting*, November 2011.
HOPE International *Program Update – Congo*, September 2011. Lancaster, Penn.: HOPE

International, 2011.
HOPE International *Rwanda Fast Facts*. Lancaster, Penn.: HOPE International, 2012
HOPE International *Savings Circle Program: Overview*. Lancaster, Penn.: HOPE International, 2011.
HOPE International *The Coca-Cola Company and HOPE International: A 5 BY 20 Partnership Proposal Prepared May 2011*. Lancaster, Penn.: HOPE International, 2011.
HOPE International *What is Spiritual Integration (SI) at HOPE?* Lancaster, Penn.: HOPE International, 2011.
HOPE Ukraine *HOPE Ukraine Quarterly Meeting – April 2010*. Lancaster, Penn.: HOPE International, 2011.
HOPE Ukraine *PAR – Delinquency Management – HOPE Leadership Summit*. Lancaster, Penn.: HOPE International, 2011.
HOPE Ukraine *Program Update – September 2011*. Lancaster, Penn.: HOPE International, 2011.
Horn, N. and Danki *IDP Rising Schools Pilot Project; End of Pilot Evaluation*. Oakbrook, Ill.: Opportunity Edufinance, 2012.
Hrywna, M. "Religious Donors Give To Secular Groups, Too." *The NonProfit Times*. http://www.thenonprofittimes.com/article/detail/religious-donors-give-to-secular-groups-too-4048
Hulme, D and P. Mosley *Finance against Poverty*. London: Routledge, 1996.
"Human Development Index (HDI) – 2011 Rankings."*Human Development Reports*. 2011. http://hdr.undp.org/en/statistics/> [Accessed 10 July 2012]
Johnson, S., and B. Rogaly *Microfinance and Poverty Reduction*. Oxford: Oxfam, 1997.
Isern, J. et al. *Sustainability of Self Help Groups in India: Two Analyses*. Occasional paper no. 12. Washington D.C.: Consultative Group to Assist the Poor, 2007.
Kimani, E., Mbaisi, J. "Microfinance Governance: K'REPSs experience of Financial Services Associations (FSAs)." Benin, 2008.
Kinetz, Erika "AP IMPACT: Lender's own probe links it to suicides: AP IMPACT: Indian lender SKS' own probe links it to borrower suicides, despite company denials." [WWW] Associated Press, 24th February, 2012. http://finance.yahoo.com/news/ap-impact-lenders-own-probe-080122405.html [Accessed 02/29/12].
Kristof, Nicholas "Moonshine or the Kids?" [WWW] New York Times, 22nd May, 2010. http://www.nytimes.com/2010/05/23/opinion/23kristof.html?hp [Accessed 02/29/12].
Lewis, Brian "Some Philanthropic Dividend Program Language: Language for strategic donors, family foundations, and Hope regional board members; language for donors; language for loan recipients." December 12, 2011.
Lascelles, D. and S. Mendelson *Microfinance Banna Skins 2011: The CSFI Survey of Microfinance Risk*. London: Centre for the Study of Financial Innovation, 2011.
Littlefield, E. et al. *Is Microfinance and Effective Strategy to Reach the MDGs?* http://www.cgap.org/publications/microfinance-effective-strategy-reach-mdgs
Lupton, R. *Toxi Charity: How Churches and Charities Hurt Those They Help and How to Reverse It*. New York: Harper Collins, 2011.
Lutzenkirchen, C. et al. *Microfinance in Evolution: An Industry between Crisis and Development*.

Selected Bibliography

Frankfurt: DB Research, September 2012.
Maes, J. and L. Reed *State of the Microcredit Summit Campaign Report 2012*. Washington D.C.: Microcredit Summit Campaign, 2012.
Marcus Taylor, "The Microfinance Crisis in Andhra Pradesh, India: W Window on Rural Distress." Food First Backgrounder, vol. 18, no.3, Fall 2012. www.foodfirst.org/en/microfinance+india
Maranz, D. "African Friends and Money Matters," Dallas, Tx.: SIL International, 2001.
Marshall, K., Van Saanen, M. (2007) *Development and Faith: Where Mind, Heart, and Soul Work Together*. Washington D.C.: World Bank.
Matthew Fuchs "Lessons Learned from Microfinance Crises: Viewpoints from Investors." *Microfinance Focus*, November 4, 2009.
Mercy Corps *The History of Microfinance*. http://www.globalenvision.org/library/4/1051
Microcredit Summit *Declaration and Plan of Action*. Washington D.C. 1997.
MicroCapital *Innovation in Food Security*. http://www.microcapital.org/special-report-alalay-sa-kaunlaran-incorporated-aski--of-the-philipppines-takes-127k-european-microfinance-award-for-innovation-in-food-security/
MicroEnsure *Microfinance Matt*ers, Issue 8, n.d. http://www.microensure.com/images/library/files/Newsletters/microinsurance_matters_issue_8.pdf
_____ *What We Do*. n.d. http://www.microensure.com/whatwedo-business.model.asp.
Microfinance Gateway *About Our Organization*. http://www.mftransparency.org/about/, 2010.
MIX Market (2010) *Microfinance in Ukraine: Country Profile* [WWW] MIX Market. http://www.mixmarket.org/mfi/country/Ukraine/ [Accessed from 31/01/12], 2010.
Myers, B. *Walking with the Poor: Principles and Practices of Transformational Development*. Maryknoll, N.Y.: Orbis Books, 2000.
Mills, P. (1989) "Interest in Interest," Cambridge: Jubilee Centre. www.jubilee-centre.org.
Mills, P. (1993) "The Ban on Interest: dead letter or radical solution?" Cambridge: Jubilee Centre, v. 1, no. 4. www.jubilee-centre.org.
Mohling, R. *Assessing Impact in Malawi*. Oakbrook, Ill.: Opportunity International, 2010.
Morgan, J. *Best Practices for National and Regional Microfinance Networks*. Paper presented at the Global Microcredit Summit, Valladolid, November 14-17, 2011.
Mosser, T. and Reed, L. *The Market for Funding of Microenterprise Development: Trends and Segments*. Oakbrook, Ill.: Opportunity International, 1996.
Murdoch, M. 'Presence: Harnessing the Power of Partnership for Client Impact', Blue Print: Shaping Opportunity's Future. Paper presented at Global Leadership Conference. Oxford: Opportunity International, 2012.
Nelson, S. White Paper. Oakbrook, Ill.: Opportunity International, 2012.
Odell, K. "Measuring the Impact of Microfinance: Taking Another Look." *Grameen Foundatio*n, 2010:1.
Opportunity International *"Reflections on Our Mission, Our Motivation and Our Core Values."* Oakbrook, Ill.: Opportunity International Network Office, 1997.
_____ *Summary of February 1998 Board Meeting*. Oakbrook, Ill.: Opportunity International Network Office, 1998.

_____ *Our Vision and Mission.* www.opportunity.org
_____ *Network Membership list,* www.opportunity.net
_____ *Bylaws of Opportunity International Network.* Oakbrook, Ill.: Opportunity International Office, 2011.
_____ *Statutes of Opportunity International Network.* Oakbrook, Ill.: Opportunity International Office, 2011.
_____ *Annual Report.* Oakbrook, Ill.: Opportunity International, 2012.
_____ *Banking on Africa.* n.d. http://www.opportunity.org/ initiatives/banking-on-africa/
_____ *Habitat for Humanity International Housing Project Proposal for India.* Special Topic, Oakbrook, Ill.: Opportunity International, 2009.
_____ *Housing and Land Title for Ghana's Poor Project Proposal.* Special Topic, Oakbrook, Ill.: Opportunity International, 2009.
_____ *Nicaragua Community Economic Development Project.* Quarterly Report, Oakbrook, Ill.: Opportunity International, 2012.
_____ *Opportunity International Bank of Malawi Business Plan: Second Phase UNCDF YouthStart.* Special Topic, Oakbrook, Ill.: Opportunity International, 2011.
_____ *Reflections on Our Mission, Our Motivation, and Our Core Values.* Special Topic, Oakbrook, Ill.: Opportunity International, 1997.
_____ "Statutes of Opportunity International." Special Topic, n.d.
_____ *Sustainable Income and Housing for Orphans and Vulnerable Children (OVC) in Africa.* Final Report, Oakbrook, Ill.: Opportunity International, 2010.
_____ *Transformation Case Studies.* Client Stories Report, Oakbrook, Ill.: Opportunity International, 1997.
_____ *Vision and Mission.* http://www.opportunity.org.
Opportunity International Bank of Malawi *Business Plan, Second Phase of UNCDF YouthStart Project Proposal.* Lilongwe: Opportunity Bank of Malawi, 2011.
Opportunity International Network Office *DNA of Transformation Lens.* Oakbrook, Ill.: Opportunity International Network Office, *2007.*
Opportunity International Australia *India Progress Report, July – December 2011*
Otero, M., and E. Rhyne. eds. *The New World of Micro Enterprise Finance.* Bloomfield, Conn.: Kumarian Press, 1994.
Prahalad, C. K. *The Fortune at the bottom of the pyramid.* August 5, 2004.
Preskill, H. and S. Gopalakrishnan. 'Fix That Fits: What is the Right Evaluation for Social Innovation.'
http://forbesindia.com/blog/the-good-company/fix-that-fits-what-is-the-right-evaluation-for-social-innovation/
Reed, L. "Commercialization: Overcoming the Obstacles to Accessing Commercial Funds While Maintaining a Commitment to Reaching the Poorest" in More Pathways Out of Poverty. Bloomfield, Conn.: Kumarian Press, 2006.
Reed, L. *The State of the Microcredit Summit Campaign Report 2011.* Washington, D.C.: Microcredit Summit Campaign, 2011.
Reed, L. *Vulnerability: The State of the Microcredit Summit Campaign Report 2012.* Washington D.C., 2012.

Selected Bibliography

Reed, L. *Integrating Faith and Practice: Facilitator Guide*. Monrovia, Calif.: World Vision International, 2011.

Reed, L. *"The Biblical Challenge to Microenterprise Orthodoxy."* Paper presented at the Christian Microenterprise Development Summit, Jomtien, 1999.

Reed, L. and Menendez, N. *"Keeping the Faith: Maintaining a Christian Mission in a Changing World.* www.wtrc-tmed.org/resources/Keeping%20the%20Faith.pdf

Rhyne, E. *"Microfinance Institutions in Competitive Conditions,"* in The Commercialization of Microfinance: Balancing Business and Development. Bloomfield, Conn.: Kumarian Press, 2002, pp. 200 – 219.

Robertson, R. *An Opportunity for All: Financial Education in Africa. Multimedia Pilot Trial White Paper.* Opportunity International, 2011

Rutherford, S. *The Poor and Their Money.* New Delhi: Oxford University Press, 2000.

Remenyi, J. *Where Credit is due: Income-generating Programmes for the Poor in Developing Countries.* London: It Publications, 1991.

Ripley, D. et al. 'Mobile Insurance Technology: A Microinsurance Game-Changer for Developing Markets.' Building Inclusive Markets: Impact Through Financial and Enterprise Solutions', SEEP Annual Conference, 2012.

Roodman, D. *Due Diligence: An Impertinent Inquiry into Microfinance.* Washington D.C.: Center for Global Development, 2012.

Salib, S. *"An Opportunity to Transform a Network"* in *International Trends Newsletter.* http://www.goinginternational.com/newsletJF98.htm

_____ *"Brief on Client Impact Monitoring Systems."* Oakbrook, Ill.: Opportunity International Network Office, 2003.

Sanderson, T. "Microfinance – Commercial or Social?" *Faith in Business*, v. 14, no. 4, 2012.

Sanderson, T. and S. Sengupta "Crossfire: 'The recent microfinance crisis in Andhra Pradesh in India.'" *Enterprise Development & Microfinance*, v. 22, no. 1, 2011.

Sen, A. *Development as Freedom.* Oxford: Oxford University Press, 1999.

Sherman, A. *The Soul of Development.* Oxford: Oxford University Press, 1997.

Sinclair, H. *Confessions* of a *Microfinance Heretic: How Microfinance Lost Its Way and Betrayed the Poor.* San Francisco, Calif.: Berrett-Koehler, 2012.

Sinha, F. "Beyond 'Ethical' Financial Services: Developing a Seal of Excellence for Poverty Outreach and Transformation in Microfinance" in *New Pathways Out of Poverty.* Sterling, Va.: Kumarian Press, 2011.

Stanley, W. *Opportunity Africa Newsletter & Opportunity Education Strategy.* Opportunity Africa Monthly Reports, Oakbrook, Ill.: Opportunity International, 2012.

Stewart, R. et al. 'Do micro-credit, micro-savings and micro-leasing serve as effective financial inclusion interventions enabling poor people, and especially women, to engage in meaningful economic opportunities in low-and middle-income countries? A systemic review of the evidence.' London: Institute of Education, University of London, 2012.

Stryjak, C. *'Will What Got Us Here Get Us There?'* Blue Print: Shaping Opportunity's Future, Paper presented at Global Leadership Conference. Oxford: Opportunity International, 2012.

Thurman, E. 'Is Interest Christian?' Oakbrook, Ill.: Opportunity International, 1996.

Todd, S. Will The Poor Always Be With Us? *Q: Ideas for the Common Good.* http://www.qideas.org/blog/will-the-poor-always-be-with-us.aspx, 2011.

Tomorrow Clubs *Tomorrow Clubs History.* http://tomorrowclubs.org/Tomorrow_Clubs_History.ihtml?id=388786, 2011.

Tongoi, D. *Mixing God with Money.* Nairobi: Bezalel Investments, 2004.

Turner, H. *Opportunity Program Strategy Blueprint.* Oxford: Global Microfinance Operations Office, 2012.

Tyndale, P. *Don't Look Back: The David Bussau Story.* Sydney: Allen & Unwin, 2004.

USAID *Gender Analysis Overview.* http://transition.usaid.gov/our_work/cross-cutting_programs/wid/gender/gender_analysis.html.

United Nations *International Year of Microcredit 2005:Building Inclusive Financial Sectors to Achieve the Millennium Development Goals.*http://www.yearofmicrocredit.org/

United Nations *Role of Microcredit in the Eradication of Poverty: Report of the Secretary General.* NewYork, 1997.

United Nations Development Fund for Women Facts and Figures http://www.womenfightpoverty.org/docs/WorldPovertyDay2007_FactsAndFigures.pdf

VisionFund International. *Bylaws.* Section 3.05. Monrovia, Calif.: VisionFund, 2003.

VisionFund International. *VisionFund's Guiding Principles on Witness to Jesus Christ* Monrovi, Calif.: VisionFund, 2010.

VisionFund International *VisionFund Microfinance Operating Policies v2.0.* Monrovia, Calif.: VisionFund, 2011.

Walden, N. and L. Baffour *Opportunity Children's Savings Account: Current Situation and Recommendation.* Oakbrook, Ill.: Opportunity International, 2009.

Whittaker, D. Speech delivered at Opportunity's Conference, Minneapolis, October 2011.

Woller, G. et al. (1999) *"Where to Microfinance?"* in *International Journal of Economic Development,* v.1, no.1, 1999.

Women's Opportunity Fund *Trust Bank Manual.* Oakbrook, Ill.: Opportunity International Network Office, 1997.

Women's Opportunity Fund *Tool Kit for Training New Loan Officers: A Resource for Trust Bank Programs.* Oakbrook, Ill.: Opportunity International Network Office, 1997.

World Bank "Can Ukraine Avert a Financial Meltdown?" http://web.worldbank.org/WBSITE/EXTERNAL/NEWSLETTERS/EXTTRANSITION/EXTDECBEYTRANEWLET/0,,contentMDK:20692620~isCURL:Y~menuPK:1544646~pagePK:64168445~piPK:64168309~theSitePK:1542353~isCURL:Y,00.html, 1998

World Relief "No Sharks or Scorpions Allowed: A Biblical View of Interest on Production Loans." *Microenterprise Brief,* no. 3, 1996.

World Vision International *An Affirmation of World Vision's Commitment to Christian Witness.* Monrovia, Calif.: World Vision, 2011.

World Vision International *Guidance on Effective Integration between Microfinance Institutions, ADPs, and National Offices.* Monrovia, Calif.: World Vision, 2011.

World Vision International *Handbook for Development Programs: The Essentials.* Monrovia, Calif.: World Vision, 2011.

Selected Bibliography

World Vision International *Microfinance Governance and VisionFund International*. (World Vision International Board resolution, WVI Board Reference: BD/07/23; BD/11/). Monrovia, Calif.: World Vision 2011.

World Vision International *Overview of Child Well-being Aspirations and Outcomes*. Monrovia, Calif.: World Vision, 2012.

http://www.microfinance.com/2010/08/20/1527/

http://www.themix.org/social-performance/indicators

ENDNOTES

[1] The term "case study" is used in a very loose manner here.

[2] There are many other small and big international CMFIs. Some of these include: Catholic Relief Services (CRS), Mennonite Development Associates (MEDA), Ecumenical Loan Church (ECLOF), endPoverty (formerly known as Enterprise Development International), and Mercy Corps.

[3] These are associations formed among a core of participants who make regular, but not necessarily equal, contributions to a fund for an agreed period of time. Participants cannot withdraw more than what they have contributed at a given point. Savings are often made for anticipated expenses such as school fees.

[4] This does not apply to HOPE as it engages in open evangelism and discipleship with its clients.

[5] Matthew 25:35-40.

[6] As it will be noted from the case studies, each CMFI in this book seems to have varying views and practices on this issue.

[7] Sherman.

[8] Of the 5 CMFIs, HOPE witnesses through both deed and word and openly proclaims the Gospel.

[9] Ibid.

[10] A study of an opportunity partner in Zimbabwe undertaken in late 1990s undertaken by Reed and Maphenduka showed that the income of the local church where clients were participating in a microfinance increased by 30%. See Reed and Maphenduka in Yamamori et al., 1996.

[11] Roodman, p. 35.

[12] Ibid., pp. 36-64.

[13] AfDB 2006.

[14] Although there was similarity in utilization as the focus was on infrastructure (roads, bridges, dams, etc.), there were differences in the way Marshall Aid to Western Europe and foreign aid to developing countries were designed and bore different results.

[15] International Food Policy Research Institute (IFPRI), Green Revolution: Curse or Blessing, www.ifpri.org/pubs/ib/ib11.pdf

[16] Amanda Briney, "History and development of the Green Revolution", geography.about.com/od/.../a/greenrevolution.htm

[17] Ibid., CGAP 2003.

[18] Mercy Corps, http://www.globalenvision.org/library/4/1051. See also Banerjee and Duflo 2011, pp. 160-61. A brief reference is made to the many politically motivated government sponsored credit schemes which ended up in the hands of the well-to-do and not being fully recovered – about 40% default. This phenomenon still goes on side by side with modern microfinance practices.

[19] Roodman, p. 74.

[20] Ibid.

[21] As will be noted in sections 1:3 and 1:4, the industry has seen more and newer innovations during the last two decades. This section relates to the foundational innovations that made microfinance what it is today.
[22] The members contributed 40% of the authorized capital. The Government of Bangladesh contributed another 40% while two state banks contributed 10% each.
[23] Roodman, p. 83.
[24] Kropp, W.E. 2002 and Isern 2007.
[25] Ibid., pp. 84-87. SHGs are also used for channeling and administering other non-financial services related to health, education, water and energy.
[26] Hugh Allen, 2002
[27] Stuart Rutherford in Foreword to Hugh Allen.
[28] Hugh Allen, 2002, pp. 1-9.
[29] Camion and White, 1999; Moser and Reed, 1996.
[30] Johnson and Rogaly, pp. 6-7.
[31] Remenyi, J., *Where credit is due: Income-generating programmes for the poor in developing countries*. London: IT Publications, 1991.
[32] Moser and Reed 1996. According to a study commissioned by the Consultative Group to Assist the Poor (CGAP), microfinance was able to attract about a total of $4 billion in foreign investment (debt and equity) by 2008. Reille and Forester, 2008.
[33] CGAP is based in Washington D.C. as part of the World Bank Group and operates on an annual budget of $10 million advising member donor countries and setting standards and tools used by the industry. Ever since its establishment, CGAP has played a critical role in developing best practice standards, developing manuals and tools, undertaking research and disseminating knowledge, training both practitioners and donor personnel and lobbying. Bateman, 2010.
[34] Mercy Corps, "The history of microfinance", posted on April 14, 2006, www.globalenvison.org/library /4/1051/
[35] The same applies to the MFIs that still operate as NGOs.
[36] Sinha, "Beyond 'ethical' financial services: Developing a seal of excellence for poverty outreach and transformation in microfinance" in Daley-Harris, S., and A. Awimbo, 2011, p.3.
[37] 2 examples include Compartamos, the Mexican MFI whose initial public offering in 2007 earned its owners $467 million. SKS, an Indian MFI had its IPO valued at $1.5 billion in 2010.
[38] Roodmand, pp.234-236. Some of the main ones included BlueOrchard, Oikocrdit, Tridos, Tripple Jump Credit Suisse, Oppenheim Asset Management and SNS Asset Management.
[39] Blue Financial Services Ltd, Annual Report 2008, Microfinance in Africa: Past, Present and Future, http://www.blue.co.za/pdf/micro%20finance%20in%africa.pdf
[40] United Nations (1997) Role of Microcredit in the Eradication of Poverty: Report of the Secretary General, New York, N.Y.

Notes

[41] Littlefield et al., 2003.
[42] Norwegian Nobel Committee Press Release, http://www.nobelprize.org/nobel_prizes/peace/laureates/2006/press.html
[43] Reed, 2011.
[44] The global projection is to reach 175 million of the world's poorest families by 2015 and aims to ensure that at least 100 million families will move above the World Bank's $1.25 per day poverty threshold.
[45] Roodman, p. 289.
[46] Naeesa Aziz, "African cellphone so get free Wikipedia access," bet.com/new, February 15, 2012.
[47] www.kiva.org
[48] En.wikipedia.org/wiki
[49] Another set up which served as a platform for sharing information, experience and best practice when different practitioners and donor officials took training together.
[50] After having served for about 15 years, Sam Daley-Harris was replaced by Larry Reed in November 2011.
[51] Microcredit Summit Declaration, 1997.
[52] Ibid. The Summit estimated that about $22 billion would be required to meet the estimated needs and indicated these to come from multilateral and bilateral agencies, grant-making organizations, the general public, banks and other commercial sources as well as interest charges and savings.
[53] www.microcreditsummit.org/about/about_the_microcredit_summit_campaign
[54] En.wikipedia.org/wiki/Microcredit_Summit_Campaign. When the first microcredit summit campaign meeting was held in 1997, microcredit was the single major product featuring the face of the industry. Today the industry offers multiple products and services and is known more as a microfinance industry than microcredit. It is not clear why even the 2011 Summit Campaign was still called the Microcredit Summit. The former is more representative and future summits should be called accordingly.
[55] http:/www.wtrc-tmed.org/content.aspx?ID=about
[56] Jenny Morgan, "Best Practices for National and Regional Microfinance Networks", paper presented at the Global Microcredit Summit, November 14-17, 2011, pp. 3-4.
[57] CGAP Strategic Directions 2008-2013: Building Local Financial Systems That Work for the Poor's Equity and Efficiency", p.6, sitersssources.worldbank.org/.../Resources/CGAP_strategy.pdf
[58] Another key institution that was provided training to both donor and practitioner communities was the Boulder Institute of Microfinance founded by Robert Christensen in 2004 built on the success of Boulder Microfinance Training Program established in 1986, www.bouldermicrofinance.org.
[59] www.makingcents.com/products_services/resource.php
www.sbaic.org/member_ profile/makingcentsitnernational/%20
[60] CYFI_Summit_Summary_Report.pdf

[61] UN, *International Year of Microcredit 2005:Building Inclusive Financial Sectors to Achieve the Millennium Development Goals*, http://www.yearofmicrocredit.org/
[62] Matthew Fuchs, *"lessons learned from microfinance crises: Viewpoints from investors"*, *Microfinance Focus*, November 4, 2009 and Marcus Taylor, *"The Microfinance Crisis in Andhra Pradesh, India: W Window on Rural Distress,"* *Food First Backgrounder*, vol. 18, No.3, Fall 2012, www.foodfirst.org/en/microfinance+india.
[63] www.sptf.info/hp-sp-taskforce.
[64] Ibid.
[65] www.themix.org/social-performance/indicators microfinance.com/2010/08/20/1527/.
[66] Chuck Waterfield, a long time microfinance practitioner and trainer, is the Founding President and CEO of Microfinance Transparency.
[67] www.microfinancegateway.org/p/site/m/template.rc/1.11.94902/ www.digital-development-debates.org/...microfinance-transparency
[68] Centerforfinancialinclusionblog.wordpress.com/...the-smart-campaign www.smartcampaign.com
[69] Microfinance in Eastern Europe and Central Asia, www.http://mixmarket.org/mfi/region/easterneuropeandcentralasia and Microfinance in Africa, www.http://mixmarket.org/mfi/region/africa, 2011
[70] Reed, 2011.
[71] The global projection is to reach 175 million of the world's poorest families by 2015 and aims to ensure that at least 100 million families will move about the World Bank's $1.25 per day poverty threshold.
[72] Mix, http://www.themix.org/publications/serach/results/taxonomy%3A32
[73] Mohnling, Ryan, *Assessing Impact in Malawi*, Opportunity International. Oak Brook, 2010.
[74] Opportunity International, *Reflections on Our Mission, Our Motivation and Our Core Values*. Oak Brook, 1997.
[75] *Handbook for Development Programs*. World Vision International, 2011.
[76] John 10:10 (GNT).
[77] In 2012, emergency relief funding was provided to help with the drought situation in Horn of Africa to assist rural farmers pay back their loans.
[78] VisionFund International mission statement.
[79] Microfinance Governance and VisionFund International. (World Vision International Board resolution, WVI Board Reference: BD/07/23; BD/11/)
[80] "The WVI President, the WVI Chief Operating Officer, the WVI Chief Financial Officer, and the President of this corporation, shall be members of the Board of Directors ex officio (with full voting rights)." VisionFund Bylaws, Section 3.05.
[81] *Guidance on Effective Integration between Microfinance Institutions, ADPs, and National Offices*.
[82] VisionFund Microfinance Operating Policies v. 2.0.
[83] Ibid.

Notes

[84] Freedom from Hunger developed the credit with education model, which couples financial services with educational topics (e.g., financial literacy, business improvements, health, etc.).

[85] Dunford C. Building better lives: sustainable integration of microfinance with education in child survival, reproductive health, and HIV/AIDS prevention for the poorest entrepreneurs. In: Daley-Harris S, ed. *Pathways Out of Poverty: Innovations in Microfinance for the Poorest Families.* Bloomfield, CT: Kumarian Press, 2002:75-132.

[86] 5 MFIs have received Platinum MixMarket awards, plus one Gold and one Silver award.

[87] www.worldvisionmicro.org

[88] Studies have shown that increasing access to finance for women will more directly impact children than a corresponding increase in access to men.

[89] Progress out of Poverty Index will be implemented by all VFI MFIs, where available, over the next 2 years to measure the % of clients living at or below the poverty line. (http://www.progressoutofpoverty.org/)

[90] Examples of indicators include, "What type of fuel does the household mainly use for cooking?" or "What toilet facility does the household have?"

[91] Child well-being outcomes are indicators developed by World Vision to measure whether children's lives are improving (see Figure 6).

[92] Overview of Child Well-being Aspirations and Outcomes.

[93] Dearborn T. *Reflections on Business and Micro-enterprise Development.* Monrovia, CA: World Vision International, 2009.

[94] VisionFund Microfinance Operating Policies v. 2.0.

[95] Ibid.

[96] "*An Affirmation of World Vision's Commitment to Christian Witness World Vision International,*" May 2011. This Affirmation addresses one aspect of World Vision's mission as expressed in the last line of its Mission Statement, "witness to Jesus Christ by life, deed, word and sign that encourages people to respond to the Gospel" and in its Vision Statement, "our vision for every child, life in all its fullness; our prayer for every heart, the will to make it so."

[97] VF's Guiding Principles on Witness to Jesus Christ (#7).

[98] "Substantial Positive change" is defined as >9.0%, "Positive change" is 3.0 to 9.0%, "No change" is +/- 3.0%, "Negative change" is -3.0 to -9.0%, and "Substantial Negative change" is < -9.0%.

[99] Reed, L. *Integrating Faith and Practice: Facilitator Guide.* Monrovia, CA: World Vision International, 2011.

[100] Lambeth Conference 1998: http://www.lambethconference.org/resolutions/1998/1998-5-2.cfm

[101] www.cct.org.ph

[102] Taken from Five Talents' Business Training Manual "God Means Business" and the Bible Study Booklet "Reproducing Talents" by Rev. Canon Peter Rwabyoma, 2002 (both

available from Five Talents UK).
[103] Bill Hybels, "The local church is the hope of the world."
[104] Archbishop of Canterbury at General Synod, 8th February 2011. See: http://www.fivetalents.org.uk/images/general/Press%20Release%20-%20Gen%20Synod%20Feb%202011.pdf
[105] Archbishop of Canterbury, quoted in Five Talents' Annual Review 2006 available from www.fivetalents.org.uk
[106] See www.anglicancommunion.org
[107] Belshaw, Calderisi and Sugden, "Faith in Development." Washington D.C.: World Bank, 2001, p. 213.
[108] William Temple, Archbishop of Canterbury, 1944.
[109] An information asymmetry occurs when one party in a transaction has more information than another, causing unfair advantage.
[110] A moral hazard is a situation where a party will have a tendency to take risks because the costs that could incur will not be felt by the party taking the risk.
[111] Quote from Deborah Meaden when describing Five Talents' work at a charity fundraising event in London, October 2008. See http://www.fivetalents.org.uk/images/general/Press_Release_Deborah_Meaden_Oct08.pdf
[112] Mothers' Union: www.themothersunion.org
[113] Chalmers Center for Economic Development: www.chalmers.org
[114] Stuart Rutherford (2000): "The Poor and their Money; Portfolios of the Poor." New Delhi: Oxford University Press.
[115] See Microfinance Transparency www.mftransparency.org for their APR Calculator.
[116] See Central Bank of Kenya at www.centralbank.go.ke
[117] More information on the operation of FSAs can be found in the paper "Microfinance Governance: K'REPSs experience of Financial Services Associations (FSAs)" by Emma Kimani and Jane Mbaisi July 2008, Benin and at www.afraca.org
[118] "The Ban on Interest: dead letter or radical solution?" 1993 and "Interest in Interest" 1989, both by Dr. Paul Mills and available from www.jubilee-centre.org
[119] Microfinance Transparency, see www.mftransparency.org
[120] See comparative data available from www.mftransparency.org
[121] Data as at Jan 2012 from Bank of Uganda, see www.bou.or.ug
[122] See www.bbc.co.uk for articles on Indian microfinance crises 2010 and 2011.
[123] Such as the Progress out of Poverty Index (PPI) developed by the Grameen Bank, and we are members of the Social Performance Task Force.
[124] For example, Milford Bateman "Why doesn't microfinance work? The destructive rise of local neoliberalism," 2010.
[125] "The importance of the informal economy for local economic development (LED) in Africa," Emma Wadie Hobson, 2011 – LED Network Africa, www.ledna.org
[126] These principles are published policy of Five Talents UK, available on www.fivetalents.org.uk

Notes

[127] Can Ukraine Avert a Financial Crisis?" 1998.
[128] Greer, 6-8.
[129] HOPE International, 2010.
[130] Mix Market, 2011.
[131] Hope International, Minutes from the Board Meeting, November 2011.
[132] Partner cannot be named for security purposes.
[133] Partner cannot be named for security purposes.
[134] Partner cannot be named for security purposes.
[135] Kristof, 2010.
[136] 2009, p. 53.
[137] 2011, p. 143.
[138] 2005, p. 113.
[139] "The Coca-Cola Company," 2011.
[140] "HOPE and Ambassador Enterprises – the 2020 Project," 2011.
[141] HOPE International, 2009, 4-20.
[142] "HOPE and Ambassador Enterprises – the 2020 Project," 2011.
[143] Excerpts from "What is SI?
[144] HOPE International (2011) *What is Spiritual Integration (SI) at HOPE?* Lancaster: HOPE International.
[145] "Hiring Christian Staff," 2011.
[146] HOPE International, 2007.
[147] HOPE International, 2011.
[148] "Program Update – Congo," 2011.
[149] "What is Spiritual Integration," 2011.
[150] Homes for Hope.
[151] SCP Overview, 2011.
[152] Greer and Smith 2009, p.156.
[153] Kinetz, 2012.
[154] Bellman, and Chang, 2010.
[155] Greer, 2011.
[156] Greer, 2011.
[157] Greer, 2010.
[158] 2008.
[159] HOPE International, 2009.
[160] MicroFinance Gateway, 2010.
[161] HOPE International, 2009.
[162] Tomorrow Clubs, 2010.
[163] HOPE International, 2010, p.15.
[164] Lewis, 2011.
[165] Lewis, 2011.
[166] Lewis, 2011.

[167] Board Strategy, 2007.
[168] *"Human Development Index (HDI) – 2011 Rankings." Human Development Report. 2011.* <http://hdr.undp.org/en/statistics/>[accessed 10 July 2012]
[169] HOPE Ukraine (2011) *PAR – Delinquency Management – HOPE Leadership Summit.* Lancaster: HOPE International.
[170] 2011.
[171] 2010.
[172] Ukraine, 2011.
[173] "Program Update," 2011.
[174] Todd, 2011.
[175] 2011.
[176] Rwanda SCA Fast Facts 2011.
[177] Moldova Update, 2011.
[178] Economy watch [www.economywatch.com] 2010.
[179] http://www.tradingeconomics.com/kenya/gdp
[180] http://www.gilanifoundation.com/homepage/eoy/2002_EoY02comment.pdf
[181] http://www.pwc.com/ke/en/pdf/Kenya-Budget-2011-2012-Press-Release.
[182] http://www.fsdkenya.org/finaccess/documents/11-06 27_finaccess_09_results_analysis.
[183] http://africa.procasur.org/wp
[184] *www.centralbank.go.ke*
[185] Faulu Kenya Board and Management Report, 2011.
[186] Faulu Kenya Client Stories: Presentation to IFC impact Evaluation delegation, January 2011.
[187] Faulu Kenya Client stories- Presentation to IFC impact Evaluation delegation, January 2011.
[188] Faulu Kenya Staff Induction Manual, June 2000.
[189] Faulu Kenya Staff Induction Manual, June 2000.
[190] Jeremiah 22:29, (NIV).
[191] Mark 13:5, (NIV).
[192] Luke 8:18, (NIV).
[193] Genesis 27:8, (NIV).
[194] Proverbs 19:20, (NIV).
[195] Proverbs 1:7, (NIV).
[196] Proverbs 23:12, (NIV).
[197] Awarded by a leading Insurance company in Kenya, the CIC Insurance.
[198] Proverbs 22:29, New International Version.
[199] Philippians 4:8, New International Version.
[200] Faulu Kenya Values Study Guides, 2010-2011.
[201] Human Resource Department Report, 2011.
[202] Staff interview form, 2010.
[203] 3 John 2, (NIV).

Notes

[204] Faulu Kenya Annual Financial Statement, 2010.
[205] http://www.fsdkenya.org/finaccess/documents/11-06-27_finaccess_09_results_analysis.
[206] Faulu Kenya Financial Education Case Studies, 2011.
[207] Jeremiah 29:11, (NIV).
[208] 3 John 2, (NIV).
[209] Matthew 13:31-32, (NIV).
[210] Lascelles, D. and Mendelson, S.
[211] A more detailed discussion on the criticism of microfinance is provided in the last chapter.
[212] Andhra Pradesh Microfinance Institutions Ordinance, 2010 quoted in Roodman, p. 255.
[213] Bateman, pp. 93-111 and pp. 202-212.
[214] Sinclair, pp. 221-222.
[215] Roodman, pp. 270 and 172.
[216] See, e.g., Bateman, pp. 28-59.
[217] Bateman, p. 202.
[218] Roodman, p. 266.
[219] Sinclair, p. 27.
[220] Bateman, p. 202, see also Bateman and Chang, *"The Microfinance Illusion."*
[221] Roodman, p. 34.
[222] Sinclair, p. xvi.
[223] See, e.g.,*"Client Protection Principles"* http://smartcampaign.org/storage/documents/2011; http://en.wikipedia.org/wiki/Financial_inclusion; www.mftransparency.org.
[224] Peter Greer and Phil Smith, pp. 141 and 146. Peter held, "microfinance is not a perfect one-size-fits-all solution, but it is an incredibly effective tool to help the poor work their way out of poverty and into a better life". He also held that it had a potential to be abused, p. 148.
[225] Sinclair, p.
[226] Sinclair, p. xvi.
[227] Bateman, pp. 34-36. This claim is made despite the limitations and weaknesses surrounding RCTs.
[228] Roodman, p. 173.
[229] Roodman, p. 184.
[230] Eric Turman, *"Is Interest Christian?"* Opportunity International, Oak Brook, 1996 and Kennet Graber, Wheaton: World Relief, 1996.
[231] Ezekiel 18:8 &17 and Nehemiah 5:7-10.
[232] Fotheringham, Paul, "Opportunity IT: Operation effectiveness initiatives – field data capture in Africa" and "Opportunity IT: Channels and partners: Mobile Banking in Africa", CEO Conference in Zanzibar, October 2012.
[233] Roodman, p. 191.
[234] The Client Protection Principles include: (i) appropriate product design and delivery,

(ii) prevention of over-indebtedness, (iii) transparency, (iv) responsible pricing, (v) fair and respectful treatment of clients, (vi) privacy of client data, and (vii) mechanisms for complaint resolution. www.smartcampaign.org/...Campaign/Smart-microfinance-and-the-clients.

[235] Financial education white paper.
[236] Ripley, "Talking Points at SEEP Savings Plenary Panel, 11-7-12", presented at the SEEP Annual Conference, November 7-8, 2012.
[237] Roodman, p. 192.
[238] The author was attending a community gathering in Malawi in 2010 where the Opportunity partner there was conducting a market research for a new product. One of the participants approached him at the end of the meeting and said in a slow voice that she was a local moneylender with 60 clients and wondered if she could borrow from Opportunity's partner for on-lending purposes because she couldn't meet the demand with the capital she had. He asked her why people would take a loan at an interest rate that is five times higher than Opportunity's partner? Why wouldn't they get it directly from the organization? Her answer was: "I am one of them. I live here. I feast and mourn with them. We are neighbours, friends and colleagues. We speak the same language. They know I am always available, flexible, empathic and have no rules. Moreover, some borrow from me to repay the loans from your organization."
[239] Roodman, p. 177.
[240] Ibid., p. 214.
[241] Ibid., p. 209.
[242] Bateman, p. 34.
[243] Bateman, p.31.
[244] Sinclair, p. 11.
[245] Lupton, 2012.
[246] Bateman, pp. 42-49; Roodman, pp. 197-214 and Sinclair, pp. 203-208.
[247] Sinclair, p. 20 and Roodman, p. 269.
[248] Gal. 3:28.
[249] According to Reed, "Maybe the first focus of financial education should not be at the client level. Maybe the appropriate starting point is for those of us employed by the microfinance industry to better understand our clients' financial needs, capabilities, and aspirations. With this improved understanding, we will be able to provide the full range of financial services they need and deliver them in a way that makes them easy to understand and utilize." Reed, http://cfi-blog.org/2012/02/14/who-needs-to-be-educated-for-us-to-achieve-financial-inclusion/
[250] Roodman, p. 201.
[251] Bateman, p. 55.
[252] Ibid., p. 136.
[253] Ibid., pp. 123-125; 207.
[254] Ibid., p. 153.

Notes

[255] Sinclair, p. 81.
[256] Roodman, p. 239 and Bateman, pp. 142-152.
[257] Lascelles, D and Mendelson, S.,
http://www.citigroup.com/citi/microfinance/data/news110125b.pdf
[258] Ibid., p. 123.
[259] Bussau and Mask, 2003 and Bussau and Getu, 2003.
[260] Bateman, p. 136.
[261] Steve Beck and Tim Ogden, "Beware of bad microcredit",
http://hbr.org/2007/09/beware-of-bad-microcredit/ar/1
[262] Ibid., p. 97.
[263] Ibid., pp. 106-107.
[264] Steve Beck and Tim Ogden, "Beware of bad microcredit",
http://hbr.org/2007/09/beware-of-bad-microcredit/ar/1
[265] HOPE is also a shareholder in the Opportunity Urego Bank in Rwanda.
[266] Roodman, p. 169.
[267] Hallie Preskill and Srik Gopalakrishnan, *"Fix that fits: what is the right revaluation for social innovation?"* http://forbesindia.com/blog/the-good-company/fix-that-fits-what-is-the-right-evaluation-for-social-innovation/
[268] Quinn Patton quoted in ibid., p. 7.
[269] 1 Tim. 6:10.
[270] Matt. 6:24.
[271] Isaiah 61:8, 42:1, Psalm 103:6 and 28:17.
[272] Micha 6:8 and Psalm 82:3.
[273] Proverbs 27:5.
[274] As pointed out in Chapter 2, there is a precedence and this is not a new call. It is more a call to encourage CMFIs to revive the CMED movement that started in 1999 and "died" 5 years later.

REGNUM EDINBURGH CENTENARY SERIES

A Learning Missional Church: Reflections from Young Missiologists
Beate Fagerli, Knud Jørgensen, Rolv Olsen, Kari Storstein Haug and Knut Tveitereid (Eds)
2012 / 978-1-908355-01-1 / 218pp (hardback)
Cross-cultural mission has always been a primary learning experience for the church. It pulls us out of a mono-cultural understanding and helps us discover a legitimate theological pluralism which opens up for new perspectives in the Gospel. Translating the Gospel into new languages and cultures is a human and divine means of making us learn new 'incarnations' of the Good News.

Mission Spirituality and Authentic Discipleship
Wonsuk Ma and Kenneth R Ross (Eds)
2013 / 978-1-908355-24-9 / 274pp (hardback)
This book argues for the primacy of spirituality in the practice of mission. Since God is the primary agent of mission and God works through the power of the Holy Spirit, it is through openness to the Spirit that mission finds its true character and has its authentic impact. This is demonstrated today particularly by movements of Christian faith in the global south which carry the good news to the heart of communities in every part of the world. Originating in the Edinburgh 2010 mission study project, the essays assembled in this volume show that today there is a renewal of the missionary impetus of the churches which is marked by its spiritual character. Here fresh motivation for mission is being found, moving people of faith to share the good news of Jesus Christ both within their own communities and by crossing frontiers to take the message to new contexts.

REGNUM STUDIES IN GLOBAL CHRISTIANITY

Contemporary Pentecostal Christianity: Interpretations from an African Context
J Kwabena Asamoah-Gyada
2013 / 978-1-908355-07-2 / 238pp

Pentecostalism is the fastest growing stream of Christianity in the world. The real evidence for the significance of Pentecostalism lies in the actual churches they have built and the numbers they attract. This work interprets key theological and missiological themes in African Pentecostalism by using material from the live experiences of the movement itself.

From this World to the Next: Christian Identity and Funerary Rites in Nepal
Bal Krishna Sharma
2013 / 978-1-908355-08-9 / 238pp

This book explores and analyses funerary rite struggles in a nation where Christianity is a comparatively recent phenomenon, and many families have multi-faith, who go through traumatic experiences at the death of their family members. The author has used an applied theological approach to explore and analyse the findings in order to address the issue of funerary rites with which the Nepalese church is struggling.

REGNUM STUDIES IN MISSION

Searching for Heaven in the Real World: A Sociological Discussion of Conversion in the Arab World
Kathryn Kraft
2012 / 978-1-908355-15-7 / 1428pp

Kathryn Kraft explores the breadth of psychological and social issues faced by Arab Muslims after making a decision to adopt a faith in Christ or Christianity, investigating some of the most surprising and significant challenges new believers face.

Proclaiming the Peacemaker: The Malaysian Church as an Agent of Reconciliation in a Multicultural Society
Peter Rowan
2012 / 978-1-908355-05-8 / 268pp

With a history of racial violence and in recent years, low-level ethnic tensions, the themes of peaceful coexistence and social harmony are recurring ones in the discourse of Malaysian society. In such a context, this book looks at the role of the church as a reconciling agent, arguing that a reconciling presence within a divided society necessitates an ethos of peacemaking.

Regnum Books International

Regnum is an Imprint of The Oxford Centre for Mission Studies
St. Philip and St. James Church, Woodstock Road, Oxford, OX2 6HR
For full listing go to: www.ocms.ac.uk/regnum